D1526990

Reckoning with the Past

Reckoning with the Past

Teaching History
in Northern Ireland

Margaret E. Smith

LEXINGTON BOOKS
Lanham • *Boulder* • *New York* • *Toronto* • *Oxford*

LEXINGTON BOOKS

Published in the United States of America
by Lexington Books
An imprint of The Rowman & Littlefield Publishing Group, Inc.
4501 Forbes Boulevard, Suite 200, Lanham, Maryland 20706

PO Box 317
Oxford
OX2 9RU, UK

British Library Cataloguing in Publication Information Available

Library of Congress Cataloging-in-Publication Data

Smith, Margaret E. (Margaret Eastman), 1949-
  Reckoning with the past : teaching history in Northern Ireland /
Margaret E. Smith.
      p. cm.
  Includes bibliographical references and index.
  ISBN 0-7391-0798-4 (cloth : alk. paper)
  1. Northern Ireland—History—Study and teaching. 2. History—Study and
teaching—Northern Ireland. 3. Group identity—Northern Ireland. I. Title.
DA990.U46S585 2005
907'.1'2416—dc22
                                        2004018660

Printed in the United States of America

♾™ The paper used in this publication meets the minimum requirements of American
National Standard for Information Sciences—Permanence of Paper for Printed Library
Materials, ANSI/NISO Z39.48–1992.

To my parents,
Polly Ann and Stuart Smith,
whose love of history and commitment to
peacebuilding prodded me early on to take
an interest in these themes

Contents

List of Acronyms

CBI	Confederation of British Industry
CASS	Curriculum Advice and Support Service
CCEA	Northern Ireland Council for the Curriculum, Examinations and Assessment
CDCC	Council of Europe's Council for Cultural Co-operation
CSE	Certificate of Secondary Education
CSPE	Civic, Social, and Political Education
DENI	Department of Education for Northern Ireland
DUP	Democratic Unionist Party
EAT	European Association of Teachers
EDC	Council of Europe's Education for Democratic Citizenship
EEC	European Economic Community
ELB	Education and Library Board
EMU	Education for Mutual Understanding
ERO	Education Reform (NI) Order 1989
EU	European Union
GCE	General Certificate of Education
GCSE	General Certificate of Secondary Education
IRA	Irish Republican Army
MP	Member of Parliament
NICED	Northern Ireland Council for Educational Development
NICIE	Northern Ireland Council for Integrated Education
PIRA	Provisional Irish Republican Army
PRONI	Public Record Office of Northern Ireland
PUP	Progressive Unionist Party
RUC	Royal Ulster Constabulary
SACHR	Standing Advisory Committee on Human Rights

SDLP	Social Democratic and Labour Party
UDA	Ulster Defense Association
UUP	Ulster Unionist Party
UVF	Ulster Volunteer Force
WEA	Workers' Educational Association

Acknowledgments

I take this opportunity to thank a number of individuals whose help, support, advice, and constructive criticism have been germane in the completion of this book. My interest in nationalism as a field of study and in the centrality of historical memory in the coalescence of nationalist loyalties grew out of discussions with Aleksa Djilas. Conversations with Stephen Van Evera encouraged me to pursue the issue of history teaching as it relates to conflict and conflict resolution. Talks with Herbert Kelman, Joseph Montville, Padraig O'Malley, and Yael Tamir put the spotlight on particular issues in the research and thus helped the framing of questions and conclusions. Hurst Hannum and Eileen Babbitt gave the project enthusiastic support at the outset and have continued to be there when I needed them in a variety of ways.

In Northern Ireland, Anthony Gallagher, Carmel Gallagher, Duncan Morrow, Brian Walker, Paul Arthur, Alan McCully, and Alan Smith gave generously of their time in introducing Northern Ireland to me, in discussing the issues addressed in this book, and in reading parts of the manuscript. Any of my failures to grasp the nuances of the subject matter are not the fault of these endlessly gracious and insightful people, but of me alone.

Finance for this research came from the William Donner Foundation's grant to the Security Studies Program at the Fletcher School of Law and Diplomacy, from the British Council, from the Hewlett Foundation's grant to the Program on International Conflict Analysis and Resolution, Harvard University, and from research grants from the Washington Semester Program at American University. I am also grateful to Brendan McAllister of The Mediation Network, Belfast, and to Brian Walker of The Institute for Irish Studies, Belfast, who on my different research trips to Northern Ireland arranged for me to have the use of office space in their institutions.

I would like to thank the faculty, staff, and students of The Fletcher School of Law and Diplomacy for their intellectual stimulation and moral support during my time there. The Program on International Conflict Analysis and Resolution at the Weatherhead Center for International Affairs at Harvard provided me with a second academic home during the early development of this project. Their seminar series allowed me to present the research to other associates and get valuable feedback. Faculty members at Boston College who permitted me to audit their classes in Irish history provided another important intellectual touchstone.

The editorial team, led by Christiane Weiss, also included Sara Fragoso and Vee Alexander. I thank all three of them for their detailed attention and superb *esprit de corps*. Three of my students, Molly Firkaly, Rose Ryan, and Abigail Stark, gave invaluable assistance in fact checking and preparing the manuscript.

Encounters with those whom I interviewed in Ireland, as well as in France, Germany, and the United States, without exception added to the enjoyment and fascination of the project. I thank all involved for their forbearance. I owe a special word of gratitude to friends in Belfast, Coleraine, Derry, Dublin, and Omagh who gave hospitality during my visits there. My parents have given me unstinting support in every aspect of the undertaking, and I owe them more thanks than I can adequately express.

Preface

Intervening in the Cycle of Conflict

This study explores how the teaching of history can reduce conflict. It responds to current interest in preventive diplomacy[1] and postconflict peace building.[2] It identifies reasons why revising history teaching is a worthwhile endeavor, why its effects may be exaggerated, and why it encounters frequent obstacles. In the process, the study links approaches to revised history teaching with their implied political visions.

Historical memories operate in a number of ways in ethnic conflicts. First, they assist group definition by supplying a "story" that gives cohesion to the group. Second, they supply groups with negative material about each other that strengthens each group's self-definition. Third, once a conflict is underway, historical material is drawn upon by both sides to articulate grievances. Because narratives exacerbate conflict, they also, as a consequence, harden group identity and thus perpetuate conflict. Many identity-based conflicts demonstrate a cycle of this kind. This study addresses the question of whether education can provide an effective means to intervene in the cycle.

Education is generally agreed to be an indicator of political realities. Whether changes in education policy can *alter* political realities is less clear. During the high water mark of nationalism and nation-state creation in nineteenth-century Europe and North America, history teaching in schools was considered the backbone of the enterprise to create a unified national mind-set. At the same time, nineteenth-century public education in the United States promoted notions of universal citizenship, the state's neutrality as guarantor of equal treatment of all citizens, and a homogenized populace. In the late twentieth century, we look back and recognize an assimilationist objective beneath the universalist ideals. American public schools paid lip service to the melting pot, but in fact promoted a national identity based on the characteristics of the dominant group: white, English-speaking, and Protestant.

Until the middle of the twentieth century, the importance of public education, and more specifically history teaching, in forging a common national identity was rarely questioned. Disadvantaged groups who became part of the U.S. melting pot learned of their rights, liberties, and responsibilities as new Americans. But in the latter half of the last century, the disadvantaged began to realize that mobilizing for group rights could help them achieve greater equity. As a result, assimilation ceased to be their goal, homogenizing forms of history teaching were challenged, and a debate over multiculturalism arose. England and Wales, like the United States, have seen heated public discussions in recent years on history standards, which are really a debate about whether education's priority should be promotion of a common mind-set and loyalty to the system or, on the other hand, awareness of the plural nature of the society.

Paradoxically, in the twentieth century, the belief, originating with Marxism and postmodernism, that culture is the product, not the source, of political and economic systems, raised the question of whether education really can effect political change. Nonetheless, generally speaking, efforts to alter a particular political landscape, be it in a progressive or a conservative direction, are usually accompanied by changes in curriculum and educational structure, with the idea that these measures will hasten or confirm change.[3] Throughout the past century, a sizeable body of people has been engaged in projects based on the assumption that culture, education, and the teaching of history can affect political life.

This book explores possibilities for coexistence in a society where two ethnonational groups have been in conflict over the character of the state, posing the question of whether and to what extent school history teaching can be a vehicle for postconflict rebuilding. It uses history teaching reform in Northern Ireland to conduct the exploration.

The choice of Northern Ireland is not random. Northern Ireland education reformers and policy makers have been grappling for some time with the question of how education can better equip the next generation to address and overcome the divided nature of the society. Their chosen policies indicate the possibilities and pitfalls.

This book is not a guidebook to history teaching reform but a "reformer's companion," showing ways of thinking about the task and the issues that have blocked the path for those who have traveled this road before. But in addition, history reform in a deeply divided society elucidates our understanding of some of the most complex situations humanity has produced. Reforming history teaching forces us to recognize what a contested society is actually like and to look carefully at the steps that allow people to move toward greater trust of each other.

The road from mutual distrust to genuine cooperation is a rocky one. When identity politics has been at the heart of the conflict, the path to mutual support becomes a dance around concepts of sameness and difference. Two groups that have long identified themselves as "not the other" may find common ground in supporting civic institutions like democracy and human rights. But at the same time they will need reassurance that their own group identity is not imperiled as they learn how to give recognition to the other.

Unfortunately, experience shows that upholding the respective differences tends to lead both groups to assert their own culture and identity, rather than show much concern for the other. It can create an artificial focus on culture, even encouraging the creation of new cultural events.

How can a postconflict society overcome this conundrum? Truly interactive pluralism is a phenomenon that Northern Ireland has yet to experience, but the need to develop it, rather than assume it will emerge on its own, is becoming more and more apparent.

This book weaves together these themes by examining education reforms and lining them up with their implied social and political outcomes. All the approaches have validity in a deeply divided society. While no one expects educators to carry, unaided, the burden of resolving a conflict such as Northern Ireland's, teachers can contribute to an outlook in their pupils that helps them address the serious social bifurcations of the past. History teaching reform offers a number of ways to do this.

Chapter One discusses international efforts to reform history teaching as a conflict prevention, or postconflict rebuilding, endeavor.

Chapter Two explores the deeper reasons why these endeavors are necessary; it examines the role of historical memory in social dynamics, in the constellation of groups and nations, and in the sense of identity of the individual.

Chapter Three tells the story of the conflict in Northern Ireland.

Chapter Four discusses the most salient narratives of the two communities in Northern Ireland and the vast debate on causes of the conflict. It then explores three responses to the conflict, which imply three visions for the future.

Chapter Five gives an account of the history of education in Northern Ireland up to the late 1960s when the "Troubles" broke out.

Chapter Six picks up the story begun in Chapter Five in the late 1960s and describes how the education system in Northern Ireland responded to the conflict.

Chapter Seven explores the way history teaching was used as an instrument of domination by the unionists and how Catholics opposed this as they asserted themselves.

Chapter Eight describes some of the principal initiatives Northern Ireland took to rationalize and neutralize the teaching of history, making the point that few of these proved to be straightforward.

Chapter Nine describes the advent of the common history curriculum and the challenges this introduced for reformers. Difficulties in enforcing instruction of the complete history of the province of Northern Ireland correlate with the continued contested nature of the state.

Chapter Ten examines the possibility of history teaching assisting in the development of alternative identifications. This approach is based on the notion that we have many layers of identity—each of us is a lake into which many streams flow. Given the fact that, over generations, two particular identifications have taken on a greater salience than the others, it asks if this is ever likely to shift.

Chapter Eleven looks at reformers' new preoccupation with education for citizenship. The themes of citizenship education might begin to provide some common ground and the beginning of a civic identity for Northern Ireland. This approach raises the knotty question of whether history teaching is being too easily demoted to a role of lesser importance.

Chapter Twelve explores the concept of "parity of esteem" as it plays out in the teaching of a history aimed at mutual acknowledgment.

The afterword recaps the lessons learned in the course of this research and discusses "interactive pluralism" as the missing ingredient, in spite of much that has been achieved.

Part One

THE BROADER PERSPECTIVE

Chapter One

Nationalism and History Teaching

During the coalescence of European nation-states in the late nineteenth century, professional historians participated in the promotion of state nationalisms, writing history that glorified their own states at the expense of others. Already in the 1880s, peace movements were protesting these chauvinist histories and their dissemination through textbooks, warning they could encourage the onset of war.[1] The concern that the enemy population is absorbing negative historical material about one's own group, a frequent assumption in situations of war or incipient war, was demonstrated early in the twentieth century, when Point Three of the Habsburg ultimatum to Serbia of July 23, 1914, called for the "elimination without delay from public instruction in Serbia, both as regards the teaching body and the methods of instruction, all that serves, or might serve, to foment propaganda against Austria-Hungary."

In the 1920s, the Carnegie Endowment for International Peace, Gilbert Murray's League of Nations Union,[2] the International Congress of Historical Sciences held in Oslo in 1928,[3] and the Universal Christian Conference on Life and Work in Stockholm in 1925[4] all promoted school textbook revision as a means of preventing further wars. The first international project of cooperation in textbook revision was undertaken by the Scandinavian countries between 1932 and 1939.[5] The first international treaty for textbook revision was in 1933 between Brazil and Argentina.[6]

After World War II, the work of reconciling accounts in school textbooks was pursued mainly by three institutions: UNESCO, the Council of Europe, and the Eckert Institute of School Textbook Revision in Braunschweig, Germany. The Eckert Institute, initially called the Braunschweig Institute, was created to oversee the rewriting of all German history texts in the wake of the war. After organizing joint projects involving West Germany with France, Britain, the United States, and Poland, the Institute went on to support other

3

bilateral projects between countries such as France and Yugoslavia, Belgium and Holland, and Mexico and the United States. Today it has projects in many countries of the former Soviet Union, Israel-Palestine, the Balkans, and South Africa.

In the case of the Council of Europe and of UNESCO, textbook revision was initially undertaken with a view to promoting a larger vision—that of European unity or of liberal internationalism. UNESCO projects have concentrated on human rights, peace education, and North-South relations.[7]

In the late 1960s and early 1970s, American social scientists began to investigate methodologies of textbook comparison.[8] The Eckert Institute and the Council of Europe have encouraged discussion on methodologies. Two comprehensive works on methodology of textbook analysis were published in the 1990s.[9]

During the 1970s and 1980s, the spate of textbook analysis and revision projects fell off. Nonetheless, some significant projects were undertaken, most notably one between West Germany and Poland, and another in South Africa.

A fairly broad literature now exists on the subject of school textbook revision as a means toward better international understanding, though most of it is descriptive, sidestepping theoretical questions about connections among history teaching, societal beliefs, and violence and, in addition, sidestepping methodological concerns and issues of application.

Since the mid-1950s, a number of scholars have written on the link between nationalism and international violence,[10] and of these a few have written on the specific role history writing and teaching plays in this nexus.[11] The fall of communist regimes has provided an impetus for a number of conferences and projects on history teaching in Eastern and Central Europe in recent years.[12] The Council of Europe has now produced recommendations for history teaching in Europe[13] and guidance on ways history teaching can promote democratic values and tolerance.[14] Interest in text analysis growing out of literary criticism and postmodernist studies has ensured that concerns about history textbooks persist.

QUESTIONS AND RAMIFICATIONS

Superficial investigation does not always show the degree to which revised textbooks have been put to use—though in the case of Germany after World War II, when all previous history textbooks were scrapped, the new textbooks obviously *were* used and played a symbolic as well as normative role in the creation of postwar West Germany. Implementation in other countries depends on the system by which education policy is formed and on the amount of autonomy given to publishers as well as to individual teachers and schools.

An obvious question to ask is whether the "decline of nationalistic history in the west," described by Paul Kennedy and confirmed by the number of projects to remove ultranationalist history in textbooks, is a contributing *cause* of reduced warfare between western European countries since 1945. Alternatively, it might be a *result*, possibly a symbolic means of demonstrating reconciliation, when the reconciliation has occurred for other reasons.

A second issue relating to textbook revision is the assumption that an agreed history, presumably with a claim to objectivity, can be reached. There is now recognition that "agreed history" in some cases leaves out items that are too hot to discuss. One of the cutting-edge issues in this field is, therefore, how to handle the hot topics. One way is to teach a variety of interpretations. Another is to acknowledge that certain elements of history have more salience for some groups than for others.[15] Yet another is to suggest that two groups experiencing the same historical events are in fact experiencing completely different historical realities.[16]

A third question is whether textbook revision can be studied in isolation from other societal processes that influence national myths. If it should be perceived *in relation to* other societal processes, what are these processes? They might include encouraging professional historians to open up elements of the national narrative to debate; studying how particular historical themes arise in popular culture and the arts; studying the way politicians use historical themes; focusing on the work of other institutions that introduce ideas about history into the society, such as local history groups or museums. Presumably, one reason textbooks get a lot of attention from scholars is that they form a discrete body of literature. This makes them a useful source of data, but it might be that ease of study creates a bias toward overemphasizing the importance of textbooks in comparison with other means of disseminating nationalist myths.

A fourth question might be to what degree geopolitical factors have affected the projects that thus far have been successful. An unprecedentedly solid Cold War political consensus in the West allowed a high level of agreement about history among West Germany and the former Allies. This facilitated agreement on textbooks. By the 1970s, European countries were looking for ways to separate themselves from that American-led consensus. West Germany was defining a foreign policy facing more toward the East.[17] The fall-off in textbook revision projects in the 1970s, while in part due to the fact that the most obvious post–World War II projects had by then been undertaken, may also have been related to this change. At the same time, "Ostpolitik" permitted a major project between Germany and Poland to reach an agreed history, which might not have been possible in the previous two decades.[18] Has it been a shared political agenda, rather than an appeal to objectivity, that has made it possible to arrive at agreement on a single history?

It is not insignificant that most textbook revision projects concern the reconciliation of histories across international boundaries, presumably to address the kind of "state-expanding"[19] nationalism characterized by Germany in World Wars I and II. The era of rivalry between Western European powers over territory ended in 1945. Official nationalisms in Western Europe needed mutual recognition and a solidification of the existing interstate system to present a united front in the Cold War. One way to do that was to enter into projects by which the histories on both sides of a boundary were made to agree.

A fifth question, therefore, is whether history revision projects undertaken internally in deeply divided societies should be understood in the same way as those undertaken across state boundaries. While old-style, state-to-state conflicts have not disappeared, intrastate conflicts were increasingly evident in the 1990s. These internal conflicts arise in situations where the governing body has failed to meet the needs of all its people for political participation, fair distribution of resources, or other benefits that would make identification with the state desirable. Negative discrimination of substate groups will lead those groups to mobilize in the name of the group. Thus, issues of group identity recognition become intertwined with other instrumental concerns, so that the conflict takes on an existential dimension. Status and legitimation,[20] as goals, are interwoven with goals of resource sharing and voice.

IDENTITY CONFLICTS

The term "identity conflict" has been coined for these types of internal conflicts for obvious reasons.[21] The push for group recognition may be instrumental to the original claim for resource sharing and voice. But if the group has a long history, it is hard to make the case that the emphasis on identity is purely instrumental. Moreover, the salience of a group's sense of identity hardens in the course of a conflict, so that leaders may have appealed to group emotions in order to galvanize followers, but in the end they find they have created a new set of social realities because the project of group recognition comes to supersede the original project. Economic concerns, for example, may be the trigger of group mobilization but, after the mobilization is achieved, the struggle for the dignity and recognition of the group may cause the group to act in ways that are contrary to its economic interests.

In these scenarios, cultural and religious differences, as well as language or racial attributes, become markers for differentiating groups. These groups develop their own narratives, mythologies, and official histories. Memory becomes a significant proxy battlefield for the conflict. Arguments about which group inhabited the land first and numbers massacred by the other group in previous wars become not only tools of mobilization but solidified elements in the people's sense of social identity.

These conflicts can be broken down into two categories: minority conflicts and ethnonational conflicts. Minority conflicts do not involve the desire to create a new state but do include the struggle for various forms of cultural recognition along with their economic and political goals. Ethnonational conflicts include the potential or desire of one group to break away and form its own state or join another state. Often groups who adopt this goal are groups who have governed themselves in the past, or at least believe this is the case.[22]

In the case of ethnonational conflicts, claims to form a separate state imply a redefinition of the existing state, undercutting the sense of identity of the remaining population in ways they find unacceptable. Because both the remaining group and the breakaway group define themselves in relation to the same piece of territory, the conflict takes on a zero-sum quality.

This zero-sum aspect is the chief reason that ethnonational conflicts tend to become intractable.[23] But there are additional contributing factors. These conflicts are usually conducted on several fronts: constitutional, territorial, resource distribution, and group psychology. That they are intrastate conflicts implies that at least one of the protagonists does not have an official military at its disposal; hence it will resort to the creation of paramilitary groups and make use of terrorist tactics, which are the long-standing weapons of the weak. The conflict is fought in localities where the grassroots population will be drawn in and will also be divided in terms of which side it supports. All this encourages pervasive suspicion and distrust in the social fabric.

As ethnonationalist tensions manifest themselves today in conflicts within state boundaries or, to put it another way, as official nationalisms are increasingly challenged by popular emancipatory ethnonationalist programs, some efforts to defuse the violent negation of the "other" by removing chauvinist language in history textbooks have been attempted domestically, emulating the kind of projects that, until fairly recently, have been undertaken only between states. Those interested in conflict resolution see the competitive narratives as a phenomenon that must be addressed. Some may even see them as an important causal factor—arguing that the groupings have coalesced around their differing ideas about history and that, if a single history could be agreed upon according to "the facts," the conflict would die down. However, to see the differing histories as a *cause* of the conflict can mean to overlook injustices in the economic or political realm. Hence, preoccupation with different histories as an approach to conflict resolution can be seen by the low power group as an avoidance tactic—a means of the elite to shift focus away from areas where its power might be more seriously challenged.

Projects to address the differing narratives in internal identity conflicts differ from those attempted across international boundaries for a number of reasons that relate to the nature of the conflicts themselves.

First, the resolution of these conflicts usually involves constitutional changes and accompanying alterations of group identity and self-concept. Second, the people on the two sides of the conflict are interacting on a day-to-day basis and, therefore, subtle forms of boundary maintenance work powerfully through the culture. They will not be easily abandoned through an intellectual exercise such as reformed history teaching. Third, history revision projects in these settings are often undertaken *while violent or quasi-violent conflict is still ongoing.* They are, therefore, more self-consciously aimed at helping *bring* peace rather than consolidating a political arrangement that follows a treaty. For this reason, it may at some point become clear that the two or more groups involved in a project to revise history teaching do not have a common political agenda beyond making peace. Even if the violence has ended and, as in the case of South Africa, new constitutional arrangements are in place, the struggle to arrive at a new sense of common history and common identity is a continuing issue and holds potential for continuing conflict. Like water seeking its own level, the way memory is handled in a society will always be an indicator of power relations. To the degree that power relations remain contested, disputes about history will continue to be intense.

We can speculate that it will be very difficult, perhaps impossible, to arrive at an agreed history in situations of ongoing ethnic conflict or indeed in the immediate postconflict phase. Moreover, history teachers will be cautious about discussing the conflict in which they live unless they are well prepared in techniques for leading controversial discussions in the classroom. They also will need to be assured that they will not personally experience intervention from parents or others who may disagree with what is being taught.

When teachers *do* manage to address the conflict in class, we will see a different kind of history teaching—not simply a forum where facts are learned, or even a place where the young are taught critical thinking, but an environment that models a form of interaction for groups who are still in the process of negotiating their identity. Beyond correcting chauvinist lies and misapprehensions, such projects must attempt to show the young how to respect, listen to, and acknowledge the views of the other group. They must address cognitive, social, and emotional aspects of the conflict by helping pupils both to understand the mind-set of the other group and to interact with people who have that mind-set. And they must underline the salience of multiple perspectives, because agreement about certain parts of the disputed history will not be possible.[24] In spite of these extra challenges, efforts to revise the teaching of history in intrastate conflict settings are now fairly widely pursued.

An additional matter for study is the link between the revision of history instruction and the broader societal healing process required after a civil war. Schools can do no more than reflect the level of a society's willingness to remember. Seeking the facts, administering justice and reparation, allowing the victims to be acknowledged, establishing forms of remembrance—these processes must feed into the pedagogy before school history can truly contribute to healthy societal memory. But this societal dynamic is an ongoing one, and there are good reasons to proceed with education reform even before the society has thoroughly addressed its history.

In the end, as their physical and psychological wounds begin to heal and as a new level of justice is instituted, it is hoped that people will become less susceptible to mobilization around reiterated historical grievance. We will explore history education's place in that process.

MULTICULTURAL CONUNDRUM

This book examines these issues in the case of Northern Ireland. It is based on qualitative interviews of historians, researchers, policymakers, and post-primary history teachers. Overall, the research uncovered the fact that in history education, as in much of the rest of the society where efforts at building community relations are being pursued, some reforms imply a determination to submerge difference, while others imply a determination to support difference. In the latter case, efforts to accept and support difference are presented as confidence-building measures that will ultimately, it is hoped, issue in a society where ethnonational difference is less important than class-based and resource-sharing concerns. Problematically, however, recognition of difference seems, on the short term, to be rigidifying the political life and grassroots relationships. Northern Ireland still stands in need of ways to recognize difference in a relational, interactive, mutually supportive fashion.

This book shows how efforts to break history's contribution to the conflict cycle can be described according to three approaches: partisanship, cosmopolitanism, and neopluralism. These categories emerged inductively from the research but they also resonate with existing theoretical work on the conflict. While each is embedded in efforts to reform history teaching, each also contains an implied political vision.

Partisan Empowerment

The first form of intervention in the conflict cycle involves a subordinate group analyzing and questioning the narratives disseminated by those in authority.

Very often, such a program will rely for its analysis on school history texts and will call for their revision. Empowerment programs of this kind can be employed in challenging the policies of a democratic state[25] or an authoritarian or oppressive regime.[26]

Partisan empowerment aims to challenge the privileged, dominant position of the elite in government, and the debate over historical narratives is a proxy arena for that challenge. The subordinate group highlights the way the prevailing narrative supports the position of the elite and confronts that narrative with an alternative narrative. It very often does this by writing its own alternative history and proposing it for schools.

Problems arise when the narratives of the dominant and subordinate groups are at some level mutually exclusive and neither leaves room for acknowledgment or inclusion of the other group's narrative. In these cases, the true aim of the exercise is not to create a more inclusive arrangement but to supplant those in power. Thus, empowerment projects may not lead to a stable resolution of a conflict but, rather, may exacerbate partisan concerns.

Cosmopolitanism

A second way revision of history teaching intervenes in the conflict cycle is in helping to develop civic culture. In this case, the broad aim is to build a common public space where identity concerns are sidelined by emphasizing the importance of civil society,[27] human rights, democratic institutions, and rational discourse. Here, the point of revising history teaching is to neutralize the power of narratives to coalesce or exacerbate group conflict. Benchmarks used to neutralize history writing are appeals to fact, objectivity, and inductive reasoning. The best examples of this approach are seen either in postconflict international relationships, such as that of West Germany with the Allies after World War II, or between countries that do not experience much dissension with each other, such as between Scandinavian or Latin American countries. Neutralization measures are also employed in situations of domestic conflict when it is hoped that finding agreement about history will diminish community dissension or violence. When they are employed in situations of ongoing ethnic violence, the assumption is that a better-educated population will prevent leaders in a conflict from co-opting historical myths to exacerbate or reinflame the conflict, though this is not usually made explicit.

While cosmopolitanism's origins are in the Enlightenment, today it is considered synonymous with modernity. It describes the cultural vision of the United States and Western Europe up to the middle part of the twentieth century, when it was assumed that minority groups and ethnic affiliations would fade in importance. Cosmopolitanism represents a world where human identity is reduced to what Ernest Gellner calls "modular man,"[28] because people find their sense of self by participating in a variety of networks—sports, amateur and professional associations, and so on—rather than through their ethnic or national identity. The problem, however, is that modernity often proves to be unsupportive psychologically and emotionally. This is because people are expected to identify with, and find their identity in, symbols that are too far removed from themselves.[29] The solution to this psychological dilemma is to seek identification with a group that can supply greater meaning and self-transcendence; hence the turning in the late twentieth century to identity concerns and identity politics.

Neopluralism

The neopluralist acknowledges different identifications rather than minimizing them and uses history teaching to support those separate identities. The challenge is to recognize the importance of the most salient communal groups in some interlocked fashion. The most likely constitutional outcome is joint sovereignty or else a power-sharing arrangement that supports the two clashing identities equally.

Here the assumption is that offering groups greater recognition will reduce their sense of insecurity and, therefore, their need to compete and fight. In a neopluralist world, we recognize that group identity, while somewhat malleable, is not wholly so. A group will seek political arrangements that support its identity, even if the identity is somewhat reframed. A failure sufficiently to acknowledge the key groups, both in the distribution of power *and* in the new narrative, will mean an incomplete solution to the conflict.

INTERACTIVE PLURALISM

In conclusion, the study argues that all three agendas have validity in the context of postconflict Northern Ireland but that, as things stand at the moment, all efforts still fall short in building a truly interactive pluralism.

Interactive pluralism implies a comfort level with difference that allows genuine interest in the outlook of the other. It implies a willingness to regard the political environment, as well as the grassroots, as a shared space. Outsiders unfamiliar with the dynamics of a deeply divided society assume that this vision is obvious and, therefore, desired by those who have already agreed that war will not be in their future. But interactive pluralism is hard, and we have few truly compelling models. It is hard because the two groups are so used to defining themselves as a negation of the other and to seeing any gain for the other as a loss for themselves.

The study makes a number of points in this connection. At the very minimum, revising history teaching can be viewed as a trust-building measure because it responds to the deep *belief* in a divided society that the other group is teaching negative history about one's own group. Nonetheless, achieving a common history curriculum has been difficult in practice, as teachers avoid teaching what feels uncomfortable to them. Revised history teaching is nonetheless worth pursuing because it can play a long-term role in helping each group understand the other's perspective on the conflict, including injustices suffered and concerns and fears that linger. But teachers will have great difficulty doing this until they see others in the society speaking in these terms and until they are given training in how to conduct this kind of a discussion. The study suggests that interactive pluralism cannot really be modeled in a classroom unless young people from both communities are actually present in the classroom. Finally, it demonstrates that a postconflict society may prefer to teach concepts of citizenship, human rights, and diversity than to engage students in the difficult discussions required in a history class that truly attempts to elucidate the power of narratives in politics and open people to the mind-set of the other. The pressure to reduce the place of history on the timetable is great. The question remains whether the reduction of history in the timetable in favor of citizenship classes will equip students sufficiently to withstand the continued politicization of narratives.

Chapter Two

The Tenacious Hold
of Historical Memory

History is our repository of information about the past and, as such, offers explanations about the present. As a repository it has the special capacity to reveal the hidden facts of injustice. More indirectly, history is critical to the creation of ethnic groups and nations, given that shared past experience, or the perception of shared past experience, is the strongest rationale for the existence of the group. In addition, history texts, monuments, museums, and other forms of public history provide a sense of stability and tradition that assist the legitimation of the existing regime. Beyond their role in group creation and legitimation, history and memory provide material for group myths that are a source of social cohesion because they supply operational codes and a system of ethics. Finally, history and memory are the containers for grievance. If grievances are not addressed, they can be a powerful tool of mobilization by political leaders.

The capacity of historical memory to coalesce politicized groups cannot be understood fully without recognizing that, simultaneously, historical memories play several critical roles in the lives of individuals. History is a way of recording and remembering traumas of past generations that have an emotional or physiological impact, and possibly a material impact, on their descendants. Trauma that has affected groups is repeatedly relived by the group, contributing to group identity while creating an ongoing sense of victimization. Because of the individual's biological dependence on the group that supports it, the individual will identify with the group in order to receive what is offered to group members, absorbing cultural elements and a shared sense of the past. In addition, in the process of developing a consistent sense of self, people use historical material to select mental constructs by which to connect inner and outer experience.

For all the above reasons, historical memories are deeply rooted in a society and are tenacious. Introducing a different history means challenging psychological and sociological patterns that are of long duration.

The instrumental purposes historical memories serve in society suggest that contentious history cannot be separated from politics and power relations. To the degree that the political life of a society remains contested, historical memory will be intertwined with that contestation. And yet the need to address the problem of contentious, chauvinist history is crucial for postconflict reconstruction and the prevention of future conflict.

Devotion to "the truth" is a core aspect of a society's dedication to justice, even if all acknowledge the difficulties in reaching "the truth." Establishing a basis of historical truth in a society places some limit on the possibilities for chauvinist leaders to distort history for political ends. A culture of historical debate makes it more likely that past injustices will be brought to light and will be addressed. Acknowledgment of the traumas of the past are a first step in mourning and are essential for individuals and the society as a whole to find healing and move forward. All these processes will assist in the development of a new narrative. At the same time, a rethinking of the past can enable intercultural understanding by helping groups remove their negative stereotypes and accept the other.

HISTORICAL MEMORY AND CULTURAL HEGEMONY

The word *history* denotes the past in general or an account of the past. Sometimes it denotes an *official* account of the past, given that, in the nineteenth century, historians generally were engaged in writing official histories. The terms *memory* or *historical memory* denote the way an individual or a society has absorbed its past. When history or memory has been shaped or molded, we give it the label *narrative.* History becomes narrative when it turns into a frame of reference for individuals or groups in their daily lives. Most written history and all memory is narrative.

In a society that upholds free speech, the work of historians is constantly shifting people's ideas about the past, casting doubt about past heroes, elevating the role of less-well-known individuals, introducing new factors to illumine simplistic notions of cause and effect, and at least implicitly raising questions about current injustices that grow out of past errors.

Open, stable government supports the process of historical debate as part of its commitment to free speech. At the same time, all governments will do their best to give a positive account of their actions. If a regime's legitimacy is fragile or nonexistent, that regime becomes more aggressive in presenting its own narrative to the society.

It has become a truism that history is an account of the past according to the winners' point of view. What this really means is that those who attain power will tell their story in a way that legitimizes their power.

For a regime to be successful in offering its own narrative to the society, the regime will not need to be involved constantly in actually writing history books: once certain assumptions have taken hold in the culture, most historians will simply absorb and restate those assumptions. Culture can, therefore, be a tool in developing social control. Cultural hegemony implies that large numbers of the population have voluntarily accepted the imposition of norms and cooperate in propagating them. Because of the regime's establishment of cultural norms, the public buys into the regime's account of the past. Soon, the historical memory of the society conforms in considerable measure to the regime's account of the past and is articulated in the written history of the society.[1]

But the truism that history articulates the winner's point of view can have much darker implications. This is because some polities are founded on a cover-up, whereby the existing regime benefits from some injustice of the past that it prefers to obscure. In such cases, the regime takes pains to disseminate a narrative that deliberately hides the truth of the past.

Challenges to the legitimacy of a regime or its moral standing involve challenges to the regime's narrative. Revolutions occur when a critical mass of the population rejects the prevailing narrative and substitutes it with another. Grievance and leadership are the *sine qua non* of a revolutionary movement but, in order to gain mass support, revolutionary leaders must have a rhetoric that articulates a new and attractive societal narrative.

Democratic societies like to think their regimes do not rely on cultural hegemony to ensure their power. Freedom of speech, after all, promotes debate and thus implies greater difficulty in obfuscating the past. But majoritarian democracy does not serve minorities in a society well. Cultural hegemony can function powerfully in democracies, and the majorities in question are generally ignorant of the extent to which this is so.

School texts, especially if commissioned or approved by those in power, are one of the most useful instruments of cultural hegemony. This scarcely needs elaboration. Regimes may not have total control over what historians write, but they usually have control of what is taught in schools. All aspects of the curriculum are of interest to the regime as it develops an economy of scale and mobilizes its workforce, but history teaching is of additional importance because it supports the narrative, and hence the legitimacy, of the regime itself.

These issues are significant in a variety of situations of political conflict.

For minority groups who live with the aftermath of trauma or injustice, the prevailing narrative of the society coincides poorly with their own historical memory. These groups, therefore, live with a twofold curse. First, the substantive ills that they are forced to live with are at least in part the result of their traumatic or unjust history; but second, the very account of that past that has entered the memory of the majority of people in the society erases or obfuscates their trauma. Revising the historical account, therefore, becomes a way to gain visibility for the group and is a first step in gaining more social assistance in dealing with the residual ills.

Second, when the mandate of a regime is poor or nonexistent, the regime will bolster its position by disseminating a narrative that supports its position. Often this involves scapegoating—creating a comparison with a negative "other" whom the society fears or dislikes. For example, a weak regime might blame its economic crisis on multinationals who are taking their profits out of the country.

A special case of scapegoating arises with regard to war. Taking a society into war can be a way for a regime to solidify its support at home, by rallying people against a common enemy. The regime will depict the potential enemy as dangerous, evil, or subhuman in order to mobilize the society and render its military willing to kill. Such a regime will therefore dig up or reinstate past instances of harm coming from that potential enemy, implying that the current conflict is a continuation of a past conflict.

Another way these issues manifest themselves is in societies where the regime is in question because a substantial minority wishes to gain political recognition or even separate itself from the existing polity. Here the regime's long-term legitimacy is particularly fragile, and rationales for its existence will be proportionally important. But, equally, those challenging the regime will put great store by *their* past, challenging the narrative of those in power, and offering their own alternative *raison d'être*.

HISTORICAL MEMORY AS MYTH

Our understanding of historical memory and its relationship to society can be illumined by a brief discussion of the role of myth in society. Myth has been, and continues to be, the subject of enormous study and discussion. Therefore, we will highlight here only a few themes that have relevance to the concerns of this book.

> Myths are dramatic stories that form a sacred charter either authorizing the continuance of ancient institutions, customs, rites and beliefs in the area where they are current, or approving alterations.[2]

The use of the word "ancient" in this definition can be misleading, suggesting myths belong *only* to antiquity. Myths, however, have relevance in any society, ancient or modern. They do, however, suggest a long-standing history and continuity by establishing a tradition and precedent that is repeated within the society in question.

We associate myth with premodern societies because those societies had an epistemology—that is, a way of understanding the world—that allowed them to regard myths as true. This does not necessarily mean that premodern societies viewed myths as *factually* true, though they did believe myths had grown out of real historical events. Rather, these societies viewed myths as true because people had attached themselves to the deeper truth of the myth and found that it resonated with their life generally.

The understanding of truth required for a myth to function in the premodern world is not allowed credibility in our modern world. Dualism, prevalent since Descartes, posits that reality is of two kinds, inner substance (the mind) and outer substance (the physical world). It rules other nonrational aspects of experience as unreal. In spite of the enormous influence of Freud in bringing to light another form of reality, namely the unconscious, current society tends to view the world according to Cartesian, dualist presuppositions. Myth, in linking the conscious mind with the unconscious and in expressing the inner world in an outward fashion, doesn't fit well with a dualist understanding of the world. Thus, in our modern world, myth is dismissed as a property of the ancients, irrational, and false. The modern world suggests to us that truth is found outside of the embrace of myth. This way of thinking may, however, cause us to dismiss a form of valid experience whose ramifications we live with daily.

Because myths take the form of stories, they can be internalized at a deep emotional level. Once it has taken hold, a myth offers a reduction in anxiety, increased self-confidence, elimination of doubts, or experience of some ultimate truth.

This story aspect to myth is important for another reason. Stories have particular significance for groups and for the building of community.

> The group's temporally persisting existence as a community and as a social subject of experience and action, is not different from the story that is told about it; it too is constituted by a story of the community, of what it is and what it is doing, which is told, acted out, and received and accepted in a kind of self reflected social narration.[3]

An additional means by which myth solidifies groups comes through ritual. Myth is closely related to ritual. Some scholars argue that myths arise out of ritual; others would say that mythical belief engenders rites that in turn validate the beliefs contained in the myth. Whatever the precise relationship between myth and ritual, scholars of myth generally agree that a myth requires an accompanying ritual in order to be a true myth.

Accounts of many historical events do not burn themselves into our present lives, but some do. Some historical events fade but, if they have been transformed into mythic events, they retain significance and also an actuality. Even in the modern world, we can find rituals that are acted out as we recite historical experiences. We could say that historical events are objective reality; when they have become myths their significance lies in subjective reality.

In addition, myths can serve as patterns by which we understand historical events. Powerful individuals look back to history for prototypical individuals on whom to model themselves. The narrative frame that we choose to give historical events is one we derive from mythic patterns.

Myth is more than metaphor. It is not a story that stands in for truth. It is not merely a *representation* of the inner life. Myth is the *actual* psychic life of an individual or group. To function as a myth, a story

> must have the power to have an effect on the realm of things. . . . It must be the kind of word which not merely designates the thing, but is the thing itself. If the word *is* the thing itself in a manner which, of course, simply remains incomprehensible to the rational, scholarly way of thinking, then it cannot be but that it is effective in the realm of things.[4]

Even if we have difficulty with this concept, we must remain open to the idea that subjective reality is not internalized only by thought processes according to the Cartesian model but by direct emotional reaction "not as remembered knowledge, but as experienced belief."[5]

While thinkers like Freud and Jung focus on myth as an internal matter, relating to the self as consciousness or will, others emphasize the impact of myth on the social order.

A myth, according to anthropologists, is a story that regulates human actions.[6] If a story functions as a myth, it governs features of the culture, functioning as a warrant or guide to activities.[7] Story and custom have a close link in all societies.

> [Myth] expresses, enhances, and codifies belief; it safeguards and enforces morality; it vouches for the efficiency of ritual and contains practical rules for the guidance of man. Myth is thus a vital ingredient of human civilization; it is not an idle tale, but a hard-worked active force; it is not an intellectual explanation or an artistic imagery, but a pragmatic charter of primitive faith and moral wisdom.[8]

Every historical change that alters social realities creates a new mythology. Thus, even though myth may be only indirectly related to historical fact, it is brought into being by the process of historical change.

But myth is linked to the past in another sense. This is because while any story can function as a myth, *foundation* stories have particular power in this regard. A myth's effectiveness lies in part in its capacity to suggest that particular actions have a historical precedent and, in the case of foundation stories, that historical precedent contributes in a major way to the group's understanding of its identity.[9] Knowledge of a foundation story supplies people with the *incentive* for ritual or moral action, as well as furnishing them with a set of indications and directions for correct performance.

Tradition possesses power because it suggests continuity. For this reason, appeals to tradition supply prestige, recognition, and therefore social stability. If a link can be made between present social forms and the idea of tradition, then these social forms are solidified. Foundation myths give tradition even more cachet and effectiveness.

Malinowski demonstrates in primitive societies how immigrant clans force an adjustment to the existing clan's mythology to account for a new state of affairs. Here myths cover inconsistencies created by historical events. They have an ad hoc role to fulfill a sociological function. Thus, the myth functions in situations of social strain, "such as in matters of great difference in rank and power, matters of precedence and subordination and unquestionably where profound historical changes have taken place."[10]

These comments are helpful in understanding the special prestige given to the endeavor of history writing in the late eighteenth and early nineteenth centuries when the "nation" was coming to birth in the wake of the American and French Revolutions. With the transition from monarchical government, whose legitimation rested on divine right of kings, to democratic government, whose legitimation comes from the people, leaders were under an increased burden to convince the people of the validity of new political arrangements. In that time of enormous social and political change, the tendency to look to the past for traditions that would offer social stability was particularly great. Leaders, therefore, supported history writing that supplied them with a foundation myth and a national story. They also encouraged the development of other traditions and symbols such as flags, parades, and national anthems. The suggestion that a new nation had a long lineage was a way to paper over the disjuncture in political arrangements and give legitimacy to new governments. In periods of war or incipient war, national leaders could use historical grievances to arouse public enmity and distrust of a potential enemy, at the same time rallying the public more firmly behind the leader.

Despite the fact that historians of our time are held to much higher standards of empiricism, objectivity, and political disinterestedness than their professional counterparts of a century ago, the partisan nature of history writing has become an accepted tenet of the world in which we live precisely because of the instrumental role it plays in constructing our political and social life. Political contests and social realignments get worked through, by proxy, in historical debates. History continues to have a legitimizing role. The only difference in our current world is that historical narrative can be a source of liberation as well as a means of asserting domination. Substate groups claiming a state of their own have turned to history as a means of claiming an independent identity and hence legitimacy.[11]

In recent years, the new literary criticism and postmodernism have urged the study of history texts and narratives as a means of highlighting hegemony of particular elites within societies or to demonstrate the belief systems that bolstered colonialism.[12] Such endeavors show the way culture and narratives are instruments of political or economic hegemony.

Indeed, postmodernism has called into question the very claim to objectivity that lies at the heart of the academic historical profession. All history, argue postmodernists, is a reflection of the interior life, the relationship to the status quo, or the linguistic proclivity of the writer. No history is irreducibly true; all history is mere narrative, and narrative is incapable of subjecting itself to critical thinking.[13]

At the same time, usage of the term *myth* has grown, so that it is now a concept with a life in popular culture. In the past, *myth* was employed in discussions of primitive societies, as an element in modern culture that solidified social relations, or else as a synonym for the word *lie*. Nowadays, it is used interchangeably with the words *paradigm* or *mind-set*. Myth creation has come to be an essential element of leadership in business and nongovernment institutions as well as in politics.[14] Leaders will gather support to the degree that they can tell a story about "who we are" that resonates with the potential followers. Today we are willing to accept a definition of *myth* as "a story that promotes a practical purpose."[15] The nature of that purpose may be legitimation. More fundamentally, myths are employed to relieve sociological strain by covering up inconsistencies.[16]

Myth, then, is a socially active but, in itself, politically neutral phenomenon. Its power to support or develop social and political programs can be used instrumentally by leaders and elites in both positive and negative ways. A list of purposes myths serve would include

- *Legitimation:* If the political organization is weak or nondemocratic, myth-making can deflect attention. This will be a particular issue if the elite fears challenge from some quarter that is unrepresented. Mythmaking can give an explanation for failed policies. It can be used to rationalize the maintenance of a peacetime army by pointing to external threats.[17]

- *Mobilization:* When a leader places large demands on his followers, or a regime on its citizens, mythmaking can help people accept this by responding to a high-sounding cause. Mobilization is necessary, for example, to pay taxes. But it can also have pernicious or chauvinist aspects, for example, in mobilizing people for an unjust war.
- *Liberation:* Historical memory allows liberation groups to mobilize around grievance or, in other ways, to challenge the narrative of those in power.
- *Recognition:* Substate groups that seek political recognition appeal to historical memory to establish their claim to the group's existence, hence the importance of the foundation story. With recognition comes status. Status will be important to bolstering the social identity of group members for psychological reasons. At the same time it will make possible the achievement of material goals. To the degree that a substate group is in an ongoing struggle for recognition, it will resist modifications of its narrative that seem to undermine the rationale for the struggle.
- *Cohesion:* Historical memory supplies the myths that create social cohesion through behavior norms and values.[18] Such myths can engender social responsibility—for example, induce people to pay taxes or join the army. They create a sense of tradition and continuity by offering cultural elements to the group. Not only holidays and celebrations, but also everyday habits, can help to solidify cultural norms.

THE SOCIAL CONSTRUCTION OF ETHNIC GROUPS AND NATIONS

Boundary Making in Relation to Ethnic Groups

A current debate among scholars with regard to ethnic groups is whether the consciousness of these groups is static or dynamic. Primordialists see ethnicity as a basic, innate category linked to kinship,[19] where the consciousness of the group is longstanding and relatively unchanging. Constructivists challenge the primordialist view, arguing that ethnic groups are in constant flux and that myths play a role in ongoing social reconstruction as well as in maintaining cohesion.

The constructivist view predominates in the field of anthropology currently. Anthropologists who study ethnic groups no longer view societies and cultures as isolated and static, nor do they focus on their historical evolution. These days, anthropologists concentrate their attention on the flux, ambiguity, and complexity of ethnic identity creation. In this view, ethnicity develops to serve instrumental goals, and ethnic categorizations have more importance in some situations than others.[20]

This dynamic understanding of ethnic groups is important for our understanding of the precise role historical material is playing in such groups. Constructivists argue that history is not *really* what it claims to be, that is, an account of the past of the group. Rather, they argue, history is assisting in the project of social construction by suggesting that the group has a longer existence than it actually has.

A related assumption is that culture is not decisive in coalescing ethnicity. This is most easily understood by pointing out that some groups may seem culturally similar, yet remain highly aware of a very relevant ethnic difference between them. And, indeed, there can be considerable cultural variation within a group, while the group remains ethnically homogeneous. Constructivists presume that ethnic group formation *precedes* the development of group culture: groups form because boundaries are created when a single difference leads to a particular form of social interaction; they coalesce because of a human predisposition to make distinctions between insiders and outsiders; and intragroup cultural forms and operational codes develop subsequently, solidifying difference. Another way to describe the relationship between culture and ethnicity is to say that culture only becomes important in ethnic identity when cultural elements are needed for the maintenance of boundaries between groups.

By this schema, the crucial objects of study are the processes by which boundaries between groups are created and maintained.[21] As groups are in consistent contact, the persistence of cultural variation between ethnic groups is accounted for by recognizing that there is a constant process of boundary maintenance underway at the meeting place of ethnic groups, where the form of the boundary may change but the boundary itself remains constant. Following this view, investigations of ethnicity focus on the relationship between ethnic groups *at the boundaries*. Ethnic categorizations can only arise if there is an interaction between two or more groups; and cultural differences are significant only if such differences have been made relevant in the social interaction.

The significance of this argument with regard to the role historical ideas play in society is considerable. Here, historical material is co-opted in the process of boundary construction. Memorials, statuary, music, parades, museums, and the teaching of history itself contribute to the goal of boundary maintenance.[22]

In such situations, the trappings of memory have an anthropological significance. These history-related rituals may stray quite far from depicting the true events of history. At the same time, it could be argued that efforts to hold people to more truthful renditions of the history for the performance of their rituals will be problematic if the more truthful accounts do not serve the boundary maintenance function as effectively.

The Constructed Nature of Nations

The relationship between ethnic groups and nations is one we easily take for granted but in fact is a matter of considerable debate.

A "nation" is defined as a group that feels a psychological bond. Beyond that, defining a nation is extremely difficult. In the end, it is generally agreed, a nation, like an ethnic group, is self-defined: the only requirement for its acknowledged existence is that the people it comprises agree that they are a nation.[23]

Nation is usually used to suggest greater politicization than would be the case with "ethnic group." Some scholars see ethnic groups as *potential* nations, having not yet developed sufficient group awareness or politicization to qualify as nations.[24] Another way to understand nations is that they refer to a psychological bond that is required for the function of states. The word *nation-state* came into use because of the belief that the political and national unit should and could be congruent. But no analytical discussion of nations and states can go far without acknowledging that this congruency rarely exists. Governments of states may attempt to develop a national consciousness that has relevance to all citizens. But this is a process that governments cannot entirely control. Several national consciousnesses can exist within a state, each with its own vision for the definition of the state.

A nation generally has a different relationship with the state apparatus than an ethnic group. One difference is seen in the United States and Canada in the case of the Native American tribes who called themselves "nations" and who, based on this status, entered into treaty arrangements with the U.S. and Canadian governments. Another difference is seen in those countries that deny some citizenship rights to ethnic minorities. *Nation*, in this latter case, is reserved for the group that lends its cultural properties to the state as a whole.

In the past, ethnic groups were studied by anthropologists, and nations were studied by political scientists. In recent years, ethnic groups have become increasingly politicized, hence clouding the difference between the two terms. Now the terms are used almost interchangeably, though the term *nation* tends to imply an aspiration to statehood or an emotional connection to an existing state.

To most people who have not thought a great deal on the matter, it is utterly counterintuitive to suppose that states' "national" identities do not grow directly from ethnic origins. But in fact, the nation is frequently understood to be a top-down creation, where ethnic categories are co-opted by the state or a political leader to create a notion of the long-time duration of group consciousness.

One form of this proposition posits industrialization as the trigger mechanism for the age of nationalism. In this view, industrialization required economies of scale and, therefore, caused a reorganization of society in order to allow the population to be fully mobilized in the economy.[25] Another explanation for national ideologies, also colored by economic determinism, posits "print-capitalism," in other words the printing press, newspapers, and the rise of literacy as the engine behind the development of the national identities of states.[26] The reader of newspapers was allowed to share the experience of people he didn't otherwise know and to contemplate a series of different things happening at the same time. This sense of simultaneity contrasted with prenationalist cultures, for which time was exclusively a matter of cause and effect, and made possible an act of imagination where people could think of themselves as belonging to a collective.

In this constructivist view of the national identities of states, the role of history writing is important in establishing a foundation story and a convincing group narrative to support the new state's claim to legitimacy. We have already pointed out that the work of professional and amateur historians was germane to nineteenth-century politics, and indeed professional historians were unashamedly committed to supporting and upholding their "nation-states." National traditions in terms of rituals, celebrations, military exercises, and forms of dress were introduced to support the idea of long-standing histories.[27] Fundamental to the exercise was the propagation of the belief that the group's existence was of long duration.

In the enterprise of creating new, agreed histories to suit the political needs of the era, it was also imperative to overlook or obfuscate certain elements of history. This was not unapparent in the nineteenth century; witness Renan's proposition that a nation is a group of people who have many things in common and who have engaged in a common act of forgetting.[28] This proposition can be taken a stage further with the suggestion that members of a nation must *acknowledge*, indeed *remember*, what it is they have formally forgotten. The creation of a nation involves a joint agreement to leave a so-called "fratricidal" past behind. History, therefore, is constructed from the present backwards and is a matter of selecting useful or relevant elements to explain the present.

> Nations . . . have no clearly identifiable births, and their deaths, if they ever happen are never natural. Because there is no Originator, the nation's biography can not be written evangelically, "down time," through a long procreative chain of begettings. The only alternative is to fashion it "up time"—towards Peking Man, Java Man, King Arthur, wherever the lamp of archeology casts its fitful gleam. This fashioning, however, is marked by deaths, which, in a curious inversion of conventional genealogy, start from an originary present. World War II begets World War I; out of Sedan comes Austerlitz; the ancestor of the Warsaw Rising is the state of Israel.[29]

This reverse order understanding of the role of historical memory in con-stellating the national identities of states has hegemony in all the social sci-ences right now. History, in this view, is not a product of the past but a response to the requirements of the present. Anthropologists and political sci-entists study how particular historical accounts are used as tools in the con-temporary creation of identity and view all historians as partisan.[30]

Thus, if culture and historical memory have relevance to group definition, it is not because they explain the existence of groups, or explain divergent po-litical aims, but because they play a rhetorical role, operating as tools of per-suasion to get group members and the outside world to accept the identity the group has adopted. Habitual patterns of social interaction cause group differ-ence; culture and historical memory uphold group difference. And the fact that history can be framed in many different ways suggests that the purpose of the framing is what is relevant, rather than an objective account of histor-ical experience. Moreover, because framing is more important than any determination to adhere to fact, incentives to ensure that rhetorical history ad-heres to fact are fairly low.[31]

We see this clearly in those contested societies where not only the leader-ship but also the very identity of the society is being challenged. In such sit-uations, political discussions often take the form of historical debates. The groups in question may each have an understanding of history that has valid-ity, and yet the two narratives have zero-sum implications for the political en-vironment. History and historical memory take on a level of importance that seems atavistic to the outsider. And yet these historical discussions are artic-ulated with intensity and seriousness. All members of the society take part.

The preceding pages have explored many aspects of history's role in soci-ety by examining the role of myth in society, the constructed nature of ethnic groups and nations, the importance of boundary maintenance, and the rhetor-ical role of historical memories in supporting group definition. Where does this leave us with regard to the role of history in postconflict reconstruction? The messages are mixed.

To the degree that historical material offers operational codes to a society, its factual base may or may not be strong. But if the factual base is not strong, correcting people's ideas may be extremely difficult, given that people are living out the stories daily in their lives. Likewise, to the degree that histori-cal material assists in boundary making, people will be reluctant to subject it to criticism or change.

On the other hand, the notion that groups co-opt history to create a ration-ale for the existence of the group, or the domination of a political party, sug-gests historical material has only a temporary hold on the society: alternative myths and narratives might work just as well.

The latter assumption is made by those who are working toward a common, postconflict rendition of history in deeply divided societies. But the project of substituting one myth with another must recognize the role that myths and narratives have been playing in the individual lives of the populace.

The next section explores why it is that individuals become so engaged in the social manifestations of history.

WHY DO THE FOLLOWERS FOLLOW?

The capacity of narratives, in the form of political ideologies, to mobilize a population is heavily dependent upon the willingness of the masses to respond to those narratives. History provides material for the narratives. But what is it about these historical narratives that arouses such a strong emotional response from individuals?

The most obvious connection between history and the individual is when the individual has experienced harm that she can remember. To the degree that this harm is not addressed, and the oppressor is not held accountable, the individual will regard history as a personal matter. She will find a way to leave that history behind, mentally block it out, or else carry it with her, constantly seeking understanding and redress. Unhealed wounds will make such a person ready to be mobilized for political action that can right these wrongs. Leaders do not need to dig far to rouse public emotions about past injustices. Leaders who articulate the group narrative in a way that acknowledges the unhealed injuries of the group will have a ready following.

But history has a personal impact that goes beyond the experience of direct harm. Shared experience is a powerful human bond. Once any group is defined, the group develops common experiences. Moreover, group membership remains important because certain material and psychological needs are met best through group membership. People then remain attached to the narrative because it undergirds the existence of the group. Protecting the narrative becomes the same as protecting the group itself.

Group members want to protect the existence of a group for such instrumental reasons as retaining a sense of security and for material benefits. But individuals also become attached to group narratives for personal psychological reasons. Groups respond to needs for belonging, recognition, and a sense of psychological security. As individuals develop patterns of thought, narratives provide elements of a person's sense of self. Moreover, narratives provide a tangible way to explain inherited trauma. In this sense, regardless of the material benefits a person derives from group membership, the person will have a strong psychological proclivity to support certain narratives to keep her own psyche intact.

The following section elaborates on the ways that narratives contribute to personal identity, thus explaining why it is that people remain profoundly attached to particular historical memories.

Identification

People's sense of self is composed of two elements: the personal and the social.[32] Social identity, in other words our sense of being part of a group, contributes something to our overall sense of who we are. For an individual who has not developed a strong sense of self, social identity can be even more important than a sense of personal identity.

The dynamic by which personal identity definition interconnects with the mores of the group is the result of a biological imperative initially arising from the infant's need to survive. In order to procure what it needs, an infant takes on the mores and attitudes of significant others.

But identification with the group meets needs that go well beyond the biological. It offers security and protection and fulfills such psychological needs as the need for meaning, recognition, and response.[33]

Researchers in the field of human needs tell us that people will go to extraordinary lengths to control their environment in order to fulfill their needs, and external constraints are not going to be effective in controlling behaviors when human needs are denied.[34] The drive to fulfill basic human needs is seen by a number of psychologists as the primary force in the lives of people, and an authority that prevents this need fulfillment will be counterproductive because it will create frustration. The message challenges Hobbes's idea that society exists to restrain evil human nature. Instead, it suggests, the evils of society develop when attempts to constrain people deny their basic human needs.

Conflict, it can be argued, arises from the struggle to fulfill basic human needs.[35] Identification with the mores and ideology of the group is a means by which the infant gains control over his life and environment so that his basic needs can be satisfied. Thus the historical narratives, as well as the cultural symbols and behaviors, that define the group become crucial to meeting an individual's basic needs.

As life circumstances change, individuals may make new identifications to secure a variety of needs. At the same time, they will seek to protect identifications already made. "Identity enhancement leads to a greater sense of well-being; identity diffusion leads to anxiety and breakdown."[36] Ultimately, a synthesis of identifications to create identity stability is crucial for psychological health. This synthesis has been described as "ideology" by Erikson. Habermas describes it as an "identity-securing interpretive system."[37]

Because a large number of people are using similar material as they create "identity-securing interpretive systems," as a group, they have the potential to act together to enhance and protect that shared identity. This ensures the continuity of group culture.

Identification can be made with the material benefactor. For the infant, it is with the provider of nurture; for groups, it is with the political entity that benefits the group. Alternatively, identification is made with the model who provides the right mode of behavior in a situation of threat. According to Freud, this would be an oedipal identification where psychological security is attained by internalizing the behavior of the parent who represents a threat. In groups, this form of identification is used when the group follows a model for appropriate behavior and attitude in a situation of threat.

Identification with the Nation

The nation, with its politicized group identity and sense of connection with an existing or future state, is able to fulfill both sentimental and instrumental needs particularly well. The group attachment to an existing or future state apparatus suggests that the group has greater power at its disposal to fulfill needs. Particularly for oppressed groups, a national ideology can meet needs for dignity and self-esteem. At the same time, at the instrumental level, attachment to the national group helps fulfill the need for security, protection, predictability, material well-being, and self-transcendence. A person will extend loyalty to the nation to the degree that it meets these needs.[38]

While the nation provides a useful ideology or identity-securing interpretive system, national ideologies do not of themselves evoke identification. A shared group identification can only come out of real experience: the dynamics of some particular situation have to render it psychologically beneficial for the individual to make the identification. Symbols have to be appropriate in supplying the response to real experience.

> [Nations] must provide appropriate modes of behavior, appropriate attitudes, appropriate ideologies, appropriate identity-securing interpretive systems, for dealing with real, experienced situations. Popular support—i.e. identification with such an ideology—comes only if it interprets and provides an appropriate attitude for an experienced reality. This experience may, of course, be politically manipulated—but a symbol or an ideology *without* a relevant experience is meaningless and impotent.[39]

The author quoted above goes on to define "national identity" as "that condition in which a mass of people have made the same identification with national symbols—have internalized the symbols of the nation—so that they may act as one psychological group when there is a threat to, or the possibility of enhancement of, these symbols of national identity."[40] Here we can see the powerful potential of historical narratives to act as interpretive systems, enhancing personal identity and solidifying the group.

Shaping the Personal Sense of Self

Another way to examine how people absorb and become dependent upon ideas about the group is through the lens of personal psychological development.

The term *cultural amplifiers*[41] has been coined to describe cultural elements that influence a child's development of a sense of self. The process of creating a cohesive and integrated self-representation, which goes on at some level for the whole of life, involves integrating images, both pleasurable and unpleasurable, wanted and unwanted, as they appear. *Externalization* is a method of helping this process along by placing unintegrated images elsewhere. Cultural amplifiers provide containers to receive externalizations.

> For an American child, a cowboy hat becomes a reservoir of a "good" fragment of the self, and wearing it provides external support to the sense of self. For Finnish children, the sauna contains aspects of their own pleasurable selves as well as the image of a warm mother, or an angry, hot father. Children learn to take satisfaction in the properties of their own ethnic group—and to consider what is shared by those of another ethnic group as "bad." In Cyprus, for example, a Greek Orthodox church may seem to a Turkish child a container of his own bad aspects.[42]

Since these cultural amplifiers, or suitable targets of externalization, are shared by the parents of most children in a group, the children will expropriate them. "Bad suitable targets of externalization become the psychological foundation of the concept of enemy in a social and political sense. As the child grows, he becomes involved in abstracting a meaning from such shared targets, developing such sophisticated concepts as ethnicity or nationality."[43] While these shared targets do not necessarily have to be historical, they can be objects that have historical significance in the group.

Thus, negative historical images of the "other" get handed down from parent to child, performing a function in the identity development of the individual. To the degree that the individual fails to integrate within herself her

negative ideas about herself, she will require these outside negative elements
to keep her sense of self intact.

As a person develops a sense of self, her interpretations of reality are constantly undergoing revision as she tries to connect her inner and outer worlds.
The person copes with this through a process of construing, that is, abstracting recurring themes and their contrasts, and shaping these into personal dimensions of awareness which psychologists refer to as "personal constructs."
Our constructs encompass all aspects of our experience, including emotions,
values, and behavior.[44]

"Core constructs" give definition to all other constructs. They dictate a person's approach to life and sense of self, allowing the person to maintain a con-
tinuous sense of identity. We resist the alteration of these constructs because
such alteration challenges our core sense of self.

> If an individual comes upon new information that elicits a construct basically in-
> compatible with or invalidating to the core sense of self, it is likely that the new
> information will be rejected or redefined in order to fit the existing, rather
> impermeable constructs. It is also likely that this process of rejection and redef-
> inition (called "aggression" by Kelly 1955) will be characterized by a high emo-
> tional charge and a great sense of urgency. In a sense, if one's core sense of self,
> the identity, is threatened by the demands, behavior, or identity of another per-
> son, then psychic or even physical annihilation will seem to be imminent.[45]

A sense of threat or victimization can therefore be experienced in several
different ways. First there is the trauma itself, then the group solidarity that it
enhances, and finally the development of a core construct of victimization.
People's sense of self is profoundly rooted in a particular view of events, and
they will feel threatened in a deep way if someone tries to make them see
these events differently.

Inherited Trauma

The most direct, personal link between the present and the distant past is the
one described in the field of psychoanalysis. An experience of catastrophe is
carried psychologically from one generation to the next and, while memory
of that event is likely to be maintained in the public arena through rhetorical
history, the personal effect can be understood as separate and profound.

A person who has experienced a trauma firsthand undergoes an injury to self-
representation too great to accept. He therefore bundles together the traumatized self-representation[46] with its object representations, affects, unconscious
and conscious fantasies, and externalizes this onto the self-representation of a
developing child. The child absorbs the traumatized person's wishes and ex-

pectations and thus becomes the repository for the troublesome parts of the older generation's psyche. If the child fails to find a way to mourn the trauma, and so deal with its accompanying shame, humiliation, and sense of helplessness, the child will pass the same patterns of self-representation down to subsequent generations. The term *transgenerational transmission* has been coined to describe this process.[47]

> When the carrier of the deposited representation grows up, he or she usually also has a conscious knowledge of the traumatic event that had befallen the parents, grandparents, or great-grandparents simply through hearing family stories. But, what influences him or her on an internal structural level is not the historical truth about the trauma, but the unconscious obligation to deal with the deposited representation.[48]

In a group, members' traumatized self-images may well refer to one and the same calamity. This is how genuine historical memories become part of the group psyche, as well as providing superficial ethnic markers or material for social identification.

The term *chosen trauma* describes the collective memory of a calamity. The word *chosen* might suggest either that the individuals in the group have exercised an option whether or not to focus on the trauma or that an elite, or leader's, choice was involved in highlighting the significance of the trauma. But in fact it means neither. Chosen traumas reflect an unconscious choice to define identity through transgenerational transmission.[49]

As time goes on, mythologized elements get added to the event. The group's interpretation of the trauma goes through various transformations. Legends get added. A group's chosen trauma can lie dormant for a time, in which case a political leader may play a role in igniting the dormant group memory. This overall process may distort the group's perception and cause new enemies to appear as old enemies. Mobilization by an elite can recharge historical memories, but this is only possible because some imprint from the past is already in place.

The collective memory of chosen traumas is more than a simple account of the past. Volkan describes it as a "shared mental representation of the event, which included realistic information, fantasized expectations, intense feelings, and defenses against unacceptable thoughts."[50] These dynamics together prepare the ground for "time collapse," in other words, literally believing that the same realities that applied in the past apply today. Time collapse really means sharing an identification with a person of long ago. For example, says Volkan, as the recent crisis in Bosnia developed, Serbs in Belgrade conflated Muslims with Turks and spoke as if they genuinely believed the Turks were going to invade Serbia; Serbs felt entitled to do to Muslims in Bosnia what

Turks in the past had done to Serbs. Bosnian Muslims had no military power; but Serbs began to see a real threat based on their own past trauma.

As a result, long past calamities retain great power in the present. People continue to retell the story, but individuals identify with the story, not simply because of frequent repetition but because of a personal connection arising from transgenerational transmission. Simultaneously, the sense of group identity becomes firmer because of the negative characterization of the oppressor group.

Victimization

Another way to understand the persistent power of group enmity is to study the psychology of victimhood. Humans maintain ties to family and other institutions, including social groups, in order to develop defenses against life's inevitable losses. A trauma that breaks those affiliations creates a wound that shatters this sense of safety, and it is extremely difficult to overcome the resulting sense of victimhood. Three components to this sense of victimization have been identified: the experience of violence, the sense of injustice, and the sense of threat of further violence and loss. Victims tend to conclude that passivity ensures further victimization. The victim feels driven to act aggressively in defense of the *self*, including the group self, in order to reduce the threat of aggression. This dynamic is at the root of much violence and terrorism.

This same victimization dynamic occurs between groups. "The egoism of victimization is the incapacity of an ethno-national group, as a direct result of its own historical traumas, to empathize with the suffering of another group. . . . Ethno-national groups that have been traumatized by repeated suffering at the hands of other groups seem to have little capacity to grieve for the hurts of other peoples, or to take responsibility for the new victims created by their own warlike actions."[51]

HISTORICAL MEMORY IN POSTCONFLICT SOCIETIES

For all the reasons outlined in the previous pages, a society that is in political and social flux is particularly resistant to altering its myths and narratives. Moreover, the reshaping of history and historical memory is never an entirely neutral matter. And yet this is not a reason to abandon the project. Changing the way history is disseminated and taught will be very difficult, but this must be pursued because the lies, the injustices, and the traumas of the society must be addressed. A more sensitive study of history should enable groups to gain more understanding of each other to assure ongoing co-operation, safety, and recognition. It is harder to be certain that such an exercise can issue in a common narrative.

Truth

The first goal of any endeavor to rewrite history must be to bring the truth into the open. Telling the truth, first of all, means acknowledgment of painful and controversial events. But a society grounded in truth telling gains for other reasons. When freedom of speech is limited and political ideologies encounter minimal criticism, leaders can expand their mythologizing to employ lies or gross exaggerations. A society that fails to challenge the lies of its leaders will soon experience other kinds of oppression. Most societies mired in profound conflict or oppressive dictatorship recognize that the death of honesty and accountability was an early stage in their downward spiral. Moreover, literature on causes of international violence cites "chauvinist mythmaking" as a significant contributor to violence and war. A key purpose for disseminating truthful history is, therefore, that if the populace knows the true facts, it will not respond to the chauvinism of aggressive leaders who are trying to rally them to war.[52]

Beyond this, acceptance of benchmarks by which truth and honesty can be established is a significant societal norm that has an impact on the legal system and is a basic protection against corruption. Historians can set a standard for truth and accuracy by requiring corroboration of evidence, citation, and primary sources and by fostering discussion, debate, and critical thinking. A historical profession that exempts no aspect of the past from investigation is an insurance against the suppressive potential of cultural hegemony.

Ironically, the notion of historical accuracy is challenged by the very concerns outlined in the first part of this chapter. In our postmodern age, truth has come to be recognized as a product of social realities and never absolute. But historians have to find a way to overcome this paralyzing truism. Most mainstream historians, consciously or unconsciously, embrace "practical realism," the acknowledgment of an inexact correspondence between language and what is being described, as an escape from total relativism.[53] All historical accounts involve some aspect of framing: this is a matter of interpretation. But holding information to a high standard of verification is a good starting place when critiquing politicized memory.

Beyond the goal of bolstering societal norms of accuracy and honesty, the commitment to unearthing the truth is key to the acknowledgment of past trauma and injustice. Societies that have misrepresented their past need to remove the veil and consider forms of reparation and healing that will allow the society to move forward creatively.

Justice

Whether they occurred long ago or recently, unaddressed injustices create a running sore that persists for generations. This is not merely a political matter, though indeed grievances are a means of mobilization of a low power group. Injustice festers in the lives of individuals. Those who suffered from it usually live with effects of the injustice long after the rest of society has tried to forget. As a result, injustice sets up a victim syndrome that can be a source of anger, aggression, flouting of the legal order, and lack of productivity.

Justice can take many forms. We tend to think of justice as a legal matter, and legal processes against those responsible for gross violations of human rights are supremely important. The court system imposes a kind of justice we could call retributive, in that someone pays a penalty through a process of punishment. But because of this possibility of punishment, justice processes based on legal mechanisms may well make it more difficult to establish the facts of the case: those who face trial will give an account of their actions that enables them to escape with the mildest sentence. This tradeoff between justice and truth has to be considered when a postconflict society attempts to find out the facts about its past.[54]

Whether or not the legal system is invoked for the sake of punishment, justice can take other forms that are less contentious, support future relationships, and make it more likely that the facts of the conflict will emerge. Restorative justice of this type includes, first of all, acknowledgment and goes on to seek forms of reparation that do not increase anger and polarization.

Historical writing can hasten these processes by bringing before the public eye past injustices and incorporating the facts that emerge in hearings or trials. Some forms of historical expression can, in themselves, be restorative, such as the creation of memorials and commemorations. When school history teaching and textbooks incorporate social injustices of the recent past, we can take this as a signal that the society has moved ahead significantly in accepting pieces of the past that have lingered in the shadows.

Trauma, Mourning, and Healing

If justice is the rational means of addressing the ills of the past, mourning is its emotional counterpart. The lingering memory of trauma suffered by individuals or groups does not fade with time, even if it goes underground for significant spells. It can place burdens on individuals and become the chief source of meaning making in groups. Collective responses to harms and injustices of the past are a frequent underlying contributor to the next battle or war. A society that wishes to move beyond its past must seek ways to lay that past to rest.

Trauma psychologists advise against repeated discussions of the traumatizing event with recent victims of trauma.[55] The traumatized victim needs time to heal without being called upon to relive the trauma repeatedly. Therapists trained in this specialization must be center stage in working with such people. It is not within the scope of this project to explore the nature of their work. One question needs to be raised, however, which is very much related: when and in what circumstances is it beneficial for a traumatized individual to participate in a group process of reexamining the past?

This question has considerable relevance for the material in the rest of this book. While postconflict societies may be capable of addressing some aspects of their immediate past, timing is crucial. It seems clear that time has to pass before these societies will be able to talk about what happened and thus to begin to mourn in public as a group. From a political standpoint, it may not be possible to discuss the past until new political realities are in place. But this is also a personal issue—if the grief is too great, people need time to shut it out, heal inwardly, and get on with their lives.

In the end, however, those who have been involved in a conflict must talk about it, and those on all sides must find a way of listening to each other. Talking and listening are needed even if the traumatic event occurred several generations previously.

> All sides must do a great deal of listening to the telling of history, especially of each group's hurts and its version of where responsibility has lain. . . . Little by little acknowledgment of the victim experience of another group can occur. . . . In this way bonds can be forged between groups, so that they can begin to substitute mutual empathy for the egoism of victimization. This connecting can serve as a model for each adversary society and, eventually, across national borders."[56]

What is being described here is a mourning process.[57] The way to ensure that present generations do not continue to participate in the traumas of the past is to make it possible for them to complete a mourning process that was not completed by their forebears. Mourning is a necessary reaction to loss and change. A group's inability to mourn can have political outcomes. It is this inability to mourn that allows memories, whether or not they have been given the subsequent gloss of mythology, to be carried into the next generation as emotional wounds. If mourning can occur, the next generation creates a new version of the event, strengthening the group's self-esteem and moving into the future without having to carry the burden of the past.[58]

Beyond talking about the past, societies can mourn their past by building monuments or museums, creating days of remembrance, or using music, art, theater, literature, or film creatively and collectively to remember.

It has been argued that joint mourning processes are an essential prerequisite for effective peace negotiations. Montville speaks of an act of "letting go" that is needed on both sides, where victimizers accept responsibility for their acts, recognize injustices done, and ask forgiveness. Likewise, victims may also have been victimizers and may have to recognize their own acts of injustice.[59] Yet peace negotiations usually occur simultaneously with the final throes of the conflict itself and are therefore unlikely to include the kind of mourning processes that are possible in the postnegotiation phase. Mourning is better understood as a continuing experience that extends well into the postconflict period.

The Search for a Single Narrative, Group Identity, and Intercultural Understanding

Emphasis on the recent construction of groups and instrumentalist uses of history in their formation can lead us to conclude that ethnic and national loyalties are impermanent and easily altered by correcting the history. Based on this notion, we can imagine that one way to move a society out of conflict is to assist in the development of a single narrative that will draw the two ethnonational groups together. Many of those who undertake revision of school history teaching and textbooks see the writing of a common history as their goal.

But ideas about the constructed nature of groups can distract attention from the continuity of the group, the primary hold that ethnic identity has on an individual,[60] and the fact that whatever its beginnings, group identity, once constellated, is a fact with social and political consequences.

In deeply divided societies, the ethnonational groups concerned live with a fear of annihilation at the hand of the other. This fear has become a core construct for individuals and is central to the group narrative. In the long run, to alter the conflict-perpetuating cycle, these fears of annihilation and the sense of victimhood that accompanies them must be acknowledged and understood, not dismissed. Without some form of acknowledgment, individuals will be utterly resistant to new ideas about the past.

In this type of society, therefore, the narratives of the several groups must at some level be honored. This does not mean untruths and injustices should be overlooked. The key point here is that often there exists more than one way of giving a true account of what happened. Contentious histories begin with the fact that several groups may have experienced history differently. Different aspects of history hold different levels of salience in the memory of the respective groups. The path to bridging this difference is to address the obfuscations of one's own group and thus give some validity to the narrative of the other.

But a further challenge arises in the course of such an exercise. For the respective narratives may well negate each other in some zero-sum fashion. What is particularly salient for one group may have a reverse significance for the other. Here we are not dealing with pure obfuscation, but with the fact that each group has adopted core constructs that are diametrically opposed to the very constructs that the other group holds dear.

It is a commonplace to note that in Irish history Protestant victories were Catholic defeats, and vice versa, and, to a considerable degree, this is true. For example, the victories memorialized in "the Sash," the quintessential Orange song—Derry, Aughrim, Enniskillen, and the Boyne—all are instances of Protestant victory (or at least heroism) in the face of Catholic assault and conversely they fit into Catholic mythology as occasions of lamentation. King William III of Orange, the man on the white horse in Protestant iconography (again, notice the thinking: white against black) serves simultaneously as the equivalent of a Protestant secular saint and as a demon figure in Catholic history. . . . Similarly, what was perceived during most of the nineteenth century as Catholic Ireland's greatest problem—the political union of Great Britain and Ireland of 1801—was for most Protestants not a problem but a much needed answer, in this case an answer to the question of how to avoid being swallowed up by the Catholic majority. Thus, for the two religious groups, the meaning of nineteenth century Ireland's most important political event, the union, was diametrically opposite.[61]

Alteration of people's ideas about history must, therefore, occur in a gradual fashion that gently creates cognitive dissonance, while not threatening the core sense of identity of self or group.

Indeed, since the several groups involved in the conflict are deeply preoccupied with the protection of their group identity, one way to reassure them in the postconflict phase is to give recognition to the narrative of each group. What this really means is acknowledging that the groups perceived and experienced the past differently, and that this fact is itself part of the history.

Part Two

NORTHERN IRELAND
AND THE TROUBLES

Chapter Three

A Brief History of the Northern Ireland Conflict

By the end of the first millennium, Ireland was populated by intermingled Celts and Vikings who had invaded in the previous thousand years. St. Patrick had Christianized the island in the first half of the fifth century. During the so-called Dark Ages, following the fall of the Roman Empire, Irish monasteries played an important role in keeping alive Christianity and the learning of Roman times. They sent Christian missions to Scotland, to other parts of Britain, and to Europe. Throughout this period, interchange between Ireland and the island of Great Britain was constant.

The Norman invasions of Ireland, beginning in 1169, mark the start of a consistent policy of the kings ruling in Westminster to extend their control to Ireland. This date has retained considerable symbolic importance in the Irish nationalist narrative. The Normans who came to Ireland from England introduced a new governmental mechanism in the person of a Lord Deputy, who acted as the King of England's representative in Ireland. During the Middle Ages, the Lord Deputy called together an embryonic Council and Parliament whose main duties were to give advice and raise taxes to support the English king. In the fourteenth and fifteenth centuries, English influence declined to the point that it was only felt in towns and in an area immediately around Dublin known as the Pale.

King Henry VII (1485-1509), the first modern English king, centralized his administration and extended English control beyond the Pale. Henry's great-great-grandson, King James I (1603-1625), took the single most important step in continuing these policies when he began to offer land in the northeast province of Ulster to those who had claims on his patronage. This new departure, which began in 1609, held a double attraction for James: not only was he developing a following who were indebted to him but the Ulster settlements seemed likely to reduce the probability of rebellion in the region. Moreover, as Britain had now become Protestant and Ireland remained Catholic, King James was concerned that Ireland could be a staging area for a Catholic invasion of England. The settlers were required to be Protestant so that plantations would reduce the hold of Catholicism in Ireland. They were expected to clear their estates completely of native Irish, build defensive works, bring in craftsmen, found schools, and build parish churches.[1] These planters came from Scotland as well as England and represented all social classes. Londonderry, known as Derry to the native Irish, was a case apart, where companies created by the guilds of the City of London received grants from King James to develop County Londonderry in a similar fashion to the joint stock ventures of the Virginia Company and East India Company.

Though the plantations did not succeed in their mission of totally evicting native Irish from their land, they alienated the local population sufficiently that they rebelled in 1641. In this uprising probably around 2,000 settlers were killed, and in retaliatory attacks numerous native Irish also died.[2] During the following decade, in the context of the English Civil War, the English army under Cromwell pursued a bloody retribution aimed at subjugating all of Ireland, which culminated in 1649 with massacres at Drogheda and Wexford. Thousands were killed, thousands more executed, and even greater numbers were sent into exile in the West Indies or mainland Europe.

The seventeenth century in English, Scottish, and Irish history is a tale of bloody competition to resolve the politico-religious uncertainties introduced by the Reformation. The two key issues were the contest between the power of the King and the power of Parliament and the contest between Catholicism and Protestantism. These issues became utterly intertwined. The crisis reached its climax in the 1680s, and Ireland was the staging ground. King James II, a closet Catholic, had been tolerated by his Protestant parliament until the birth of his son in 1688, whom he baptized Catholic. The vision of a future Catholic monarch at the head of the Church of England was unacceptable to Parliament. In 1688, Parliament deposed James and called in his nephew and son-in-law, the Dutch Protestant Prince William of Orange, to rule jointly with his wife (James's daughter), Mary. James attempted a comeback, bankrolled by the Catholic Louis XIV of France, and succeeded in raising a pro-Catholic army in Ireland. His ultimate defeat, at the Battle of the Boyne in Ireland, is the basis for the Protestant parades that take place every July 12 in Northern Ireland to this day.

After James's defeat, legislation was passed in Westminster making it impossible for a Catholic to inherit the throne or for a monarch to be married to a Catholic. Creating stability was now the priority, and stability was perceived to be served by suppressing Catholicism.[3] In 1691, King William signed the

Treaty of Limerick, guaranteeing religious freedom to Catholics in Ireland and security of tenure on their land, but the treaty was broken immediately. A series of acts known as the Penal Laws, passed in the late seventeenth and early eighteenth centuries, severely restricted the religious, educational, professional, and civic life of Catholics. Bishops were outlawed; Catholic orders were banned; priests had to register or flee. Catholics could not buy, inherit, or lease land, own a horse valued over five pounds, hold government franchises, or belong to trade guilds unless they took the Anglican communion. Catholics' control over education of their people was severely curtailed. At this time in Europe generally, state religion dictated the practice of the people, and the Treaty of Westphalia (1648) allowed religious minorities five years' grace in which to move to another state.[4] In Ireland, however, those refusing to follow the state religion were a majority, not a minority, and their numbers and geographical position made it unthinkable for them to go elsewhere.

During the eighteenth century, an elite class, known as the "Ascendancy," blossomed in Ireland. They worshiped in the "established" church (in other words, the church linked to the British crown), which was Anglican.[5] They owned large amounts of land in Ireland, dominated the Dublin parliament, and retained strong links with England.

The late eighteenth century saw a move toward parliamentary reform in Dublin, undoubtedly prompted by ideas in America and in France. In this context, the Penal Laws were gradually lifted by legislation in 1778, 1781, 1782, and 1793, but Catholics still could not own land, vote, or run for political office.

The first attempt to define and assert a modern Irish nationalism came just before the end of the century and was led by a Protestant, Wolfe Tone, whose republican vision, modeled on the French definition of the nation, included all confessional groups. Tone's 1798 uprising failed miserably, in part because French troops coming to his aid failed to link up with him. But the episode was enough to convince Westminster that Ireland needed to be held under closer control. In 1801, with the Act of Union, the Dublin parliament was closed down, and Irish elected representatives went to Westminster.

In the course of the nineteenth century, the idea of Irish nationalism became increasingly linked with Catholic and ethnic Irish concerns so that, by midcentury, Irish nationalism was ethnic rather than civic in character. In the 1820s, 1830s and 1840s, Daniel O'Connell, the first European political leader to understand and use tactics of broad political mobilization, headed this movement. In 1829, his campaign for "Catholic Emancipation" succeeded in bringing Catholics into the representative political system, and this was followed shortly afterward by success in gaining a reduction of 25 percent in the tithe paid by all Irish to the Anglican Church.

O'Connell went on to lead the first of a series of attempts in the nineteenth century to overthrow the "union," in other words to remove Ireland from the jurisdiction of the Westminster parliament. O'Connell's Repeal Movement of the 1840s aimed to accomplish this by parliamentary means. His natural successors were the Home Rule movement of the 1870s, 1880s, and early 1890s. Neither the Repealers nor the Home Rule movement envisaged complete independence for Ireland but rather a relationship with Britain something like that of Canada, which had attained dominion status and its own parliament in 1867.

Other Irish nationalist movements, most specifically the Fenians and the Irish Republican Brotherhood (later renamed the Irish Republican Army [IRA]), aimed to overthrow the union with Britain by use of force.

The rise of these revolutionary movements was assisted by the galvanizing effects of the Great Famine of midcentury. The Irish had become heavily dependent on the potato because growing enough potatoes to feed a family did not require very much land. In a country of rapid population growth, where landowners often cultivated wheat for export, the potato was a solution for tenant farmers whose plots were small. But when the potato crop failed, wheat continued to be exported, leaving the ordinary people with no alternative food supply.

The blight that rotted the roots and leaves of the potato plants in 1845 had been seen before, but what was unusual was that the following summer the blight returned. The British Prime Minister tried to respond by lifting the grain tariff to allow free trade of grain. He also brought shiploads of corn from America to Ireland. But efforts to distribute this food fell pitifully short of what was needed. The price of grain rose, and profiteers at the ports did very well in the crisis. Tenant farmers who were unable to pay their rents were thrown off their land.

The British government's response to the famine was largely overseen by Charles Trevelyan, an official who took the decision to limit public distribution of free food and instead to institute public works projects that would employ people so they could pay for food. Money to finance these public works projects was not sent to Ireland from the British government itself; rather, relief works were to be financed in Ireland. This placed a level of pressure on the Irish economy that it was unable to bear. Soon public works projects broke down altogether, and people were forced to go to soup kitchens where contamination often spread dysentery.

At least a million people out of a population of 8 million died in the famine, and a further 1.5 million emigrated. In a ten-year period, the population dropped 35 percent. That the British government mismanaged its response to the famine is clear, though it would be incorrect to say that it did nothing.

Westminster contributed some seven million pounds in aid, or just under half of the total amount paid in famine relief. From one point of view it was the first time a European state had done as much to cope with a natural disaster; from another, it was a pitiful response, considering that the annual tax revenue of the United Kingdom at this time was about 53 million pounds,[6] and the United Kingdom was the preeminent world power.

Catholics suffered more than Protestants, partly because Ulster, where many Protestants lived, happened to be less hard hit but also because Protestants were overly represented in the ruling, landowning class. The famine, or "Great Hunger," left subsequent generations of Catholics shocked and embittered not simply because of the loss they experienced but because of the callous nature of Britain's response. The famine, therefore, added to the bitter feeling of Catholics toward Protestants and created a body of immigrants in the United States who were committed to send money back home to finance movements for Home Rule or independence for Ireland. More generally it contributed to Catholics' already growing sense of political identity, which was coming to define Irish nationalism.

The 1880s were a crucial turning point in Irish politics and in the development of the character of Irish nationalism. Charles Stewart Parnell, a Protestant, became the spearhead of the Home Rule movement. The likelihood of success for the movement grew exponentially when Parnell gained the support of the Liberal Prime Minister Gladstone for the cause of Home Rule. Home Rule failed to pass in Westminster in 1886, however, because the Liberal Party split over the issue. Home Rule failed again in 1893, largely because of the disarray in the Irish Parliamentary Party following Parnell's citation as corespondent in a divorce case by the husband of the woman he had been living with for some years.

The period had been a watershed in Irish politics not only because of the near passage of Home Rule. Land reforms of 1879 had tripled the Irish electorate by giving tenant farmers the possibility to purchase their land and thus, as landowners, gain the vote. As a result, in 1885 not only large numbers of Catholics but the Catholic Church itself were for the first time fully mobilized in an election campaign. The Church's involvement alienated many Protestants from the cause of Home Rule. Unionism, that is, the belief that Ireland should remain part of Britain, took hold as a political philosophy during this period at a new level of intensity.

Protestants, concentrated in Ulster, turned away from Home Rule in the late nineteenth century for two principal reasons. First, Belfast and Ulster had grown remarkably during the century, and Belfast was now one of the premier ports of the British Empire. Business links with London, Liverpool, and Glasgow were considerable, and the Ulster owners of these businesses increasingly perceived their future to lie not with a devolved Ireland but with England. Second, Ulster Protestants, who were profoundly anti-Catholic, were concerned by the increasing identification of Irish nationalism with Catholicism. Moreover, Protestants recognized they would be reduced to minority status in a predominantly Catholic Ireland that had achieved Home Rule. The irony of the 1880s is that the very process that so successfully mobilized Ireland to support Home Rule created a new source of opposition. And the fact that the minority opposed to Home Rule were concentrated in one area intensified their views and made them more difficult to ignore. After the 1880s there ceased to be sufficient unity of will within the island to accept Home Rule.

Despite this resistance, the British parliament passed Home Rule for Ireland in 1912. Ulster Protestants were now so opposed they prepared for civil war by importing arms and training a paramilitary army—the Ulster Volunteer Force. Catholics started their own paramilitary unit—the Irish Volunteers. The crisis was staved off by the outbreak of World War I and an agreement to postpone Irish Home Rule until the war was over. An insurrection in Dublin on Easter Monday of 1916, to be known to history as the Easter Rising, protested the postponement of Home Rule and called for full independence. It was put down within a week, and the British authorities executed fifteen of the leaders. This act hardened more moderate opinion in Ireland. In elections at the end of World War I, the party calling for complete separation from Britain, Sinn Féin, won overwhelming support, except in Protestant majority constituencies. The Sinn Féin victory further alienated the Protestants of the North. Civil insurrection was sharpening the crisis. The British authorities adopted the same compromise position they would resort to in India in 1947—partition.

CREATION OF THE STATE OF NORTHERN IRELAND

The 1920 Government of Ireland Act established separate administrations for the North and the South, keeping both entities under the final authority of the British crown. This act was to prove unacceptable to the South and become a dead letter there, but in the North it was to be the foundation of the polity of Northern Ireland. According to the Government of Ireland Act, North and South were each to have their own parliament. A Council of Ireland was to be formed to liaise between the North and South, with the idea that the two would move in the direction of unity in the future. In addition, a Boundary Commission was set up to review the positioning of the border, which had "temporarily" excluded parts of traditional Ulster to ensure the North a Protestant majority. Although the Protestant majority in Northern Ireland proceeded to create their new state, the apparent fluidity of the arrangement fed their sense of insecurity.

The Government of Ireland Act was not accepted in the South, because the Sinn Féin party was advocating the creation of an independent Irish republic that would encompass the entire island. By this time, the military arm of Sinn Féin had organized itself into the Irish Republican Army (IRA). The IRA's two-year guerilla war against Britain ended with a treaty between London and Dublin in 1921 that created a devolved state in the South, the Irish Free State, with dominion status. The treaty's acceptance of partition triggered a civil war between the extreme (i.e., antipartition) and moderate Irish nationalists that ended in 1923 with the victory of the moderates. In the mid-1930s Prime Minister De Valera ended the Free State's status as a dominion and made Ireland merely "externally associated" with the Commonwealth. De Valera also altered the South's official stance toward the North: a revamped constitution of 1937 stated in Articles Two and Three that the Irish nation had jurisdiction over the whole island and that the laws of the Irish state applied only in the twenty-six counties of the South, "pending reintegration of the national territory."

From 1923 Dublin consciously undertook the task of nation-building by shoring up the distinctive elements of Irish nationalism. The link between the Catholic Church and the Irish state was strong, and the Irish constitution legally enforced the social values of Catholicism. The new Irish polity promoted the Gaelic language and Gaelic culture and encouraged the teaching of an emotive, anti-British history in schools. During the depression, under De Valera's leadership, it pursued an economic policy of autarky, and during the Second World War was neutral, further alienating Northern Protestants.[7] In 1948 Ireland declared itself a republic and severed all constitutional ties with Britain.

When it joined the European Community in 1973, Ireland was categorized with the poorest of the European economies. European money was therefore pumped into the Irish economy in the subsequent quarter century, and by the mid-1990s Ireland's had become the fastest-growing economy in Europe.

The North was not unaffected by the Irish Civil War. In 1920, northern Catholics, who had traditionally been strongly nationalist, that is, supportive of a united Ireland, and who comprised one-third of the population of the North, made clear their opposition to the creation of the new statelet. The IRA in the North committed acts of violence, and the security forces retaliated. Unionist authorities created an Ulster Special Constabulary to maintain order. Recruitment was based on the old Ulster Volunteer Force, and no effort was made to recruit Catholics. Thus a paid Protestant paramilitary force, sanctioned by Westminster, was created to keep the peace. Between July 1920 and

July 1922, 303 Catholics, 172 Protestants, and 82 members of the security forces were killed. In addition, between 9,000 and 11,000 Catholics were driven from their jobs in Belfast, 23,000 Catholics were forced out of their homes, and about 500 Catholic businesses were destroyed.[8]

A Special Powers Act was invoked in 1922, initially because of the civil war and its spillover into the North. This meant no *habeas corpus*, home searches permitted, and the death penalty for possession and use of explosives. The act was renewed annually until 1933, when it was made permanent. To Protestants, the law seemed reasonable: their argument was that only those who wanted to rebel would find it otherwise. To Catholics, the Special Powers Act was one more sign of oppression.

In subsequent decades housing and job discrimination to the disfavor of Catholics were rife, and boundaries for electoral districts were heavily bent to maximize the strength of the dominant political party. As in all parts of Great Britain, voting in local elections was open to rate payers only; in other words, you had to own a dwelling or pay rent in order to vote. Entrepreneurs had an additional six votes for every company they owned. These practices were abolished in Great Britain in the late 1940s but remained in Northern Ireland until the late 1960s.

Northern Ireland's government proceeded not unlike that of a one-party state. Westminster was determined to get Irish affairs out of British politics and established the convention that matters pertaining to Northern Ireland were to be discussed in Belfast, apart from a small number of issues reserved for Westminster's handling, even though Northern Ireland continued to send elected representatives to Westminster. Poverty, joblessness, and the housing shortage were the worst in the United Kingdom during the depression and into the 1950s. When the Labour government was elected in Britain in 1946, bringing with it the welfare state, nationalization of health services, and a sweeping education act, all the people of Northern Ireland benefited, but these changes had enormous significance for Catholics, somewhat reducing the intensity of their interest in unification.

In the 1950s the antipartition movement had reached its lowest ebb. The Nationalist Party's attempts at peaceful constitutional agitation had achieved nothing. Temporarily, this gave new energy to the IRA for an offensive that began in December 1956 and continued sporadically until 1962, when the IRA called its men off active service, embraced a more traditional Marxism, and abandoned the use of violence.

By the early 1960s the North's economy was facing a serious slump. Harland and Wolff was still the largest shipbuilding unit in the world, but it had failed to make the changes necessary to respond to international demand for oil tankers and bulk carriers. The linen and aircraft industries were also in decline. In addition, technical progress in agriculture was creating further un-employment. The entire United Kingdom was adjusting to the loss of its imperial markets and the Second World War's drain on its resources. But Northern Ireland continued to trail the rest of the United Kingdom on most measures of prosperity.[9]

THE CRISIS OF 1968-1972

Captain Terence O'Neill, elected Prime Minister of Northern Ireland in 1963, introduced economic reforms and attempted more open relations between the two communities and with the South.[10] Some Protestants resented these moves both because they distrusted O'Neill's policies of centralized planning and because they saw their own power threatened. Soon, in addition, O'Neill's inability to deliver on the reforms he had promised alienated the mi-nority whose hopes he had raised. It was in this context that the civil rights movement came into being, emulating the civil rights movement in the United States and the student revolution in France and calling for justice in housing, jobs, and voting rights for Catholics.

The first civil rights marches occurred in the summer of 1968. In January 1969, a march from Belfast to Londonderry emulating King's march from Selma to Montgomery was ambushed several miles from Derry by loyalists (extreme Protestants) throwing rocks, many of whom were later identified as local, off-duty members of the Special Constabulary. During the season in July when Protestants hold their traditional marches, Catholics threw bottles at the marchers. In August, the Royal Ulster Constabulary (RUC, in other words, the police) invaded the Catholic section of Derry—the Bogside—smashing doors, throwing stones, and singing sectarian songs.

The RUC was overwhelmed by the requirements placed upon it to keep the peace. The situation deteriorated in August 1969 both in terms of the level of violence and of the number of towns involved. Guns became part of the fight-ing in Belfast on the night of August 14-15 when Protestants rushed into the Catholic area of the Falls, throwing petrol bombs as they went. Later evi-dence showed that the Special Constabulary had given support to this attack. Six people were killed in Belfast during that week, and twelve factories and over one hundred houses were destroyed. On Friday, August 15, the British government agreed to send British troops to Belfast to keep the peace. The troops were initially welcomed by the people of Belfast, both Catholic and Protestant.

The ad hoc nature of the decision to call in the British army marked the be-ginning of a series of problems at the heart of the Northern Ireland conflict relating to the security forces. One of the main problems was establishing the relationship between the British army on the one hand and the local police— the RUC—on the other. London proceeded to take increasing control over security, disbanding the Special Constabulary and creating from it a new army regiment of locally recruited soldiers. The RUC was disarmed and demilitarized, and the army assumed the chief peacekeeping role even though the Northern Ireland government retained the principal policy-making power.

In August 1971, at the recommendation of Stormont, internment (i.e., imprisonment without charge) was introduced; but this measure only increased the level of disturbance and violence. The deteriorating situation caused British Prime Minister Edward Heath to decide to transfer responsibility for law and order to Westminster. In response, the Prime Minister of Northern Ireland resigned, and direct rule began. The Northern Ireland government was suspended, and the Stormont parliament was shut down. Northern Ireland continued to send elected representatives to Westminster, but now ministerial appointments to Northern Ireland portfolios were made by the British government and sat in the British Cabinet.

HARDENING OF THE CONFLICT

During the early years of the Troubles, investigation into civil rights abuses brought a new level of acknowledgment of these social ills. Most notably, the Cameron Commission, appointed by the O'Neill government in 1969 to investigate the disturbances of 1968, concluded that in certain areas, ward boundaries for local government produced a permanent unionist majority, even when this bore no relation to the numerical strength of the unionists in the city. The Cameron Commission also recognized the nepotism of unionist-controlled local government councils.[11] As a result civil rights legislation was passed to address discrimination on housing and voting, and a Fair Employment Agency was set up in 1976[12] to address job discrimination.

But by the mid-1970s the conflict had moved beyond the concerns of the civil rights marchers. Reunification was now part of the Catholic/nationalist political program. The ready availability of Irish nationalism as an ideology and the proximity of the Republic as a compelling alternative government made this turn of events almost inevitable. The Northern Ireland conflict quickly became a contest of two nationalist ideologies: one claiming the whole of the island of Ireland on behalf of a Catholic/Gaelic nationalism, the other claiming that Northern Ireland rightfully should remain part of the British state. Compromise seemed increasingly impossible.

This rigidification of the conflict was assisted by the violent acts of paramilitaries, the police, and the army. In August 1969, Catholic militants criticized the traditional IRA for its failure to defend Catholics from attacks by Protestants, who were in some cases assisted by the police. The IRA, restrained by its recently adopted nonviolent stance, was taunted by Catholics as the "I Ran Away." At the end of 1969 the IRA split. The new Provisional IRA that emerged as a result aimed to give teeth to the IRA as an effective source of protection for Catholics. The Provisional IRA (PIRA, though over time the initials IRA have come to be used to refer to this group) perceived the British troops brought in to keep the peace in 1969 as the traditional enemy and urged violence against the British and against Northern Ireland security forces who supported British presence. The introduction of internment only exacerbated the situation, which sharpened further when British paratroopers fired on a group of unarmed Catholic civil rights marchers in Derry on January 30, 1972, killing fourteen. The incident, known as Bloody Sunday, remains etched in the minds of Catholics as confirmation of British injustice, the more so because the subsequent official inquiry into the incident whitewashed the paratroopers' responsibility.[13]

Paramilitaries supporting the unionist side—referred to as loyalists to distinguish them from moderate unionists—had also been mobilizing since the mid-1960s, initially in response to O'Neill's reforms and later as a defensive response to the activities of the Provisionals. The PIRA has received considerably more attention than the loyalist paramilitaries because it has gained the reputation of being perhaps the most sophisticated terrorist organization in Western Europe[14] and is known to be responsible for the deaths of many more people. In addition, following the implementation of the Good Friday Agreement, the political party to which the IRA is linked, Sinn Féin, holds Cabinet office, causing unionists to complain that Sinn Féin Cabinet members have a private army at their disposal. But loyalist paramilitary activity increased in the early 1990s, and in 1992 and 1993 loyalists were responsible for more deaths than republicans.[15]

In the mid-1970s both the PIRA and the security forces shifted their policies. For the PIRA this took the form of pursuing a war of attrition against security forces and British authority figures while at the same time developing an overt political organization. In the case of the security forces it meant giving more responsibility for security to Northern Ireland. In addition the security forces adopted the policy of "criminalization," in other words treating those arrested for paramilitary activity as criminals rather than political prisoners. The policy set in motion a reaction of protest by the prisoners in Long Kesh Prison (also known as the Maze), a prison specially built to hold paramilitary prisoners. The prisoner protests culminated in the hunger strikes of 1980 and 1981, when ten republican inmates died. The death of the hunger strikers aroused new support for the IRA in the general population and pushed the government of the Republic to become more involved in trying to resolve the situation.

At least 3,600 people have been killed in the conflict since 1969 with considerably greater numbers maimed and psychologically traumatized. Areas where mixed populations of Catholics and Protestants were living in the 1960s have changed in their demographics as one or other community has moved out. The Northern Ireland economy, unhealthy to begin with, declined severely during the Troubles and was held together by an annual British subvention that by 1993 had risen to £3 billion. Over time the conflict generated a culture of its own: by 1996 about one-third of all employment in Northern Ireland was government related, with a high proportion of those jobs relating to the Troubles.[16]

ATTEMPTS TO REACH A SETTLEMENT

With the exception of a brief interlude in 1974, known as the Sunningdale government, Northern Ireland was under direct rule from Westminster from 1972 until the implementation of the Good Friday Agreement of 1998. The period was punctuated by a series of attempts to find a solution to the problem or, at a minimum, to stop the fighting and lay the groundwork for future discussions. Soon after the conflict began in earnest in 1969 the British government unequivocally stated that Northern Ireland would not cease to be part of the United Kingdom without the majority consent of the people of Northern Ireland,[17] and this remained a consistent British policy. At the same time the British government sought to give Dublin some role in the process of governing Northern Ireland. As talks evolved, the role envisaged for Dublin increased in importance. This created a sense of insecurity for Protestants.

For the sake of simplicity the main political parties involved will be enumerated here. On the unionist side the more moderate Ulster Unionist Party (UUP) is currently led by David Trimble, who served as First Minister from 1998-2002. The more extreme unionist party is Ian Paisley's Democratic Unionist Party (DUP), which, in the November 2003 elections, outstripped the UUP. On the nationalist side, the Social Democratic and Labour Party (SDLP), led by Mark Durkan, supports unification with Dublin by constitutional means.[18] Sinn Féin, the more extreme party supporting unification, is the nationalist party with the largest following. Led by Gerry Adams, Sinn Féin traditionally has had links to the IRA and has not been willing to condemn outright the IRA's violent acts. Sinn Féin was only permitted to be part of the peace talks of the 1990s when the IRA was on ceasefire. At the center is the Alliance Party, the only party that draws significant numbers from both communities. It is a unionist party in that it maintains that constitutional change can only come by consent, and it has never drawn enough support to be significant in the political equation. A number of smaller parties have played a significant role from time to time.

Five key moments in the twenty-five-year span of negotiations over the future of Northern Ireland deserve to be highlighted.

The Creation of the Power-Sharing Executive of 1974

This plan, the achievement of William Whitelaw, the first secretary of state for Northern Ireland after the installation of direct rule, has been called the "most successful of the British political initiatives within the province" prior to the developments of 1996-1998.[19] It consisted of an "Executive" designed on the basis of proportional representation, which included moderate unionists, the SDLP, and the Alliance Party. Elections for a Northern Ireland Assembly six months earlier had delivered a majority of candidates supporting the concept of a power-sharing Executive. However, the majority of unionists elected to the assembly were opposed. The power-sharing Executive had, meantime, been installed, but in May 1974 loyalists staged a strike, known as the Ulster Workers' Council Strike, which brought the province to a standstill, most notably by enforcing electrical power cuts. Paramilitary organizations played a significant role in bringing about this strike. The Wilson government in London criticized the loyalist strikers but did nothing to halt the strike. Unionist members of the Executive gradually resigned until the entire experiment fell apart.

The Anglo-Irish Agreement of 1985

Both the British and Irish governments increasingly felt the need for better cooperation with each other in their efforts to control the repercussions of violence in the North and to bring a settlement. This process assumed new energy in 1980 when Prime Ministers Thatcher and Haughey agreed on a new level of close cooperation that would include Anglo-Irish studies on issues of joint concern. The joint studies recommended the establishment of an "Intergovernmental Council" of ministers whose brief would be to review British and Irish policy toward the North. The council met thirty times between November 1983 and March 1985 and resulted in the Anglo-Irish Agreement, signed on November 15, 1985. The agreement accepted categorically that the problem was a joint problem of Britain and the Republic. It laid down stipulations for an ongoing intergovernmental conference to address political, security, and legal matters and promote cross-border cooperation. The agreement also provided a mechanism for raising international economic support for Northern Ireland. Several articles were designed to act as catalysts to push the North toward a devolved, power-sharing government. Local politicians were not, however, to be involved in the actual workings of the intergovernmental conference.

Unionists felt betrayed by the fact that the agreement had been made over their heads by the British and Irish governments and that it gave Dublin the right to a consultative role with regard to policy in the North. On one occasion in 1985 between 50,000 and 100,000 loyalists gathered to demonstrate against the agreement in the Belfast city center. Loyalist paramilitaries became more active and caused statistics of violence to rise in the late 1980s and early 1990s.

The Brooke and Mayhew Talks, 1989-1992

Peter Brooke, appointed secretary of state for Northern Ireland in July 1989, capitalized on the tensions following the Anglo-Irish Agreement and called for an alternative agreement that would include all parties. To reassure unionists, he agreed to hold the next round of talks during a gap between meetings of the intergovernmental conference and sent the Anglo-Irish secretariat elsewhere during that time, thus removing for unionists the sense that the intergovernmental conference had some special influence on the next round of talks. Brooke articulated the negotiation in terms of three "strands." Strand One referred to the internal political relationships in Northern Ireland; Strand Two referred to the relationship between the Northern Ireland parties and the Irish government; and Strand Three referred to Britain's relationship to the island of Ireland. The Brooke talks began in mid-April 1991 and bogged down the following autumn. They were significant because they established the principle of the three strands and the acceptance that nothing would be agreed in any one strand until everything was agreed in the talks as a whole. They also proved to be an important educational experience for the participants, helping some of the local parties learn about negotiation and helping build some trust.

Sir Patrick Mayhew succeeded Brooke as secretary of state in the spring of 1992 and resumed the talks in April 1992. As they proceeded, the talks were forced to tackle more specific, substantive issues and thus became more difficult to pursue. They bogged down again in the autumn of 1992.

During the subsequent year leading up to the Downing Street Joint Declaration of 1993, a number of shifts in the political equation began to be felt more strongly. First, since the Anglo-Irish Agreement of 1985, unionists were recognizing their marginality both in Northern Ireland and as a minority in the United Kingdom. Simultaneously Sinn Féin was also feeling more marginalized. Loyalist violence, on the increase since the Anglo-Irish Agreement, was forcing Sinn Féin to recognize the limitations of the armed struggle. Moreover, Sinn Féin had lost credibility after an incident in Enniskillen in 1987 when an IRA bomb killed eleven participants in a Remembrance Sunday ceremony. Sinn Féin began to look for opportunities in the political process and realized this would mean abandoning some long-standing positions.

Gerry Adams's leadership was important in the search for a new stance for Sinn Féin that took it beyond the rhetoric of an absolutist, sacrificial political struggle. One sign of change was the decision of Sinn Féin to accept and use the seats it won in the Republic of Ireland's elections of 1986. This was the first time since partition that Sinn Féin had recognized any Irish elected assembly and taken its elected seats there. Several months after Enniskillen, John Hume of the SDLP initiated talks with Sinn Féin, and in a letter to Gerry Adams on St. Patrick's Day 1988 Hume criticized the IRA for harming the people it claimed to protect and for allowing its methods, strategy, and rhetoric to become more sacred than its ultimate cause. In the talks that followed between Hume and Adams, Hume underlined that Britain no longer had any long-term interest in remaining, and succeeded in moving the discussion about self-determination onto a new level of political reality. The document *Towards a Lasting Peace*, published by Sinn Féin in February 1992, acknowledged that unionist fears would have to be addressed and that British withdrawal would only be accomplished through cooperation with both the British and Irish governments.

The Downing Street Joint Declaration of December 15, 1993

Signed by the British and Irish Prime Ministers, this document was the result of the various political shifts referred to above. It was a statement of principles, not structure (which had been the case with the Anglo-Irish Agreement). The document restated Britain's assurance it had no selfish strategic or economic interest in Northern Ireland and the Republic's acceptance of a unionist veto on unification. It promised Sinn Féin a place at the table if the IRA renounced violence.[20]

Nine months later, on August 31, 1994, the IRA announced a total cessation of military operations but refused to use the word "permanent" and refused to accept the Joint Declaration as a solution: "A solution will be found only as a result of inclusive negotiations."[21] Loyalist paramilitaries announced a ceasefire six weeks later. The Joint Declaration had launched a Forum for Peace and Reconciliation to "make recommendations on ways in which agreement and trust between both traditions in Ireland can be promoted and established."[22] Sinn Féin participated in this body's weekly meetings from the outset in October 1994. This was invaluable in allowing Sinn Féin to become a party in an ongoing democratic discussion. The Framework Documents of February 22, 1995, moved the process ahead further by laying out arrangements for devolved structures in all three relationships.

The stumbling block that had arisen meantime was that of laying down of arms, usually referred to in this context as "decommissioning." Although the Joint Agreement had not made provisions for disarming paramilitaries, the British government wanted this in order to keep unionists on board in the process. U.S. Senator George Mitchell was put in charge of an Independent International Commission on Decommissioning to examine this question. Its recommendations—that decommissioning proceed in tandem with peace negotiations—were announced in February 1996. Prime Minister Major then called for an election in Northern Ireland to select party representation for future multiparty negotiations. These negotiations, chaired by Mitchell, became the arena where the Good Friday Agreement of 1998 was hammered out. The IRA, which had broken its ceasefire in February 1996, adopted it once again in summer 1997, in time for Sinn Féin to be included in the talks.

The Belfast Agreement of April 10, 1998

Many of the elements that emerged in previous talks reappear in this document. The three strand structure stands. The document recognizes the differing political aspirations of the parties as "equally legitimate." It restates that Northern Ireland will remain part of the United Kingdom and will not cease to do so without the consent of a majority of people in Northern Ireland, but that if such a majority does express a wish for Northern Ireland to join the Republic, the government of Great Britain will support and execute this decision. It includes draft legislation to amend the Irish constitution, removing its claim to the territory of Northern Ireland. Strand One sets up a devolved government in Northern Ireland through an elected assembly and executive authority based on proportional representation. Assembly members register their identities—nationalist, unionist, or other—in order to provide a measure of the representation of the two communities at any given time. The system of voting within the Assembly ensures that key decisions are taken on a cross-community basis. Strand Two creates a North/South Ministerial Council that brings "together those with executive responsibilities in Northern Ireland and the Irish government, to develop consultation, cooperation and action within the island of Ireland." Participation in this council is "one of the essential responsibilities attaching to relevant posts in the two Administrations." Strand Three sets up a British-Irish Council whose membership includes representatives of the British and Irish governments and of devolved institutions in Northern Ireland, Scotland, and Wales, as well as representatives of the Channel Islands and the Isle of Man. It meets at summit level twice a year and in "sectoral formats" on a regular basis. In addition, Strand Three sets up a British-Irish Intergovernmental Conference which brings together the British and Irish governments to promote cooperation at all levels.

The agreement further declares that the government will pursue policies for sustained economic growth: addressing environmental, transport, and infrastructure needs; developing rural areas and rejuvenating cities; and addressing employment equality. The government will promote the use of the Irish language in public and private situations and remove restrictions upon its use; and it will require the Department of Education to facilitate Irish medium education. One clause speaks of the "sensitivity of the use of symbols and emblems for public purposes and the need in particular in creating the new institutions to ensure that such symbols and emblems are used in a manner which promotes mutual respect rather than division," and goes on to say that arrangements will be made to monitor this issue and consider necessary action. With regard to security, the British government undertakes to ensure the early return to normal security arrangements in Northern Ireland and will continue to consult on firearms regulation and control. With regard to policing, the agreement lays down general principles and establishes an independent commission to make recommendations for future policing arrangements in Northern Ireland. Both governments agree to provide for an accelerated program for the release of prisoners. All parties to the agreement reaffirm their commitment to the total disarmament of paramilitary organizations. Parties undertake to bring schemes into force by the end of June 1998 to facilitate decommissioning within two years.

Since the signing of the Good Friday Agreement in 1998, much of the above has been put into effect. Following the report of the Patten Commission with regard to policing, a new Police Service of Northern Ireland has been created, with recruitment of Catholics and Protestants in a fifty-fifty ratio. The British military presence has been reduced but not eliminated. The vast majority of prisoners imprisoned because of the Troubles have been freed by a general amnesty.

Current difficulties over the implementation of the Good Friday Agreement largely swing on decommissioning and policing. The fact that the IRA has taken only a few steps to lay its weapons beyond use arouses distrust and disillusionment in the unionist community, which is unwilling to accept Sinn Féin as a partner in the coalition of the Executive while the IRA retains its weapons. Sinn Féin has been critical of the police reforms and has refused to take a place on the policing board, because, it argues, Britain still retains too much power over justice and security in Northern Ireland. In elections of November 2003, the more extreme parties of both the unionist and nationalist communities won more votes than the moderates.

Direct rule by Westminster, reintroduced in October 2002, remains in force as this book goes to press.

Chapter Four

Narratives, Explanations, and Visions for the Future

Northern Ireland's history, the history of the conflict, and debates about the causes of the conflict have become intertwined in the narratives of the two communities. While a host of contributing causes present themselves, the conflict can be characterized quite simply as the clash of two ethnonational programs that seem to be incompatible.

This chapter lays out three possible responses to ethnonationalism in Northern Ireland, both in terms of explanation and in terms of prescription for the conflict. These three responses—ethnonational partisanship, cosmopolitanism, and neopluralism[1]—also represent three visions for the future of Northern Ireland. They can be elaborated not only in political terms but also in terms of their implications for historical narrative and for history teaching. They supply the structure for subsequent chapters that examine approaches to history teaching reform according to these prescriptions.

COMMUNITY NARRATIVES

The Northern Ireland conflict operates at the top echelon of politics but also permeates the grassroots. The layered nature of the conflict makes it all the more difficult to explain it. The past remains very much part of the present in Northern Ireland. Even if present grievances are to some degree addressed, past grievances do not disappear, because they have become core elements of the identity of the respective groups. At times, narratives take on a mythic character and are acted out ritualistically. Both groups have a narrative that not only gives an account of the community's own past but also states that community's view of the cause of the conflict. Debates about the causes of the conflict take on a life of their own.[2]

The Unionist Narrative

Increasingly, over the past four decades, unionists, who are nearly all Protestants, have been describing themselves as British.[3] They equate Britishness with a certain pride in the strengths of the British Empire and Commonwealth and with the rule of law, rational government, and parliamentary democracy. Some unionists would say that the Catholic Church's strong connection with the government of the Republic is precisely what British democracy rejects.

In historical terms, the unionist narrative is drawn principally from two key military events of British history in which the Ulster Protestants played a central role.

The first, the Siege of Londonderry (or Derry, as the nationalists prefer to call the town), took place in 1688-1989. King James II of England, a Catholic, was driven from his throne the previous year by his largely Protestant parliament after he gave his infant son a Catholic baptism—implying that his heir would also be Catholic. James fled to Ireland to raise Catholic support to regain his throne. During the ensuing fighting, Protestants in the area of Derry sought refuge in the walled town, and, as the story goes, the Apprentice Boys of the city closed the gates on the attacking Catholic army. After living some weeks under siege in increasing hardship, the military governor of the town, Colonel Lundy, suggested that they surrender. His proposal was met with horror, and Lundy was forced to remove himself from the town by night in shame. The siege was lifted not long after with the arrival of English ships. The following year, James was definitively defeated at the Battle of the Boyne, an event that ushered in the reign of the Protestants William and Mary, and increasing domination of Ireland, especially the Catholic Irish, by Britain.

Every year, the unionists of Londonderry and other towns of Northern Ireland recall this event with an Apprentice Boys' march and a burning of Lundy in effigy. The idea of "no surrender" is central to this historical commemoration and, over centuries, has become central to unionism itself. In 1985, at the time of the Anglo-Irish Agreement that gave Dublin consultative powers on the future of Northern Ireland, the Protestant/unionist community hung a banner across the Belfast City Hall, saying "Belfast Says No." The word "no" reverberated over past centuries, recalling the stalwart refusal to give in at the Siege of Derry. "No surrender" has become part of the unionist moral code—an expression of strength of character and rectitude, etched more deeply into the unionist mind-set every year through the reenactment of the siege.

A second key event for unionists is the Battle of the Somme, one of the worst of the appalling battles in northern France in World War I. On the first day of this battle, approximately 22,000 British soldiers were killed, of which 2,000 were from the 36th Ulster Division in what later became Northern Ireland.[4] The 36th Ulster Division was largely comprised of men who had earlier signed up for the Ulster Volunteer Force, a paramilitary organization formed to oppose Home Rule from Great Britain. The name "Ulster Volunteer Force," or "UVF," was revived in the 1960s by a loyalist (extreme unionist) illegal paramilitary organization. This new UVF has constantly used imagery from the Battle of the Somme to suggest continuity in its existence and cause and to remind its followers of the sacrifices made by Ulster unionists on behalf of Great Britain.

Unionists see the recent Troubles arising from the Republic and Northern nationalists' intention to unite Ireland. For decades, unionists argued that Articles Two and Three in the Irish constitution—clauses that claimed the entire island as the rightful territory of the Republic—were proof of Dublin's intentions and gave encouragement to the Catholic minority in general, and the IRA in particular, to resist acceptance of Northern Ireland as a legitimate entity. A small body of unionists perceives Irish nationalism as a "front" for the enterprise of re-Catholicizing all Ireland and all Europe. The overwhelming Catholic ethos of the Republic has been a huge obstacle in the minds of unionists to any thought of unification, and unionists assume that the Republic's proximity makes Northern nationalists believe their cause to be more viable than it otherwise would be.[5]

A paradox for unionists, and a source of their insecurity, is the fact that the government of Great Britain has not consistently taken their side in the conflict. This dynamic adds to unionists' sense of victimhood. They were sent as the spearhead of Protestantism in an alien land where they were attacked by the locals, they argue, and subsequently they were abandoned by those who sent them.

The Nationalist Narrative

The nationalist narrative is one of victimization of a wholly different kind. Nationalists identify with the native Irish who experienced the coming of the Normans from England in 1169 as a colonizing event. They see the continued British presence as a series of acts of oppression, in which Britain attempted to wipe out the Catholic faith.

Republicans (extreme nationalists) take inspiration from the 1798 rising of Wolfe Tone and claim that their vision for Ireland, like Tone's, is a civic nationalism where confessional differences are irrelevant.

The nadir of colonial Irish history was, for nationalists, the Great Famine of the 1840s, when at least a million out of a population of eight million perished. Britain's callous mishandling of the famine became the core element in anti-British sentiment. Nearly seventy years later, in 1916, another

Catholic/nationalist martyrdom took place, when fifteen men who had masterminded a rebellion against the British authorities in Dublin were convicted of treason and executed. Their leader, Padraig Pearse, has in some accounts taken on the characteristics of a slain Christ figure. Sixty-five years later, in 1981, Bobby Sands, the first of the hunger strikers to die in the Maze prison in protest against British handling of the Troubles, came to be seen as another martyred personality whose death was blamed on the British and thus an incarnation of Pearse.

That the root cause of the Northern Irish conflict lies in Great Britain is axiomatic to most nationalists in the region. Britain is responsible for encouraging Protestant settlements in the first place and for a series of discriminatory acts against Catholics beginning with Cromwell's massacres, the Penal Laws, and the Act of Union that reneged on its promise of Catholic voting rights. Britain is believed to have encouraged the separate aspirations of the Protestant community in the nineteenth century as part of a "divide and rule" policy in order to maintain British control. Britain is considered responsible for Ireland's economic underdevelopment as well as for a policy of cultural and political oppression. In the 1918 election, when the Irish Independence Party won 79 out of 105 seats, showing three-quarters of the population wanted complete separation, British authorities responded with partition. Between 1920 and 1972, Britain pursued a laissez-faire policy in Northern Ireland that allowed the unionist oligarchy to discriminate against the Catholic minority.

A refinement of the nationalist narrative, the traditional Marxist interpretation of the conflict, finds the locus of blame in British imperialism. Britain balked at giving independence to Ireland because it feared that this would be the beginning of the breakup of the Empire. James Connolly, one of the leaders of the 1916 Rising, who first articulated the Marxist interpretation of the Irish conflict, saw the struggle for independence from the British Empire as a workers' struggle. True Marxist that he was, he believed that the distinction between Catholics and Protestants would disappear after independence. Partition, he argued, kept alive the national question and prevented the true concerns of class interest from emerging and being addressed. Partition, therefore, removed all hope of uniting the workers.

Challenges to the Traditional Community Narratives

Now that the South has removed Articles Two and Three from its constitution as a result of the Belfast Agreement of 1998, unionists cannot argue with quite the same force that the Republic is inciting the conflict, though unionists remain fearful about Dublin's current role in Northern Ireland's government.

In fact, there are many indications that the people of the South and their government have great ambivalence about the idea of welcoming the North into the Republic. The Articles remained because the political cost of abandoning them seemed too high, not because they matched the aspirations of the Dublin government. With regard to the Catholic Church's control of temporal matters, in the last twenty years a groundswell of opinion in the Republic has rejected the notion of state-sponsored Catholicism. Apart from all this, there is the argument that nationalism existed in the North before partition and was strengthened by the discriminatory treatment of Catholics by unionists after 1920.

Some elements of the nationalists' anti-British view of the conflict have also had to be revised in recent years. Nationalists now generally accept that there are two distinct peoples in Ireland. In addition, many recognize that partition happened because of the desires of Northern Protestants—the British had agreed to Home Rule without partition—and that the Irish Parliamentary Party and the Liberal Party (the principal parties in Ireland and Britain supporting Home Rule) failed from early on to recognize the strength of unionist opposition. Likewise, nationalists are now more willing to acknowledge that they underestimated unionist fears of the Catholic nature of the Irish state. The promise in the Belfast Agreement that Britain will support unification if a majority in the North so wills makes the notion of the British as solely responsible for the conflict less tenable than in the past.

Despite the reduced sway of old "British culpability" arguments, there is no question that the British state, by continuing its constitutional guarantee to Northern Ireland, allowed unionists to believe in the viability of their worldview. Britain's support of internment in the early 1970s, its security policies and cooperation with the RUC, and Westminster's habit of placing Ireland low on its list of priorities have confirmed stereotypes nationalists have of the British.

OTHER SOURCES OF THE CONFLICT

While the above discussion about causes places blame for the conflict on outsiders, some scholars see internal causes as more salient.[6] Others search for a model of interaction between external and internal causes.[7] Still others move away from the external-internal dichotomy altogether and describe, for example, a "system of relationships" that has shown both continuity and change over time.[8]

Culture

One of the many cultural issues explored with regard to the conflict, and indeed the one that got the most attention in the Belfast Agreement, is the marginal status of the Gaelic language in the North. But the fact that Gaelic is spoken by such a small percentage of people North and South makes it hard to accept that it plays more than a symbolic role. Another cultural argument describes the Ulster Protestants as "precontractarian," meaning that they are prenational and their difficulties arise from the fact that they are not able to find in any identity the means of characterizing themselves as a nation.[9] A similar argument with regard to nationalists comes from the Irish revisionist historians, who argue that Northern Irish nationalists demonstrate the most dated aspects of Irish nationalism—"its autarkic economic vision, its Gaelicist exclusivism, its Irish Irelandism, and above all its cult of violent redemption"[10]—and suggest that this is the basis of the mentality of the IRA. Other cultural arguments maintain that both groups in Northern Ireland are affected by a culture of violence for a number of reasons including distrust of the modern state, which leads to a willingness to support extragovernmental forms of policing, and a patriarchal society that upholds military values. Still others attribute constitutional stalemate to the tradition of elected officials behaving as intransigents rather than demonstrating creative leadership or statecraft.

The most compelling cultural argument is that the two communities demonstrate two "mind-sets," which in many respects are mutually exclusive. These worldviews are perpetuated by patterns of social separation—limits on intermarriage, place of residence, and separate school systems.[11] Participation in cultural activities peculiar to one's own group and the use of intellectual property—museums, rituals, and history writing—also contribute to this differentiation process.[12]

One of the points often used to challenge cultural arguments is that there are many cultural *similarities* between Catholics and Protestants. But in fact, this argument goes a long way toward *explaining* the conflict. In order to set up effective boundaries, groups need to find and emphasize differences. But if available differences are few, the task of boundary maintenance is more onerous. "The more cultural differences there are, and the deeper they are, then the greater the likelihood that collective identities will be secure rather than threatened."[13] In other words, the tension in Northern Ireland comes in part from the difficulty the groups have in maintaining their sense of separateness.

It is true, however, that much of the time the two communities seem quite happy to tolerate each other's cultures. The argument that the conflict results purely from a clash of cultures fails to account for the violent dynamics of the conflict, underestimates the rationality of the agents, and underplays the importance of political institutions.[14]

Religion

Though the conflict in Northern Ireland is fought between two communities with different religious orientations, the argument that the conflict is about religion is hard to sustain. Ecumenists believe the conflict is the result of churches stressing their differences. Liberals in general believe that religion makes people more inclined to be violent. Some see Protestantism as responsible for the conflict because of its centrality to unionism: Protestants see the unionist regime as a bulwark against Catholicism. Others believe that the Roman Catholic Church plays a greater role than Protestantism because of the level of control the Vatican exercises in the Republic and the decline of Protestant population in the South through emigration or because couples of mixed marriages are obliged to bring their children up Catholic. Some unionists believe that nationalism involves a project to eradicate the Protestant religion.

Arguments against the notion of religion as the essential causal factor are the decreasing religiosity of Northern Ireland and the lack of correlation between the areas where the conflict is greatest and the level of religious conviction of those who live in those areas. Relations between the Protestant and Catholic churches were improving when the Troubles began in the late 1960s. IRA members are not particularly religious, and there are no Catholic clergy in politics. Religious explanations fail to recognize the differences in historical experience and economic and political power. Because religion is the key ethnic marker, its importance gets exaggerated. People belong to religious communities regardless of the level of their religious convictions because the religious label is an ethnic label. For this reason, neither ecumenism nor secularization will bring peace.

The cultural argument that currently carries the most weight among academics is the anthropological view that the churches play a considerable role in reinforcing the social boundary between the two communities through endogamy and educational segregation.

Economics

Liberal economic arguments see ethnic conflict as a reaction to economic problems such as recession, protectionism, economic rivalry, or other impediments to free trade. They suggest that groups fight to gain economic equality or that nationalist identities grow from material interests. They assume the solution to the conflict is to increase general prosperity through investment, equal opportunity in jobs, and free trade or simply to make it clear that proceeding with the conflict is not profitable. The poor state of the Northern Ireland economy during the Troubles made it hard to refute these arguments.

But liberal explanations cannot account for the fact that the poor are not always challenging the system or the fact that groups pursue ethnonational conflicts even when it is against their economic interests to do so. While it is generally acknowledged that economic disparity plays a role in ethnic mobilization and ongoing rebellion of a lower power group, the role economics plays in an ongoing conflict is complex. One clear way economics feeds the conflict is in the fact that unemployment makes participation in paramilitary groups additionally attractive.

Lack of Cross-Cutting Loyalties

Political scientists often refer to the Northern Ireland problem as the result of a lack of cross pressures. Ideally, individuals should belong to a number of groupings that compete for their participation and loyalty in different ways, and political parties should include representatives of many of these social groups. In Northern Ireland, religious affiliation, school, and place of residence provide no alternative groupings to political affiliation, and indeed these groupings tend to affect others such as sports, women's groups, boy and girl scouts, and so on. This is a compelling argument.

Lack of Possibility for Consociationalism

Consociationalism, otherwise known as power-sharing or proportional representation, is thought by some to be the most attractive solution for the government of conflicted plural societies.[15] It builds on the balance of power model: several smaller groupings can find common cause in balancing the influence of a larger group. But in the case of Northern Ireland, it is problematic because the several segments of society fall into two unalterable blocks that are unequally balanced. In addition, the lack of society-wide loyalties or common external threats makes it difficult to see common causes that can hold differing parties together in some common enterprise.

Explanations That Link Internal and External Factors

The role played by Britain is crucial to understanding the conflict, but this should be examined in terms of its interplay with domestic realities. A helpful distinction between British imperialism and British colonial policy shifts the argument away from traditional Marxist assumptions and toward an examination of the societal structures that developed during the colonial era. Frank Wright has coined the term *ethnic frontier* as a description of Northern Ireland comparable to parts of former Yugoslavia, Cyprus, and Lebanon, where two broad national communities are competing for sovereignty. In Northern Ireland this is a direct result of British colonialism: Britain is responsible for introducing into Ireland a settler community whose group identity preordained that it would have a different national allegiance from the natives. In such situations the actions of external powers are important—

if one group seeks the aid of one outside power, the other group will seek the aid of another. Belgium and Switzerland are fairly stable because outside powers have not intervened on behalf of "co-ethnics." This has left the ethnic groups inside Belgium and Switzerland to behave like cultural minorities rather than ethnonationalist groups. The best hope in ethnic frontier situations, Wright said, is to make sure that the external powers cooperate with each other to contain the conflict—a vision that began to be enacted in the Irish situation with the Anglo-Irish Agreement of 1985 and has continued to the present.[16] This is why Northern Ireland is in a much better potential position to control its conflict than are Cyprus, Lebanon, or Israel-Palestine.

The corollary to characterizing Northern Ireland as an ethnic frontier is to describe it as a British state-building failure. The large numbers of settlers in the seventeenth century made it impossible for these settlers to gain the loyalty of the people of the area—a prerequisite for state-building. Plantations ruined the potential for co-optation of local elites. Repeatedly, for example, with regard to the Treaty of Limerick of 1692 and the withholding of Catholic Emancipation in 1801, the Protestant Ascendancy prevented policies that might have drawn the native Catholics into the governing process. When Catholic mass mobilization did develop, it had a separatist program.

The role of settler colonialism in undermining state-building explains Britain's initial failure to incorporate Ireland into the British state. In turn, unionist treatment of Catholics under the Stormont regime greatly assisted their failure to integrate Catholics. This failure to absorb Catholics of Ireland into the British nation-building project at an early stage meant that Irish Catholics would, almost inevitably, develop their own ethnonationalist program.

A Clash of Rival Ethnonational Programs

To suggest that the Troubles have been the most recent stage of a four-hundred-year conflict is to bow to a historical essentialism that is not only inaccurate but lends itself to partisan arguments. But to deny the conflict's connection with the past is to give away too much. Ruane and Todd solve this by describing an ongoing "system of relationships" in Ireland that have undergone both change and continuity.[17] They see a set of differences—religion, ethnicity, settler-native status, nationalism versus unionism, civility vs. barbarism—that interlocked with structures of dominance, dependence, and inequality, to solidify the relationship. The relationship took different forms in different historical periods: colonization, the eighteenth-century Ascendancy, the union, partition, direct rule. But the system of relationships had continuity from one stage to the next.

McGarry and O'Leary have also proposed an interactive model to describe the way the various elements have contributed to Northern Ireland's dilemma. They argue that in analyzing the conflict in Northern Ireland, religious, cultural, and economic explanations are inadequate of themselves unless they are cast as contributing elements in the coalescing of group loyalties that contain political aspirations. Religion and culture, which act as markers in the conflict, should be understood not in terms of what they represent substantively but because they give people evidence of shared experience or common origin and therefore a means of recognizing potential friends and strangers:

> A common intellectual failing has been the conversion of the 'markers' which distinguish the two groups with distinct national identities into factors that are claimed to have crucial explanatory content in their own right. Typically religion and/or a range of other cultural differences are said to explain the conflict, violence and stalemate. . . . The fundamental failing of this perspective is that it forgets that ethnic groups can maintain themselves and continue to fight with each other even in the face of significant acculturation—whether that acculturation is occasioned by secularism, linguistic homogenization, or other cultural dilution. Acculturation, the sharing of culture, does not necessarily lead to assimilation, a sharing of identity, either in Northern Ireland, or elsewhere.[18]

The most plausible explanation of the conflict in Northern Ireland, argue McGarry and O'Leary, is one that draws together both external and internal factors. Northern Ireland is a conflict zone where internal and external elements have contributed to marking off the communities, mobilizing the communities, or exacerbating the conflict but where the principal expression of the conflict is the *political* rivalry of the two ethnonational groups. Settler colonialism began a process that denied the dignity of one group by another, coalesced Protestant-Catholic difference, and encouraged the development of nationalist programs. A long-accumulated history of confrontation has supplied a rich catalog of narratives and symbols to characterize the conflict.

These rival nationalisms confront each other over the territory of Northern Ireland, whose mixed population contains a significant body of people supporting each national vision. Personal identity, political loyalty, ideas about security and threat, and religious cultures, all knit together by a sense of history that gives each worldview cohesion, contribute to these ethnonational ideologies. In the end, however, ethnonationalism is a phenomenon that stands separately from the sum of its parts. Therefore, addressing its various contributing elements does not necessarily reduce the animosity between the groups.

Understanding the conflict as an ethnonational conflict suggests why economic arguments have relevance but in the end are inadequate to explain the conflict. Economic inequality helps group differentiation and political mobilization, but ethnonational communities are ultimately engaged in political projects rather than economic projects, and repeatedly show willingness to sacrifice the latter for the former.

Ethnonationalism also suggests that cross-cutting loyalties will not reduce the likelihood of conflict. The cross-cutting loyalties argument fails to recognize the high salience of ethnonational attachments. Removing other sources of social division leaves national loyalties intact.[19] This is clear from the fact that secularization, or the diminished use of the Irish language, has not reduced the conflict in Northern Ireland. Likewise, class loyalties are not strong enough to trump nationalist loyalties, especially when it comes to elections.

PRESCRIPTIONS FOR THE CONFLICT

Having characterized Northern Ireland as an ethnonationalist conflict, McGarry and O'Leary analyze the "meta-conflict," as follows:

cosmopolitan perspectives,
* which declare that the conflict is not primarily about rival nationalisms, or*
* maintain that national divisions are relatively mutable and capable of being transcended sooner rather than later;*
ethno-national partisan arguments,
* which accept that the conflict is indeed about nationalism but believe that it flows directly from a unilateral assault on their community's right to self-determination; and finally*
neo-pluralist arguments,
* which maintain that the conflict is focused on two competing and equally legitimate demands for self-determination.* [my italics][20]

This typology has been elaborated by other analysts of the conflict.[21] With some tweaking it provides a useful framework for this study, where we are examining, among other things, the way that history reform plugs into various long-term political visions. To each of these arguments can be attached implicit explanations, stances toward the conflict, and prescriptions. In addition each of the arguments has implications for the role that narrative plays in the conflict.

Partisan Arguments

Those who rely on partisan explanations have a zero-sum understanding of the conflict and vision for its solution: they believe the conflict will be resolved when their own group's right to self-determination is respected. Their prescription is to seek the victory of their own group and discount the aspirations of the other group. They legitimize this prescription by characterizing their own group as the low power or victimized group. This description fits people on both sides of the Northern Ireland conflict because of the "double minority" phenomenon embedded in the conflict. Catholics perceive themselves as the minority in the North, while Protestants perceive themselves as the minority in the whole island.

The partisan political agenda is one of group empowerment. Each group seeks reassurance that it controls its affairs. The ultimate satisfaction of that search, and therefore the purest solution to the aspiration for power, is the total control of the mechanisms of government.

But partisans see narratives as a crucial proxy arena where the contest for power can be engaged. Their total belief in their own agenda will cause them to use the term *history* rather than *narrative* as they tell their story and to understand their advocacy of their own history as a battle to bring *true* history to the surface. It would be a mistake to view such undertakings cynically, because in many cases projects of this kind are completely legitimate, bringing to light sufferings and injustices of the past. The cause of an oppressed group is one of partisan empowerment. Part of the program is to ensure that the story of the oppressed group is acknowledged in societal memory and in written history. The problem arises when partisans challenge the other group's narrative and replace it, or suppress it, with their own alternative narrative. When their own political project is their primary concern, partisans are in danger of being unable to hear the genuine concerns articulated by the other group. This can lead the "dominant" group to characterize themselves as victims of the "oppressed" group. The political goal of empowerment can therefore feed an escalatory cycle where each side in the conflict believes its own group's survival depends on suppressing the other group's narrative as well as the other group's entitlement to a say in the governing process.

Cosmopolitan Arguments

Cosmopolitanism can be synonymized with modernity as it has come to be understood in the West in the past three centuries. Cosmopolitanism is a worldview that grows directly from Enlightenment philosophy, which proposed that universal values should be applied to every individual and which therefore sidelined notions of group recognition that had been accepted in the past. Cosmopolitans assume that ethnonationalist issues are not fundamental social categories. They see one or the other of the elements involved in ethnic conflict—economic disparity, religious intolerance, or cultural difference—as the *reason* for the conflict. Their pre-scription for the resolution of the conflict is to address whichever of these elements they have chosen to believe is the problem and, subsequently, to work toward finding common ground.

Cosmopolitanism comes in many varieties, and one way to differentiate them is in their attitude to culture.

Assimilationists. The universalist vision that emerged in the eighteenth century with the Enlightenment was supported by, and in turn supported, political and economic developments in the modern era, where growth of cen-tralized states depended on economies of scale and hence a homogenized cul-ture. This imperative toward homogeneity[22] that is so characteristic of the modern state gets described idealistically as a civic nationalism, where all substate groups have equal importance. In reality, it usually involves assimi-lation, where substate groups are expected to diminish in importance and eventually disappear.

Cosmopolitans in general do not advocate changes of sovereignty, and cer-tainly the assimilationist brand does not. Assimilationism is a form of dis-guised partisanship supporting the status quo and the dominant group. True cosmopolitans must find a way to get around this problem by advocating a so-lution that requires change from both communities.

Rationalists. Another cosmopolitan outlook emphasizes the importance of institutions and norms of rational thinking to protect the rule of law, interest-based politics, empiricism, and democracy.[23] Its adherents will seek to reduce the pull of particularist loyalties by encouraging intergroup contact and co-mingling. They will label group difference as a cultural or minority matter that need not affect the definition of the state. These people usually belong to the well-educated liberal center. A small and distinct group consists of traditional Marxists who, like other cosmopolitans, discount the fundamental importance of ethnonational divisions, though their "universalist" prescription—working-class empowerment—is different.[24]

Fragmenting Identifications. Whereas the rationalists ignore identity, a third cosmopolitan approach opts not to ignore ethnic difference but to oper-ate comfortably in a world that is a mosaic of various cultures. This type of cosmopolitan helps to affirm cross-cutting loyalties by nurturing alternative identifications. The underlying assumption here, as far as Northern Ireland is concerned, is that characterizing Northern Ireland society in terms of two ho-mogeneous blocks is actually artificial. The constructed nature of groups and identifications tells us that existing ethnic identities are shifting and mal-leable. A truly cosmopolitan person recognizes that many elements inform an individual's sense of self. Such a person can act from a variety of inner im-pulses relating to a spectrum of cultural backgrounds and can move smoothly from one particular environment to another, functioning with ease in all of them.

Legalists and Human Rights Advocates. While this group has much in common with the rationalists, its focus on human rights has created an interesting new dynamic within cosmopolitanism. Rights used to be understood as universals, with equal applicability to all human beings. But in recent decades, we find that human rights principles of dignity and equality have led us to recognize group rights as deserving of recognition. Ironically, the acceptance of group rights reinstates group difference as something to be honored in human experience. Cosmopolitanism, therefore, leads in the end to its antithesis. We will look at this in Chapter Twelve.

As far as historical symbols, myths, and narratives are concerned, supporters of this view see them as problematic contributors to ethnic conflict and try to reduce their power. They do this by subjecting all history writing to the test of empirical fact and rationality and by urging schools to teach students to observe proper research practices and to engage in critical debate.[25] They see the academy as crucial to the enterprise, because of its power to model and uphold proper practices of research and critical argument. They believe that intellectual endeavors can be held accountable and therefore that a "common," agreed history should be possible, even if this takes some time to reach.

Neopluralist Arguments

Neopluralists, according to McGarry and O'Leary, recognize the fundamental importance of ethnonational difference and look for ways that two or more ethnonational ideologies can, simultaneously, be supported and respected. In contrast with cosmopolitans, who by definition marginalize particularist concerns, this group rejects the sterility of a political life stripped of the transcendent attachments that ethnic loyalties offer. Thus they are reordering the pieces of the puzzle so that identity can be given more play. They will look for ways to recognize difference while simultaneously supporting cohesion. They will try to square the circle, to give full recognition to the several groups in conflict, but at the same time to get around the constitutional impasse implied in an ethnonational conflict. The phrase *parity of esteem*, which first appeared in the Opsahl Commission Report of 1992–1993[26] and is expressed in the Belfast Agreement, sums up the neopluralist approach.

Advocates of this vision maintain that while identity *is* malleable, once a group has been engaged in a struggle for status, the group identity hardens, especially when blood has been spilled in that campaign or when the group sees the possibility of attaching itself to a state identified with its group. Thus, they argue, nothing short of political recognition will satisfy such groups, and it is naive to hope otherwise. The conundrum, therefore, is how to give two or more groups in one polity equal political recognition. Critics of the approach argue that it sets up a self-fulfilling prophecy: the more recognition given to group identities, the less such groups will be satisfied with anything short of political recognition.

Those who support the notion of parity of esteem see the problem as one where the two communities are too insecure to shift in their outlook and need to be made to feel more secure before they will move forward. Each group's fear arises because of genuine physical threats. But the sense of threat also arises because of a visceral awareness that cultural, and hence psychological, boundaries are not strong enough for the group to maintain its sense of cohesion. Neopluralism tries to offer all salient groups psychological reassurance, with the hope that in the long term this reassurance will be less needed. The emphasis on single community work in the community relations field is a good example of parity of esteem pursued at the grassroots.

Here, political solutions are explored that grant ethnonational status to both groups. The best choice would be joint sovereignty and, failing that, power sharing. At the level of narrative, this approach seeks ways to give equal validity to the narratives of the two groups simultaneously.

Long-term societal outcomes that confer equal validity are hard to envisage. They imply a postmodern acceptance of several realities simultaneously. But neopluralism as a "way station" on the road to a cosmopolitan Northern Ireland has considerable currency right now in Northern Ireland.

The real question for Northern Ireland, therefore, is how do people make the transition from being preoccupied with their own outlook to the place where they can include the outlook of the other in their worldview?

Interactive pluralism is, presumably, the bridge. So what does interactive pluralism involve in practice? The research uncovered some examples, though it also demonstrates that we are only at the beginning of discovering what this means.

IDEAL TYPES

Table 4.1 that follows lays out the positions just described. The positions should be understood as *ideal types*, developed to assist analysis. They should not be understood purely as good or bad. Each expresses important concerns that arise in conflict situations. In the real world of the conflict in Northern Ireland, these arguments overlap. In different phases of the conflict one may have more relevance than the others.

Table 4.1. Prescriptions for the Conflict and Their Implications for History Teaching

Prescription	Strategy	Manifestation in Society	Approach to Use of Narrative	Expression in History Teaching
Partisanship (empower own group; seek victory of own group by defeating other group)	• Keep the status quo—the unionist strategy • Reunite Ireland—the nationalist strategy	• The conflict as we have seen it	• Replace other group's narrative with own group's narrative	• Teach no Irish history; the group narrative is the British narrative (metaphors of siege, etc.) • Teach about the oppression of Britain, the Heroes of the Easter Rising, etc.
Cosmopolitanism (build a civic culture inorder to neutralize ethnonationalist tendencies; shift focus to other universal values; emphasize alternative identifications)	• Promote social integration	• Integrated schools, contact programs, intermingling	• Create a neutered narrative by subjecting all history to rational objective criticism	• Strong focus on history teaching in schools • Hold textbooks to high standard of fact • Restore omissions • Focus on process, debate, and interpretation • Challenge taboos • Emphasize complexity of history to undermine rigid ideas about political myths and identity
	• Promote an intellectual culture based on rationality and objectivity to enable the public to reject chauvinist mythologies about their own group or others	• Support the growth of historical profession through journals, conferences, academic freedom • Use media to introduce objective ways of speaking about the conflict		
	• Promote economic justice	• Ensure equal opportunity of housing and jobs		• Teach more technical and business subjects so school leavers are more able to get jobs • Recast history as the "people's history," hence promote economic, social, and local history

(continued)

Table 4.1. Prescriptions for the Conflict and Their Implications for History Teaching (*continued*)

Prescription	Strategy	Manifestation in Society	Approach to Use of Narrative	Expression in History Teaching
	• Promote institutions of civil society	• Human rights, just legal system, and an end to gerrymandering, encouragement of democratic structures		• Teach about human rights and democratic institutions
	• Appeal to alternative identities (local identity, Ulster identity, European identity)	• Society of Ulster Local Studies • Workers Educational Association • Adamson, Hall, PUP UDA • Develop links with EU and Europe	• Diminish the importance of the salient narratives in the conflict by focusing on alternatives	• Take children to local places of interest, do projects on their town, etc. • Teach local history in schools • Teach European history and politics; link schools with European schools by e-mail, etc.
Neopluralism (support the recognition of two identities and outlooks)	• Establish equal validity based on entitlement	• Create political structures that give both groups fullest political recognition	• Encourage cultural observances of all groups	• Recognize divergent interpretations • Recognize parallel cultural patterns
Interactive pluralism	• Establish equal validity based on sharing	• Modify power-sharing to reduce its centrifugal tendencies	• Encourage processes where the two groups can listen to and acknowledge each other's story	• Recognize complementary nature of the narratives • Recognize different perspectives or historical consciousnesses • Acknowledge faults in one's own group that have harmed the other

The table goes on to show the different prescriptions that arise from the various arguments. Each of these prescriptions has a political agenda in the wider society, a view of the "right" role of narrative in society, and a set of implications for history teaching.

Subsequent chapters of this study treat each of the prescriptions for the conflict described here and explore the implications of each for actions taken with regard to history teaching in Northern Ireland.

Ultimately, the capacity for parity of esteem to rigidify rather than resolve the conflict has to be addressed. This research shows that what is lacking in the neopluralist vision is an expression of mutual commitment to work interactively with the "other." Key to resolving the political impasse in Northern Ireland, and to finding a way reformed history teaching can model a mind-set for the new Northern Ireland, is to explore interactive pluralism. Only the very first indications of such an approach can be seen in history teaching in Northern Ireland.

Chapter Five

Education in Ireland and Northern Ireland: 1537–1972

As far back as the 1500s, education was viewed as a means of indoctrination that had political implications. The Penal Laws of the eighteenth century seriously curtailed educational possibilities for Catholics. As a result, Catholics resorted to "hedge schools" to educate their children.

In 1831, the United Kingdom created a national school system for Ireland. Though initially welcomed by both Catholics and Protestants, from the outset the system was subject to tensions with regard to religious instruction. Both confessions encouraged creation of their own schools in response. By the early twentieth century, only 25 percent of schools in Ireland had interdenominational mixing, down from 50 percent a half century before.

The Northern Ireland government, established in 1921, again tried to create a national school system, which again was thwarted by both communities: Protestants succeeded in getting a requirement for Protestant religious instruction in state schools, while the Catholic Church insisted on retaining its own schools. The result was a segregated education system.

In the late 1960s, Catholic schools received more government funding in exchange for accepting some local government representation in school management. Other reforms also reflected a more progressive vision by the education authorities. It was at this time that history teaching became an open topic of discussion.

PRE-1920 IRELAND

The part played by education in the Irish conflict is as old as the conflict itself. Schools have traditionally been run by their respective confessional communities. As long as religion has been an issue in the joust for power, education has been a focal point of that competition. An account of education policy cannot be separated from political history.

As the Reformation proceeded in lockstep with Tudor administrative changes of the early sixteenth century, King Henry VIII (1509-1547) ordered Anglican clergy in Ireland to set up schools to teach English and Protestantism there. The Parish Schools Act of 1537, mandating all those in Holy Orders to keep an English school within the vicarage where they were situated, included stipulations on the use of the English language and on the discontinuance of Irish forms of dress and wearing of hair.

One professional historian argues that the Parish Schools Act was designed to ensure the loyalty of the Anglo-Irish who lived in the Pale and to recapture the allegiance of the English who had already been assimilated into Irish society—that the legislation was not aimed at the native Irish.[1] Another view of the matter is that the measure was designed to create schools "whose main objects were to propagate an alien tongue and an alien church [and which] represented a political and religious challenge to Irish Catholics."[2]

If Henry Tudor's aim was to suppress Irish Catholicism, he had no initial success; in fact it is unclear whether any parish schools were built during Henry's reign.[3] But during the seventeenth century, as the English launched the Ulster plantations and extended their hold in Ireland by other means, a number of trusts and societies founded schools with the explicit aim of propagating Protestantism.

Under the Penal Laws of the eighteenth century, it was illegal for a Catholic to be educated in a school that did not teach the Protestant faith. Catholics were forbidden to run their own schools, to tutor their children at home, or to send their children abroad to be educated. Catholic resistance took the form of the "hedge" school. These illegal classes were carried on by Catholics in barns or in open country, with lookouts posted to spot approaching authorities. They were believed by some Protestants to be transmitting Gaelic culture. In fact, they were often attended by Protestants, which suggests that if they had a Catholic thrust, this was not so in an exclusivist sense. Though the hedge schools predated the development of nineteenth-century Irish Catholic nationalism, they ensured the continuance of a body of educated Catholics and contributed to Catholic morale and self-respect.

When the education provisions of the Penal Laws were removed in 1782, Catholics could start their own schools on the proviso that school masters take an oath of allegiance to the Crown and accept no Protestant pupils. Catholic orders began founding schools to supplant the hedge schools. But no aid for starting Catholic schools was forthcoming from the state: state monies for education went to charitable societies, which, in the British Isles, tended to have an explicitly Protestant focus. Indeed, many of these societies engaged in aggressive proselytizing in the first three decades of the nineteenth century. Hedge schools therefore continued, renamed "pay schools," because children were to pay the master a penny a week.

During this period, Catholics received assistance from the one charitable society that was nondenominational, the Kildare Place Society, or Society for Promoting Education of the Poor in Ireland. This organization, for a time, came close to creating the basis of a successful national school system. It published a set of books for its own use, provided teacher training, and had an efficient inspection system. By 1831, it had 137,639 school children in its charge.[4] Catholics regarded the Kildare Place Society as a significant light on the horizon, a means by which schooling for Catholics could be financed. In the 1820s, however, presumably responding to the growth of Daniel O'Connell's campaign for votes for Catholics, members of the Kildare Place Society began giving some of the Society's income to Protestant proselytizing societies. O'Connell protested, but in vain. Nonetheless, O'Connell *was* successful in his broader goal, and in 1829 "Catholic Emancipation" gave Catholic landowners voting rights.

National Schools

In 1831, legislation in Westminster established a state school system for Ireland. It was the first system of universal public education in Europe. The creation of the national schools came from a genuine convergence of interest of two groups who were otherwise on divergent courses. The British authorities and the "Ascendancy" (the Protestant elite within Ireland) aimed to draw Catholics into allegiance to the state and Crown. Catholics favored the idea because of their need for educational funding. Both groups wanted an end to the hedge schools: the Protestant elite because they believed these schools imparted "barbarity" and "treason"; Catholics, because they wanted state financial support to school their children.

The "national" schools of the new system were primary schools going up to age fourteen. They were to be run by a manager, usually the local Protestant or Catholic clergyman or, preferably, by joint Catholic and Protestant managers, and to be open to children of any denomination. Indeed, they were to make an effort to *attract* children of all faiths. The schools would be owned by trustees. Local communities would supply one-third of the building costs, and the rest would be supplied by the Board of Commissioners of National Education, an interdenominational body that would also oversee choice of textbooks and curriculum. Religious instruction would be offered separately to Catholics and Protestants by the clergy of their own faith outside official school hours. Each teacher was to be "imbued with a spirit of peace, of obedience to the law, and loyalty to his sovereign."[5]

In most European countries, the introduction of a national school system came in the wake of the industrial revolution, the growth of towns, the decline of agriculture, and the removal of education from volunteer societies of the church. In Ireland, no industrial revolution and no decline in agrarian life, and very little decline in the close link between the family structure and the economy, had taken place. It seems fairly clear that the British authorities, habituated to viewing Catholics as a potential source of rebellion, introduced the national schools to offset the new influence that Catholics would have in political life as a result of emancipation. The quotation at the end of the previous paragraph underlines that "loyalty" was a central aim of these schools.

Despite the original vision to remove the Irish school system from the influence of sectarian politics, this is not what came about. The churches quickly pushed the new national system in a more denominational direction by forcing a series of compromises. Initially, opposition came from the Protestant churches. The Church of Ireland (Anglican) interpreted the policy of religiously mixed education to be a challenge to the supremacy of the Established Church[6] and decided to form its own school system, which deteriorated over the next forty years for lack of funds and by the end of the century had, for the most part, disappeared. The Presbyterians, particularly concerned that the proposed national system would give Catholic priests the right to come onto the premises of Protestant schools, thus according de facto recognition to Catholicism, insisted on greater power being given to school managers to control who would have access. This concession was the first major compromise by the Board of Commissioners of National Education.[7]

The Catholic Church was initially more supportive of the new system but became increasingly critical. In 1836, the Christian Brothers withdrew their schools from the system. By 1840, the Catholic Church was calling for more overseeing rights to be given to priests with regard to religious and moral instruction in national schools. In 1850, in a significant departure from the original concept of national schools, a decree by the Synod of Thurles pronounced that only schools run by Catholics were suitable for educating Catholics.

This more aggressive insistence by Catholics on the right to educate their own took place in the period immediately following the Great Famine, a time when the Catholic Church under Archbishop Paul Cullen was becoming more outspoken. By the 1885 elections, a Catholic-based nationalism was firmly in place, which eventually achieved Home Rule for Ireland in 1912. This should not, however, lead us to assume that Catholics had a homogeneous point of view about nationalism or about historical narratives. Secret societies, such as the Fenians, were advocating a revolutionary nationalism to which the Catholic authorities were opposed.

But in 1850, an additional preoccupation of Catholic prelates was the intertwining of secularization and growing state power that was affecting all of Europe in the late nineteenth century. In countries like France and Italy, the state was interfering much more in a variety of aspects of people's lives. The Church's response was to harbor and disseminate a suspicion of state intentions. Protestantism could therefore be characterized not simply as the religious ideology of British power but as a halfway house on the road to a secular society. This threat of secularization gave strength to Ireland's deeply conservative Catholicism.

While the original plan for the national schools had envisaged that as many as possible would be under joint management of Catholics and Protestants, this was not enforced by the commissioners, and by 1852, only 175 out of 4,795 schools were under joint management. Moreover, there were not enough Protestants in the school system to make mixing possible to any great degree. 1867 was the year when the greatest number of schools in Ireland had interdenominational mixing—57 percent. By the 1912-1913 school year, the number was down to 25 percent.[8]

By 1880, Ireland had the most literate peasant society in Western Europe,[9] but the school system had long since ceased to be nondenominational, despite the government's assertions to the contrary. "The National Schools," commented J. C. Beckett, "did a great deal towards abolishing illiteracy, but almost nothing toward increasing mutual understanding between Irishmen of different faiths."[10] With the horizon of the twentieth century looming, sectarian politics continued to plague the education system, and the issue of teaching the Irish language, funding for schools, and the role of local authorities would become the main points of discord.

Irish Language

After the defeat of the second Home Rule bill in the House of Lords in 1893, Irish nationalism found an outlet in cultural forms. W. B. Yeats had spearheaded an Irish cultural renaissance in poetry, art, and theater. The Gaelic League, founded in 1893, went on to promote the Irish language, arguing that language and nationhood were synonymous, that national resurgence follows awakening of interest in native speech, and that Britain's way of asserting power over subject peoples had been to remove their language. The League proved to be an effective recruiting ground for the nationalist political program. Nationalists believed re-Gaelicization would happen easily and that education would be the vehicle.

From the 1890s, the principal controversy in schools was over the teaching of the Irish language. The conventional belief of nationalists was, and continues to be, that hedge schools taught Irish and the national schools obliterated its use. Others argue it is not clear that Gaelic culture was strongly emphasized in the hedge schools[11] and that Irish was already rapidly going out of style in the early 1800s. What *is* clear is that the numbers of people speaking Gaelic fell sharply from the 1830s. The famine and emigration undoubtedly contributed to this. But the question remains as to whether the national schools deliberately stamped out the Gaelic language. Akenson says the Board of Commissioners of National Education were, in the 1830s, "not hostile to the Irish language, but unaware of it." There was no rule against its use, he says; rather, hardly anyone considered it might be used.[12] But minutes of the Board's meetings for 1834 and 1844 show requests for teaching of Irish in a specific school. The commissioners refused the requests. Again, in 1855, 1857, and 1858, one headmaster's requests to use Irish in an Irish-speaking area did not meet with a positive response. Perhaps the authorities did not take Gaelic seriously, but surely they were not unaware of the issue.

In 1879, Gaelic was introduced as an optional school subject: a system was set up to give extra fees to teachers to teach Irish outside school hours. In 1883, Gaelic became permitted in schools as a means of elucidation. In 1893, it became permitted as a medium of instruction. In 1899, the issue was greatly publicized by the clash of views between, on the one hand, two dons of Trinity College, Dublin, who tried to discredit the case for use of Irish as a subject in intermediate schools and, on the other, Dr. Douglas Hyde, founder of the Gaelic League, who supported Irish language education.[13] Hyde won the debate, and Irish was given a larger place in the Intermediate Board's examinations. But, even more significantly, the subsequent numbers of pupils taking Irish in schools greatly increased. In 1909, the Irish language became a requirement for matriculation to university.[14] By 1919-1920, 80 percent of secondary school exam candidates took the Irish language exam.[15] After partition, the Republic continued to make Irish compulsory for university entrance.

Funding

At much the same time, growing concern, particularly coming from Protestants, about a shortage of funding for schools led to a proposal to bring local authorities into the school structure so that local taxes could be allocated toward schools. The first push in this direction came in Belfast in 1904 and was linked with the rapid growth of the city in the previous decades and the attendant drain on the reserves of Protestant schools. Catholics opposed drawing local authorities into the structure of schools because they feared the local authorities would interfere in the management of the schools. The issue arose again in 1918-1919 and was again defeated due to Catholic opposition.

The desire to draw local authorities into the running of schools as a means of addressing finance, religious instruction, and, to a somewhat lesser extent, Irish language and culture were to remain the principal foci of education policy-making debate in Northern Ireland after partition in 1920. From 1920, the same issues would be addressed in the context of a competition for power between the Catholic minority in Northern Ireland and the Protestants who were asserting a British identity for what they believed to be a British state. As in the nineteenth century, history teaching would be considered so delicate a matter that it would rarely be talked about.

STORMONT: 1920-1972

In June 1921, Lord Londonderry, the first minister for education of the new Northern Ireland state, declared that he supported a nondenominational, state-run school system. At this time of great flux in Ireland, when no political settlement had yet been reached in the South, Northern Catholics viewed partition as a temporary way station en route to an independent Ireland. They therefore understood Londonderry's policy as a denial of the inevitable and registered their nonacceptance in several ways.

First, the Catholic Church declined representation on the committee designing proposals for future educational structure. This committee, established in September 1922 and chaired by Robert Lynn, gave representation to all unionist and Protestant groups. It therefore proceeded with a homogeneous concern to ensure Northern Ireland's relationship with Britain and to utilize education in creating a new national identity for Northern Ireland. The Catholic Church believed the committee's agenda was to undermine the influence of Catholicism in general and Catholic schools in particular.

Second, Catholic clergy and teachers initially refused to be placed under the charge of the Northern Ireland Ministry of Education, insisting that they would continue to take orders from school authorities in Dublin. Until late in 1922, Dublin cooperated, paying Catholic teachers. Eventually, Dublin refused to continue the arrangement, and Catholic teachers went onto the payroll of the Northern Ireland government.

The Education Act of 1923

Following the recommendations of the Lynn Report, the Education Act of 1923 set up a school system for Northern Ireland.

School Management. The new system urged all schools, of whatever denomination or status, to transfer their management to education committees that were part of the local government system. Schools that complied would be eligible for full government funding. Many schools, especially Catholic schools, declined these terms. The result was three classifications of schools:

- *"Transferred" or "controlled" schools:* These schools had handed over control to the local authorities and thenceforth would be run by the local authority and receive all their finance from the state. The schools that fit this category were either existing schools previously owned and run by Protestant churches or newly created schools. By 1937 half of all Protestant primary schools had gone this route, and ultimately most others did as well. These schools were attended almost entirely by Protestants.
- *"Voluntary four plus two" schools:* This was a midway position for schools that wanted to retain some control over their management. These schools got their name from the required ratio of local authorities to be represented on their boards of management: two members were named by the local education authority, and four were named by the trustees of the schools. These schools received payment of salaries and half their running costs from the state and were to negotiate their capital costs with the state. Some Protestant secondary schools and grammar schools went this route.
- *"Voluntary" schools:* These schools did not place themselves under the local authority. They received full salaries and half their running costs, but no capital costs, from the state. These schools were not subject to the state's requirements with regard to religious instruction. But they *were* subject to the state's requirements with regard to textbooks and school inspection. This ended up being the designation of most Catholic schools as well as some Protestant grammar schools and Free Presbyterian primary schools.

Funding, in other words, varied in proportion to the extent that the school was under the jurisdiction of the local authority. As an issue of public accountability, this was understandable—the more accountability, the more public funding available. The problem was that inevitably, given Catholic reluctance to accept influence of the local authorities, who were overwhelmingly Protestant, schools with a mainly Protestant student population were the only schools that got full funding. The Catholic Church and Catholic community had to raise all capital costs for their schools over and above the taxes they paid to Stormont.

Religious Instruction. Religious instruction could take place on the school premises, but was to be outside compulsory school hours. It was no longer a required part of the curriculum. Local authorities were not to provide the religious instruction; rather, clergy of the various denominations were to be brought in to teach it. School managers were instructed to provide "moral education" in the course of the school day. The religious denomination of teachers was not to be taken into account in hiring.

Irish Language. The Irish language was to be available as an optional subject only from Standard Five (fifth grade) instead of Standard Three, as had been the case previously. As a result of lobbying from the Gaelic League of Northern Ireland, in 1928, new regulations reversed this and allowed Irish as an optional subject from Standard Three. In 1933, however, grant money for teaching Irish in elementary schools was withdrawn.

Education Policy 1923-1972

While Catholic opposition to the Education Act of 1923 would come as no surprise, the strength of Protestant opposition was unexpected. Protestant complaints were directed against two aspects of the act: no religious instruction in school hours, and the requirement that religious denomination of teachers not be taken into account in hiring. The Protestant Churches and the Orange Order put pressure on the prime minister to amend the act just as he was facing an election in 1925. With the Boundary Commission's report soon to be delivered,[16] Prime Minister Craig could not risk the potential loss of support involved in holding fast to the Education Act. He therefore rushed through an amendment to the Education Act in March 1925, to the effect that local education committees could require Protestant religious instruction in controlled schools. This was the moment when state schools became de facto Protestant schools.[17] Not the remotest possibility remained that the Catholic Church would permit its parishioners to send their children to these schools.

In 1930, a new Education Act increased the Protestant clergy's presence on local authorities' school management committees by allowing Protestant clergy who were former school managers to have an automatic place on these committees. In addition, it allowed school managers a veto over appointments of teaching staff who were not qualified on religious grounds to be teaching in the school. Thenceforth, all teachers hired by state schools had to be willing and able to give religious instruction and, as a result, Catholics, as well as people of no religion, were unlikely to be hired by state schools. At the same time, this act made a gesture in the direction of Catholics: 50 percent of building costs of Catholic schools were now to be met by the state. This move was a salve to the conscience of the state authorities, but was considered totally inadequate by Catholics.

Having succeeded in establishing Protestant religious instruction in state primary education, zealous members of the Protestant community went on to push for compulsory teaching of religion in state secondary schools, which, in this case, the government resisted.

Education in the entire United Kingdom was revamped at the end of World War II. Most significantly, the Butler Education Act of 1944, and its Northern Ireland counterpart, the Education (NI) Act of 1947, entitled all children to some form of secondary education and raised the school leaving age to fifteen. The Butler Act introduced the "eleven plus" exam, taken by all children upon the completion of their primary education. Those who passed were to be the ones selected for grammar schools.

Under this act, as in 1930, the government made a gesture to Catholics to appear to balance its concessions to Protestants: grants to cover capital costs of voluntary (i.e., Catholic) schools went up to 65 percent without placing additional requirements on the management structure. The gesture still fell far short of Catholic aspirations. Another progressive element of this legislation was a "conscience clause," to the effect that candidates for teaching jobs did not have to be willing to teach religion, reversing the 1930 ruling.

During the 1950s and 1960s, many new schools were built, but in every year between 1948 and 1971, always more state schools than voluntary schools were built. In 1958-1959, twice as many state schools were built. While it is true that the Catholic population was smaller than the Protestant population, the Catholics had a greater need of new schools. The requirement that Catholics put up 35 percent of the funds for constructing new schools surely impacted this statistic. Nonetheless, generally speaking, relations between the government and the churches settled down during this period, and if the old issues didn't go away, they were referred to with less acrimony. Debates about history teaching, on the other hand, became more open during this period, as will be described in Chapter Seven.

In the 1960s, the United Kingdom was beginning to pull itself out of the shadow of World War II, and Northern Ireland Prime Minister Terence O'Neill was moving on his twin goals of economic expansion and greater openness to the Catholic community. In 1969, the state undertook to pay full maintenance costs of all voluntary schools and raised the amount contributed for their capital costs to 80 percent. Schools that accepted the terms for this increased support would be called "voluntary maintained" and would accept a little bit more local government input in their management. Forty-five grammar schools and 234 primary and secondary intermediate schools took this new status. The term *maintained schools* continues, to this day, to be used to describe Catholic schools in Northern Ireland, just as the term *controlled schools* refers to Protestant-dominated state schools, a small example of the use of euphemism to create an outward veneer of nonsectarianism.

Changes in the public examination system in this period also reflected a mood of reform. Most notably, the task of formulating exams was taken away from employees of the Education Ministry and was given to a new Northern Ireland General Certificate of Education Committee. While this did not entirely remove the exam system from the influence of the ministry, it distanced it somewhat by ending inspectors' involvement in the exam process.

SIGNIFICANT REFORMS PREDATING THE TROUBLES

Education in Ireland has always been a focal point of the contested nature of the society. For both Churches, retaining control of religious education and funding issues has been the primary matter for concern as far as education policy is concerned. The Irish language and history teaching were also matters of concern because of their significance for the power balance, but they always had a lower priority. Both communities resisted the notion of integrated, national schools in the nineteenth century. Again, after the formation of the Northern Ireland province, the vision of a state school system for all was thwarted by both Protestants and Catholics.

Nonetheless, reforms were beginning to come to the system even before the Troubles began in the late 1960s. Most notable was the 1947 act that guaranteed education up to age fifteen for all children and up to age eighteen for those who passed the eleven plus exam. In addition, funding to Catholic schools increased in 1969. Moves to take the external examination system out of government control had particular significance for history examinations. We will discuss reforms in school history teaching in subsequent chapters.

Chapter Six

The Education System Responds to the Troubles

When considering education's contribution to the conflict, some people argued that overt or latent curriculum differences in the separate school systems assisted the development of different mind-sets. Others saw the problem as one of social separation per se, to which the separate school systems had contributed. Still others blamed social and economic inequities that made it harder for Catholics to find jobs or make their way up the social ladder, and which were merely exacerbated by segregated education.

Legislation in 1989 laid down a common, required curriculum for all schools. In addition, new policies have been, and are being, introduced to reduce social inequities in the education system. Some integrated schools have been created as an optional alternative to segregated education.

Whether or not schools have contributed to the social conflict in Northern Ireland, the idea that schools could help change attitudes is now completely embraced by education authorities. Education policy change has been speeded by the availability of progressive ideas about education from England, the Continent, and the United States.

THE EDUCATION SYSTEM

The State's Responsibility for Education

Between 1921 and 1972 the Northern Ireland government had full responsibility for education. In the post-1945 period the unionist government opted for a policy of parity with practice in Britain on education and welfare measures, even though their conservative political outlook tended to be antithetical to the

89

interventionist measures that developed in the postwar period. Under direct rule, the chief political office became the secretary of state for Northern Ireland, a Cabinet post in the U.K. government, appointed by the British prime minister and based in Westminster. The secretary of state appointed a team of three to five junior ministers, one of whom had responsibility for education among other matters.

Under the Belfast Agreement of 1998, responsibility for government and civil service was put back in the hands of the devolved government, except for criminal justice and policing. Between 1998 and 2004, this devolved government has been suspended several times due to disagreements between the main political parties. In these cases, the government was returned to Westminster. Therefore, education policy has in principle been wholly returned to Northern Ireland, though at the time of writing, Westminster is back in charge.

In the past, local government completely controlled the school boards of state schools. Now five regional agencies or Education and Library Boards (ELBs) have this responsibility. Some 40 percent of places in ELBs go to officials elected in District Council (i.e., local government) elections, and the rest are filled by appointment of the Education Ministry.[1]

Initially, Catholic schools were run by independent boards. In 1969 the Catholic Church agreed to accept a minority of publicly appointed representatives onto their school boards, in exchange for which Catholic schools have received more state funding. Since 1990, Catholic schools have had the option of being totally funded by the state and almost all have taken this option.

ELBs delegate the budget to the various schools under their aegis—both Catholic and state schools. In addition, they give curriculum support and training to teachers by appointing field officers in each subject.

The Department of Education for Northern Ireland (DENI) is the civil service arm responsible for education. DENI's responsibilities comprise inspection of schools, curriculum, and examinations. Until 1989, no mandatory curriculum was set down by DENI. Teachers saw curriculum design as part of their professional role, though they bowed to the advice of inspectors, who pay periodic visits to classes. Following the inception of statutory curriculum requirements in 1989, however, the Council for the Curriculum, Examinations and Assessment (CCEA) has been charged with the creation and enforcement of curriculum requirements.

Schools

Northern Ireland divides its secondary level pupils into two tiers by administering an exam to all children at the end of their primary education. Those who pass the "eleven plus" exam are eligible to attend grammar schools, which prepare students for the Advanced Level exams (A-Levels) that are required for university admission. Grammar schools in Northern Ireland are considered to be of exceptionally high quality.

Those who do not pass the eleven plus attend "secondary modern school" or "high school." Many of these schools take children only through to age sixteen, and pupils who take their final exams at sixteen leave with a General Certificate of Secondary Education (GCSE).[2]

The eleven plus exam might seem to reward merit but in fact has been a means of perpetuating class distinctions. There is a real and perceived class difference between secondary and grammar schools. An additional criticism of the system is the fact that failing the eleven plus can be such a blow to self-esteem that it becomes a self-fulfilling prophecy: young people who fail the eleven plus can lose the incentive to do well.

In 1999, Northern Ireland had 970 primary schools, 166 secondary schools, and 70 grammar schools.[3] Since 1981 a number of integrated schools, catering to Catholics and Protestants together, have been started, which now number around fifty and encompass about 5 percent of the enrollment in Northern Ireland.

Teacher Training

Four institutions in Northern Ireland train teachers: Queen's University, the University of Ulster, and two colleges of education—Stranmillis College (recently promoted to university status) and St. Mary's College. Like the broader education system, and for the same reasons, the two colleges of education are de facto religiously segregated. Stranmillis is a state-run institution, although it does employ a significant number of Catholics on the staff. But Catholic primary schools' requirement that their teachers possess an approved certificate in religious education training means that few Catholics attend Stranmillis except when they are pursuing postgraduate specializations not offered elsewhere. In the early 1980s, the Catholic Church vetoed a suggestion to amalgamate the state and Catholic training colleges into a single college.

In the past, a concurrent education and history degree was offered at the University of Ulster at Coleraine for those planning to become history teachers. Though this is no longer offered, a significant number of prospective history teachers, nonetheless, study at Coleraine. Some history teachers have reached their positions by other routes: by taking education degrees and teaching first in primary schools, by studying politics, or by taking their degrees in England or Scotland.

Textbooks

Traditionally, primary and secondary schools would submit lists of textbooks they proposed using in the coming year for DENI's approval. This continued into the 1970s. In the case of grammar schools, prior approval was not required: inspectors would simply take note of what texts were being used in schools. Inspectors had the power to prohibit books deemed unsuitable, but no authority was exercised to enforce the use of certain texts. Often books for grammar schools were prescribed by the bodies administering A-Levels. This does not mean that schools did not feel they were under some coercion. Most schools chose to use previously approved texts to avoid ruffling feathers.

Because of the freedom of choice that was permitted, it is difficult now to establish what texts were used in schools in past decades. Moreover, the freedom of teachers to create curriculum and teaching materials means that textbooks are not necessarily a good indicator of what was being taught. Textbooks have, therefore, had limited usefulness for study of the mind-set propagated by schools in Northern Ireland before the Troubles broke out.

REFORMING EDUCATION IN RESPONSE TO THE CONFLICT

In the late 1960s, those trying to explain the outbreak of violence often cited the curriculum in general and the history curriculum in particular. But calls for change did not get taken up immediately in any serious way.[4] Often such ideas met with accusations of "social engineering," a frequently used phrase to register reservations about proactive education policy.

Indeed, the idea that education had any role at all to play in *improving* community relations was greeted with considerable suspicion in the 1970s. Both Protestants and Catholics had reservations: Protestants feared an unwelcome new agenda that questioned old ways; Catholics feared that education would become a more efficient instrument of the state.[5]

Early responses to the conflict addressed, even if they did not wholly solve, the civil rights issues of housing, local government, and employment. They were slower to act with regard to education. In the mid-1970s, DENI began to allow piecemeal curriculum development projects and occasionally encouraged them. Most significantly, in 1982, a full thirteen years after the first person was killed in the Troubles, DENI issued a circular, a copy of which was sent to every teacher, announcing that schools must play a role in building better community relations.[6]

Meantime, individual teachers were taking initiatives to bring new programs to schools. These can be broken down into three general categories, which vary according to people's explanations for the conflict and their beliefs about education's appropriate role. Academic research, policy initiatives, and efforts by volunteer groups with regard to education after 1972, reflect an interplay among these three sets of assumptions.

- *Cultural hypothesis:* The animosities grow from different mentalities passed on in schools that teach very different material to their pupils, especially in the way they inform pupils about the other community. This happens through the formal curriculum, but also through the "informal curriculum"—school assemblies and extracurricular activities—and through the "hidden curriculum"—the set of attitudes and values passed on through school symbols, teachers' use of language, and attitudes toward outsiders.
- *Social differentiation hypothesis:* School segregation contributes to the divisions, but not because of what is taught in schools; rather, segregation emphasizes group difference and perpetuates ignorance and mutual suspicion. This position sometimes overlaps, or gets confused, with concerns about hidden curriculum.
- *Social justice hypothesis:* The divisions arise because one group has been discriminated against in the past, and vestiges of that discrimination remain. Catholic schools' smaller per capita income from the state has traditionally made it harder to pay for the necessary equipment for science teaching. This has perpetuated the strong tilt toward humanities teaching in Catholic schools and contributed to the difficulties Catholic school leavers have in finding jobs. An additional facet of this argument criticizes the selective system, that is the eleven plus, for the way it discriminates against the less privileged.

Any organized account of reform measures taken in the last thirty years obscures the ad hoc social environment in which people were working; nonetheless, it is useful to think in broad terms of three intervention strategies that have been taken since 1972, in response to the three hypotheses laid out above. These are curriculum, addressing the cultural hypothesis; contact programs and integrated schools, addressing the social differentiation hypothesis; and strategies to equalize opportunity, addressing the social justice hypothesis.

ADDRESSING THE CULTURAL HYPOTHESIS THROUGH CURRICULUM REFORM

An open debate about the degree to which curriculum was responsible for the conflict was launched in 1975, when a research project funded by the Ford

Foundation concluded that in overt educational content the schools showed little difference.[7] The study, nonetheless, demonstrated differences in the "hidden curriculum" propagated by segregated schools through use of symbols, assumptions, and vocabulary of teachers.

Ten years later, a qualitative analysis of the two systems reached similar conclusions and elaborated on the way that the broader culture of the schools confirm or contribute to a sense of difference between the communities.[8] The author cited, for example, the Catholic teacher who said the Protestant school flies the Union Jack (the British flag) to demonstrate Protestant power over Catholics, and the Protestant teachers who believed that the Catholic symbolism in the Catholic school was retained to spite Protestants; he thus argued that there is more cognizance of symbols by those observing them than those displaying them.

The author of the latter study, Dominic Murray, maintained that schools *reflect* difference rather than *cause* it. He dismissed the importance of history as a means of establishing identity, and therefore the need to scrutinize history teaching, though it must be remembered that his research had been carried out in two primary schools, where history teaching would not have played a significant role. Murray made it clear that he understood identity to mean identity with social institutions, in this case the government and government departments in Northern Ireland, or with values. He argued that what happens with schools is what happens more broadly—Catholics identify with the church authorities, and Protestants identify with the state authorities.

Nonetheless, Murray advocated curriculum reform to help change attitudes. He argued that *playing down* the existence of different cultures perpetuates the problem. On the Protestant side especially, the need for cultural identification goes with a deeper need for self-preservation. He therefore recommended teaching tolerance of the *values of others*, especially through social studies classes. This argument was an early expression of the issue that continues to confront education policymakers to this day: how much to encourage the explicit discussion of difference.

Even though the two studies emphasized that the curriculum content of the two school systems was not that different, by focusing on the hidden curriculum they both argued that subtle messages in schools confirmed the respective mind-sets. In this way, they left room for the argument that curriculum reform could make a difference if it taught the next generation to have greater understanding of the other group.

In the 1970s, individuals acting with limited DENI support launched several curriculum development projects emphasizing conflict resolution, and peace education, and developing contributions to the mainstream curriculum. No overarching philosophy or plan lay behind them. In retrospect, their value lay in the fact that a group of teachers took ownership of the issue at hand and gained some experience in new forms of teaching. Together these projects "began a process and established a context which made future developments possible."[9]

In 1982, following DENI's memorandum calling all schools to contribute to community relations,[10] DENI created a body to initiate, support, and coordinate activities in curriculum development for better community relations. Many teachers who had been developing new curriculum became part of this Northern Ireland Council for Educational Development (NICED). Their first task was to come up with a term or phrase to describe the kind of curriculum they sought to encourage. They adopted the term *Education for Mutual Understanding* (EMU), as it was considered less controversial than some of the alternatives (for example, "peace education" or "community relations education").[11]

Over the next five years, the EMU program encouraged schools to introduce community relations themes into the classroom on a voluntary basis. DENI circulated guidance material on EMU to schools; the ELBs appointed EMU Field Officers to give support to teachers; and a variety of agencies and charitable trusts supplied advice and funding to teachers. Teachers were, at the end of the day, the ones who chose whether or not to pursue such programs. This respected their autonomy and ensured that no one felt pushed further than they wanted to go.

Cataloguing these projects ended up being a community relations project in itself. *Education for Mutual Understanding: A Guide*[12] included every suggestion that had ever arisen on the subject of schools' role in promoting good community relations and introduced procedures for the promotion of EMU. The guide provided interested teachers with a more coherent set of options as they set out to develop new programs.

Summarizing the work of the previous years, in 1989 the Ministerial Working Group on Education for Mutual Understanding defined the program thus: "Education for Mutual Understanding should enable pupils as an integral part of their education:

- to learn to *respect* and value themselves and others;
- to appreciate the *interdependence* of people within society;
- to know about and understand what is shared as well as what is different about their *cultural traditions*;
- to appreciate how *conflict* may be handled in nonviolent ways."[13]

ADDRESSING THE SOCIAL DIFFERENTIAL
HYPOTHESIS THROUGH GREATER CONTACT

Contact Schemes

Both the 1975 and 1985 studies mentioned above highlighted the problem of little if any significant contact, much less cross-fertilization, among schools. A further 1984 study, designed specifically to measure the extent of contact between schools, found very little contact.[14] In recognition of this problem, a series of ad hoc programs encouraging contact between Protestant and Catholic schools were undertaken in the early 1980s. In 1987, DENI began offering financial assistance to schools for contact programs.

The "contact hypothesis," the notion that social contact between majority and minority group members will reduce prejudice, has generated a body of critical and supportive literature in recent years relating not only to Northern Ireland but to other protracted conflicts.[15] Broadly in Northern Ireland, contact projects have included joint holidays for Catholic and Protestant children, school outings to museums, and more proactive reconciliation activities.[16] Contact schemes are an understandable response to the social differentiation hypothesis, though they can be criticized for failing to be sufficiently analytical about the nature of the contacts and the kinds of effects they are designed to have.

One of the continuing areas of confusion with regard to school contact programs is whether they should engage the children, or the teachers for that matter, in any explicit discussion or acknowledgment of difference. They are not usually designed to do so. It is nonetheless assumed that contact programs address the problems of the "hidden curriculum" and so help to undermine stereotypical thinking about the other group. In some cases, contact programs are conducted by teachers who are strongly engaged in the process of confronting difference and building new relationships. But it takes a creative and bold team of teachers to make that happen. The teachers must be self-aware about their own prejudices and capable of talking about these matters to young people. The average teacher does not know how to do this. Contact programs, therefore, should not be understood to be the same as EMU programs, where some open discussion of difference is required.

Teachers interviewed for this study split fairly evenly in their opinion of whether or not children benefit from joint outings. Several teachers called contact programs "artificial," saying that the children do not mix or get to know one another. Others had anecdotes about how the pupils from the different schools had kept in touch and remained friends. One teacher said the only contact program that works well is one where a group has to cooperate in performing a task.

While many of those organizing contact schemes cited Murray's findings in *Worlds Apart* as the rationale for their projects, an analysis of Murray's conclusions quickly reveals that Murray did not simply advocate more *contact*. Murray's book calls for a new culture of *discussion* in schools. While he calls for more contact, he is also saying that the curriculum should help each group appreciate the values of the other and help each group to feel acknowledged.

The confusion between EMU, which is supposed to foster discussion, and contact schemes, which are not explicitly doing so, did not escape the attention of education policymakers and researchers. By the mid-1990s, it had been recognized that schools were counting their contact programs as a fulfillment of the EMU requirement. Thus, schools were finding a way to duck the task they found most difficult, namely to have open discussions about difference.[17]

Integrated Schools

A significant change in the picture in Northern Ireland since 1981 has been the introduction of integrated schools.

Talk about the need for integrated schools started at the outset of the conflict.[18] The General Assembly of the Presbyterian Church and the Annual Synod of the Church of Ireland passed resolutions guardedly supporting the notion. The Catholic hierarchy has remained opposed. Among the laity these generalizations break down. Some Protestants like to think of their schools as nondenominational state schools, and so they support integration, believing it would simply mean Catholics attending state schools. But Catholic supporters have the impression that they support the integrated school movement more than Protestants do.

All Children Together, founded in 1974,[19] was a key step in mobilizing parents who did not want their children to experience segregated education. The organization promoted debate and discussion and lobbied successfully for legislation allowing state schools to become integrated. When it became clear in the late 1970s that legislation was not providing sufficient impetus to make existing schools convert, some All Children Together parents worked together to create one prototype integrated school. Lagan College opened in 1981 with twenty-eight pupils in a Boy Scout hut in Belfast.

Now there are fifty integrated schools, and every community in Northern Ireland has an integrated primary school within a reasonable distance. About 5 percent, or 16,500, of Northern Ireland's school children now attend integrated schools.[20]

The integrated schools are managed and staffed by people of both communities. They welcome children of any or no religious belief and have worked out procedures for the religious instruction for those of both Christian denominations. They originally committed themselves to retain a 60:40 balance in pupil enrollment between the two communities and to reflect both cultural traditions in their curriculum.[21] In recent years, however, it has become accepted that integrated schools can have a greater imbalance than 60:40.

Because these schools are being created from scratch rather than conversion, the financial burden of starting them has been considerable. Committees composed mainly of parents raise the money. Much of the financing has come from educational trusts and foundations, most significantly the three Quaker foundations, Nuffield, Cadbury, and Rowntree, and from the European Union. In the early 1990s, the funding system was streamlined by bringing all the trusts together to make one interest-free loan fund—the Integrated Education Fund—with the idea that once a school got going, DENI would take over the costs and buy the school building.

Legislation passed in the 1990s further encourages the conversion of existing schools to integrated schools. While this approach seems reasonable because it will reduce costs and because overall enrollment is down, Protestant (i.e., state) schools are more likely to convert, and seeing the numbers of their schools fall may feed unionist paranoia.

The integrated school movement is viewed with skepticism in some quarters, mostly because it seems doubtful it will attract more than a small percentage of the population. Some critics reason that it caters only to those families who were not taking sides in the conflict and that in many cases the children attending come from mixed marriages. Claims that integrated schools are secular or that they serve the middle-class population only, have been refuted by the evidence, but many in the population still believe them. An additional concern is that integrated schools draw the liberal-minded away from mainstream schools, with the result that the liberal pupils are not present to influence the hard-line members of their own community; the outcome, it is argued, will be a less liberal society. Many suspect that parents send their children to integrated schools when the children have failed the qualifying exam for grammar schools and that children who do gain entrance to grammar schools will not be sent to integrated schools, though anecdotal evidence does not confirm this. President of Ireland Mary McAleese, who was, until 1997, a pro-vice-chancellor of The Queen's University in Belfast, expresses reservations about integrated schools because she believes children should not be the ones to carry the burden of a problem their parents have been unable to solve.[22]

Secondary school teachers recognize that the creation of new integrated schools means secondary school enrollment in other types of school will drop, therefore causing teacher layoffs, but that those teachers losing their jobs will not necessarily wish to teach at integrated schools. The high turnover of principals of integrated schools and the acknowledged risk that a teacher who has taught at an integrated school will not be able to get a job elsewhere, are indications of the stress this movement places on the teaching profession in these schools. Moreover, while the high level of parent participation in the creation and running of these schools is one of their features, some teachers and principals feel this can get out of hand once the school is operational.

All these concerns are voiced regularly, and many relate to the inevitable debates that arise with the creation of a new institution. The more fundamental question is whether these schools do create better understanding and whether they will benefit the society. It will be some time before research can give any answers on this. Those teaching at integrated schools demonstrate profound commitment and pride of achievement. This optimism surely has an impact on the outlook of students.

The strongest argument against integrated schools is that they are an unrealistic option for the vast majority, given the widespread opposition to them. Attention, it is argued, should therefore be given to solutions that have wider applicability.

ADDRESSING THE SOCIAL JUSTICE HYPOTHESIS THROUGH EQUALITY OF OPPORTUNITY AND TREATMENT

Equity in School Funding

A 1987 review of the employment situation in Northern Ireland by the Standing Advisory Commission on Human Rights (SACHR) demonstrated that Catholics were twice as likely to be unemployed as Protestants.[23] This finding showed up the ineffectiveness of the 1974 Fair Employment Act and resulted in new and more stringent employment legislation—the Fair Employment Act of 1989.

A subsequent study found that a higher proportion of Catholics than Protestants left school with low or no qualifications and that a higher proportion of Protestants took science subjects at school and university.[24] Studies of school financing pointed to the extra financial burden carried by Catholic schools, by virtue of the fact that at that time they received only 85 percent of their capital funding from the government. In addition, government funding for Catholic schools' recurrent costs proved to be a lower figure *per capita* than that received by Protestant schools. It was recognized that, for a number of reasons, Catholic schools are less inclined to approach the government for funding.[25] The smaller size of some Catholic school premises and the subsequent difficulty in providing specialist teaching space could also contribute to these statistics.

SACHR therefore recommended that DENI monitor the impact of current policy on the separate school systems, that it review arrangements for capital grants, and that it increase the number of places available in Catholic grammar schools. The Educational Reform Order of 1989 required funding for Catholic schools that is equal to that received by state schools.

COMMON CURRICULUM:
THE EDUCATION REFORM (NI) ORDER 1989

A sea change in education policy and content came in the late 1980s, with the introduction of a required, common curriculum for Northern Ireland's schools.

The special circumstances that brought about this decision were particular to the British political situation at the time. The Thatcher government in Westminster was beginning, by the late 1980s, to move the British education system in a more conservative direction. It decided to lay down more stringently defined curriculum requirements than had ever been the case in British education. This went ahead with the passing of the Education Reform Act of 1988 for England and Wales. The separate legislative process for Northern Ireland presented an opportunity to enact tailor-made reforms for the province.

Even if most curriculum specialists did not think that curriculum greatly differed in the two school systems, they recognized the symbolic importance of efforts to ensure that curriculum in all schools was the same. This was really a gesture of empowerment toward Catholics.

Ironically, a conservative policy in the United Kingdom had liberalizing repercussions in Northern Ireland. In many countries, a common curriculum would imply the state's imposition of a mind-set to encourage national cohesion. The Education Reform (NI) Order 1989 (ERO) incorporated a number of progressive measures aimed to address community relations needs. It drew on projects pursued in Northern Ireland in the previous twenty years, summarizing and acknowledging the work that had gone before and defining clear goals for the future. Its stipulations included the following:

- *Curriculum:* Standardized requirements were laid down for all school subjects, including history and religious instruction.
- *Cross-curricular themes:* All teachers were to incorporate six "cross-curricular themes" into their teaching. Two of these, focusing on career opportunities and technology, were designed with the social injustice hypothesis in mind, to cre-

ate more options and a sense of opportunity for students. Two other themes, Education for Mutual Understanding (EMU) and Cultural Heritage addressed the cultural hypothesis. Elements of earlier EMU programs were made compulsory and incorporated into all subjects across the board.

- *Funding of integrated schools:* The government undertook to finance integrated schools once they had passed a certain threshold of external funding and enrollment.
- *Funding of Catholic schools:* Catholic schools that agreed to allow more government representation on their boards would be eligible for full capital funding from the government.
- *Introducing market economics into the education system:* Grammar schools could now accept any number of pupils and would receive a government subsidy for every pupil they accepted.

CURRENT ISSUES IN EDUCATION

The ERO created considerable optimism among policy reformers. Curriculum developers had a mandate to include twentieth-century Irish history and to develop EMU. The integrated schools movement saw the new funding stipulations as a mark of government confidence in them. Catholic schools had been brought fully into the system.

Over time, quirks emerged. Problems with regard to the history curriculum will be discussed in a later chapter. As far as EMU was concerned, schools continued to concentrate on contact programs as a way of fulfilling their EMU requirement, sidestepping the harder task of openly discussing the kinds of topics intended for EMU.[26] Market economics in education allowed grammar schools to siphon off the top tier of pupils in secondary schools. The serious and growing dearth of good, motivated pupils in secondary schools demoralized teachers and pupils. The belief that schools need to offer more to, and expect more from, students who had not passed the eleven plus seemed to be losing out to market forces. While Catholic schools were enjoying the benefits of full capital funding, the government had raised the hurdle a new integrated school had to cross to make it eligible for government funding. This was in part because total numbers of school children were falling, so that it was not justifiable to lay out government money for new schools.

Curriculum

Recognizing that the themes of Education for Mutual Understanding and Cultural Heritage had not on the whole enabled teachers to discuss controversy and diversity in a classroom setting, a curriculum review completed in 2003 underlined the need for greater educational focus on tolerance, diversity, and democratic values.[27] The new plan was to teach these topics through a mandatory class in Local and Global Citizenship. The new syllabus had four sub-themes: Diversity around Me, Exploring Ethnic Diversity, Understanding Sectarianism, Human Rights and Social Responsibility. The curriculum was arrived at after consultations with representatives of a wide number of groups in the community, as well as with teachers.

Contact

The integrated school movement continued to grow at its own pace and benefitted from encouragement from the U.S. State Department and the International Fund for Ireland, both of which identify this as an area that they believe deserves international assistance.

School contact programs continued, though the energy behind the initial scheme fell off. New plans emerged to set up more official linkages between schools.

Social Justice and the Selective System

Following the election of the Labour government in 1997, DENI commissioned research on the effects of the selective system. This research concluded that the system was socially divisive and while it created conditions that allowed a minority of schools to achieve very high academic results, it also produced a long tail of low-achieving schools.[28] Other research suggested that the high stakes tests used to select pupils contained significant technical flaws[29] and called into question their reliability and validity. As a consequence of the research findings, the minister of education established a Post Primary Review Body, chaired by former ombudsman Gerry Burns, to offer recommendations on future arrangements. The Burns Report[30] recommended the end of academic selection and the establishment of formal networks of schools to create cooperative, rather than competitive, relationships among schools.

The recommendations of the Burns Report were controversial and excited considerable opposition from sections of the elite grammar school sector. Interestingly, however, the Catholic bishops indicated that while they were opposed to their schools being obliged to come under the proposed arrangements, they were in favor of the end of academic selection. The Department of Education carried out a consultation on the recommendations of the report.[31] The fact that over 200,000 response forms were returned by members of the public to DENI is one indication of the degree of engagement the issue created.

Since no consistent pattern of opinion emerged from the consultation, the minister of education decided to establish a Post Primary Review Working Group. Businessman Steve Costello chaired the Working Group and most of its members represented educational interests. Their task was to bring practical suggestions for a way forward, given the results of the consultation exercise. The Costello Report was presented to the minister in November 2003 and published in January 2004.[32] The report confirmed the view that academic selection at age eleven years should end and that future postprimary arrangements should be characterized by cooperation among groups of schools, although in a less formal way than that proposed by the Burns Report. The minister of education accepted these recommendations and announced that the last selection test would be held in 2008.[33]

ONGOING PROCESS

In spite of the fact that Northern Ireland's education system was better placed than that of many postconflict societies to introduce reforms, this has been a drawn-out and ongoing process. Subsequent chapters will focus particularly on reforms in the teaching of history and evolving interest in teaching about citizenship as an alternative approach to addressing problems linked with the conflict.

Part Three

Partisan Prescriptions

Chapter Seven

Domination and Empowerment

Given the fact that elites use historical narratives to coalesce or hold on to power, subordinate groups can be expected to respond in kind. Subordinate groups will analyze history teaching to demonstrate the failure of the ruling elite to include them in its definition of the nation. They will encourage their own historians to develop a narrative for their group. And they will pursue a campaign for the recognition of that narrative as part of their program of liberation. In response, those representing the mind-set of the dominant group will analyze texts of subordinate groups to demonstrate their intention to rebel. Thus, in protracted internal conflicts, debates about history and school history teaching policies become an arena where the political contest is pursued. A group's success in disseminating its own history and having it more widely adopted is an indicator of that group's power.

This chapter examines the capacity of history teaching to be an indicator of power relations in Northern Ireland and a tool in the political program of the subordinate group. It looks at two successive regimes: first, the period of the national schools under British authority, 1832-1920; and second, the school system of the Stormont regime of 1920-1972. After exploring whether indeed history teaching was used by the state to assert its power, the chapter examines how, and with what success, protest politics made use of this fact.

The use of history teaching policy as a tool for imposing the dominant culture first by Britain in the period before 1920 and afterward by the unionists under Stormont, is confirmed but only in the narrowest sense. British authorities tried to minimize the amount of history taught in schools; Stormont authorities accentuated British history but left schools some leeway in what they taught.

The idea that Catholic schools propagated an aggressive Irish nationalist history is also difficult to prove as a general matter, despite many confirmatory anecdotal accounts. In some cases, Catholic schools refrained from teaching any Irish history.

The Catholic protest strategy of challenging the lack of adequate Irish history in schools generally correlated with increasing self-confidence of Irish nationalism. But by the mid-1970s, as the Troubles passed their five-year mark and the Sunningdale government failed, nationalist politicians stopped taking this particular tack, presumably because the security situation had become a greater preoccupation.

Nonetheless, reforms in the teaching of history proceeded. A deconstructionist spin might suggest that these reforms were an overdue response from the education authorities, granted by the authorities once the subordinate group had demonstrated its power by other means, through the civil rights movement and all that followed in the 1970s. Alternatively, we could view the reforms in history teaching and the civil rights movement as parallel responses to new, liberal thinking in Europe and the United States in the late 1960s.

THE NATIONAL SCHOOLS OF THE NINETEENTH CENTURY

As described in Chapter Five, a national school system was established in 1831, just two years after Catholic emancipation gave male Catholic landowners the vote. The system was run by an interdenominational body — the Commissioners of national education — with religious instruction offered after school hours. From a religious standpoint, Britain was not attempting to impose its culture. Britain's efforts to neutralize the issue of history teaching in the national schools, however, can be interpreted as a strategy to engender loyalty to the British Crown.

From inception of the national schools in 1831, the Commissioners of National Education recommended textbooks to schools and by midcentury had produced quite a number of their own. The commissioners' recommended books were not compulsory, but they were very widely adopted. Use of other books required special permission from the commissioners, who were willing to use their veto power. An added incentive for using the commissioners' books was that a certain number were donated to the schools and freely renewed every four years (after 1848 every three years), and those that were not free were priced low.

The books published by the commissioners have been described as the best set of school books produced in the British Isles before 1860.[1] They took the form of a basic reading series called *The First Book of Lessons*, *The Second Book of Lessons*, and so on, and covered grammar, arithmetic, geometry, mensuration, geography, agriculture, and natural philosophy. Other readers included geography, English grammar, and biblical history. All textbooks were filled with moralizing and religious references. History lessons appeared rarely in these books. And very little material relating to Ireland, apart from basic geography, was covered. Akenson describes *The Fifth Book of Lessons*, the most advanced of the texts, which devotes fifteen pages to history from 1500 to 1835. It leaves out the Reformation, Ireland's union with Britain in 1801, and O'Connell's movement for Catholic emancipation.[2]

A number of the commission's books were written by Church of Ireland (i.e., Anglican) Archbishop Richard Whately, a fellow of Oriel College, Oxford, who had earlier remarked that the aim of the national schools in Ireland was to make of every pupil "a happy English child."[3] The second resident commissioner of national education, Alexander MacDonnell, frankly allowed that a major aim of the lesson books was to inculcate loyalty and reverence to the law.[4]

In midcentury a school inspection system was instituted, and inspectors' comments on the teaching of particular subjects were thenceforth included in the yearly reports of the commissioners. These official reports do contain views on the teaching of history and specifically of Irish history. Reports in 1855 and 1859 register inspectors' complaints on the absence of history teaching.[5] To one of the complaints, the commissioners replied:

> [We] have long been anxious to introduce . . . a work on history; but [we] have been unable to find any work extant which would be suitable for united education. . . . Steps should be taken as soon as possible, towards the compilation of an historical work, which should contain no matter that could give just cause of offence, either on religious or political grounds, to persons of any denomination in Ireland. . . . The compilation of a work on history is felt to be a task of a very delicate and difficult nature.[6]

Yet no official support was given to the development of such a history textbook. Between 1838 and 1894, the National Board inspected about seventy books containing historical material. Thirty-two of these were books being used illicitly, that is, without the permission of the National Board. Of these, thirty were rejected when permission to use them was sought.

In correlation with increased Catholic self-confidence and rising nationalism of the second half of the century, the Catholic Church began to complain about the lack of Irish history in schools. Addressing the Powis Commission February 24, 1869,[7] Cardinal Paul Cullen commented, "National School books are sadly deficient in Irish history . . . ; our history is not so disreputable as to be unfit to be studied by our children."[8] And the following year Walter Scott Coward, an assistant commissioner to the Powis Commission, testified about the "un-Irish character" of books approved by the National Board in which "the absence of any Irish history . . . [was] an attempt to destroy the feeling of nationality, and was the feature which provoked most resentment."[9] In response, the Powis Commission report urged, "in all schools the use of any suitable books should be allowed without any privilege or preference for the books of the Commissioners of National Education."[10]

This pronouncement changed nothing. In 1872, a payment-by-results scheme was introduced, which meant that certain subjects would now be listed for examination, and Treasury grants to schools would be calculated in relation to exam results. History was not a listed exam subject; it was included in geography and English.

An interesting aspect of the national schools' policy toward history teaching is that it was apparently nondiscriminatory. A list of history textbooks refused sanction by the commissioners includes more books on English and British Empire history than on Irish history.[11] This fact does not necessarily undercut the argument that the purpose of removing history as a school subject was to remove the opportunity for teachers to use Irish history "as a cover for subversion."[12] Rather, the commissioners seem to have assumed that teaching British history would have led to more insistence upon the inclusion of Irish history as well.

Nor should the omission of British history be taken as an indication that there was no attempt to inculcate a sense of British nationality and loyalty to the Crown in the national schools. Other school subjects could do this. The absence of material about Ireland in literature, geography, and so on, still suggests the national schools were bent on removing possible sources for Irish nationalism. Certainly, nationalists and republicans of the twentieth century interpreted the policy thus. Padraig Pearse commented:

> It is because the English education system in Ireland has deliberately eliminated the national factor that it has so terrifically succeeded. For it has succeeded— succeeded in making us slaves. And it has succeeded so well that we no longer realize we are slaves.[13]

Many people argued, during the late nineteenth century and subsequently, that the policy of refusing to teach Irish history actually brought about that which it was designed to prevent. Addressing the Powis Commission in 1870, Robert Sullivan, author of *Geography Generalized,* which included a number of entries on European history, said that the absence of history textbooks fed "feelings of disaffection which exist in the country, by sending the pupils of the National Schools to other sources of information."[14] Another inspector who testified to the Powis Commission suggested that the paucity of Irish history in approved textbooks was sending some teachers to "dangerous sources" and contributing to the growth of Fenianism.[15] A century later John Magee, a lecturer in St. Joseph's College, Belfast, echoed this belief in a seminal article in 1970. Commenting on the two mind-sets of the two communities, Magee suggested that the problem went back to the era in the nineteenth century when no history was taught in schools, and people were forced to turn to popular history.[16]

Outside schools, Irish history books were being published and were being read. These were often highly charged renditions of the nationalist narrative. Mitchel's *Jail Journal*, *Speeches from the Dock*, and *The Spirit of the Nation* were published cheaply and sold at markets and fairs. As the Home Rule movement gathered steam, journalists turned to history writing to give justification to their cause. The best known of these was A. M. Sullivan, whose *Story of Ireland*, published in 1870, described Irish history as a struggle to regain freedom lost 700 years before and was enormously popular among Catholic nationalists. The book was, naturally, refused sanction by the commissioners for use in schools.[17]

It may be jumping to conclusions to suggest that had there *been* history classes in schools, people would have paid less attention to the partisan political histories that were being published. But given that there were none, knowledge of history was clearly gained in settings of political and religious homogeneity and through politicized history books. Irish nationalism produced impassioned writers who wrote liberation history. Protestant historians, especially in Ulster, wrote about the experience of plantation among a hostile, backward people, where a sense of siege was a daily reality. Both groups described themselves as victims:

> Protestants and Catholics—unionist and nationalists, call them what you will— had a completely unbalanced view of the past, and, because of the manner in which their mythology had been acquired, had no knowledge at all of the historical basis of each other's point of view.[18]

These histories contributed to two group identities whose sense of the past was entirely at odds, apart from their mutual belief in a history of continual intergroup conflict.

The Commissioners of National Education finally sanctioned an Irish history textbook in 1897, P. W. Joyce's *A Child's History of Ireland*. The book was largely a political history that attempted to respect different political points of view. The author wrote in the opening:

> I have tried to write soberly and moderately, avoiding exaggeration and bitterness, pointing out extenuating circumstances where it was just and right to do so, giving credit where credit is due, and showing fair play all round . . . Perhaps this book . . . may help foster mutual feelings of respect and toleration among

Irish people of different parties, and may teach them to love and admire what is great and noble in their history no matter where found.[19]

This policy departure suggests the authorities were coming to the conclusion that amid the increasingly politicized public uses of history, they would do better to offer schools an attempt at a balanced, middle-of-the-road history than none at all. The policy's timing was interesting. Coming, as it did, during the growth of the Gaelic language movement, this decision may have been designed to thwart the increasing influence of nationalism in education.

THE STORMONT REGIME 1920-1972

Government Policy

The Lynn Report of 1922 that designed the Northern Ireland school system made the definitive recommendation that history teaching in all schools that received any government funding should reinforce a sense of British identity and instill loyalty to the constitution of Northern Ireland. History was not to be taught in the first two years of primary school. It was to be an optional subject for the final three years of primary school and central to the curriculum of secondary schools. Definitive evidence of the government's intention to limit the teaching of Irish history for political reasons appears in cabinet minutes of November 22, 1922, where Louis McQuibban, the permanent secretary, is recorded to have said he agreed with the recommendation that for the top three years of primary schooling, history and Irish language should be mutually exclusive subjects "in as much as the kind of history that would be taught in schools where it is desired to foster the study of Irish would be likely to have a bias of a very undesirable kind."[20] Protestants, it seems, believed their own history teaching was unimpeachable. The Lynn Report articulated the significance of history teaching as follows:

> It is obviously important that every citizen should become acquainted with the history of his native country, and for this purpose the children in our schools should acquire an elementary knowledge of the history of Great Britain, and of Ireland and especially Ulster as part of the United Kingdom. In senior classes the subject should be extended to include the history of the British Empire and some knowledge of the outstanding events in modern history.[21]

The intention to use history teaching as a vehicle to guarantee unionist power is further elucidated in the same report:

> All State-aided schools should aim at cultivating a spirit of respect for law, and obedience to constituted authority, and no aid should be given or continued to

any school in which principles are inculcated subversive of the authority of the State.

No books should be used in State-aided schools to which reasonable objection might be entertained on political grounds.

All teachers should as a condition of their recognition be required to give an undertaking to carry out faithfully the regulations of the Ministry. Further . . . the duties of citizenship should be included in the instruction given to pupils in the schools. . . . In addition, we consider it desirable that the Ministry should encourage in all State-aided schools the flying of the Union Jack on suitable occasions.[22]

The focus on loyalty must be understood in relation to the fact that the boundary and identity of the new state were still being challenged.[23] Two members of the Lynn Committee considered the section on loyalty in the Final Report too weak and lodged a reservation, declaring in part:

Not only should the flag be flown over every State-aided school, but even the youngest children should be assembled at very frequent intervals and taught to salute the flag, thus inculcating loyalty in the children and preparing the soil in which the seeds of Civics, as they grow more advanced, could be planted.[24]

With regard to textbooks, the report required primary schools to submit to the inspectorate for approval a list of textbooks used:

We think that the powers of the Ministry to regulate and supervise the books used in schools should be very strictly exercised in the matter of historical text books and readers. No book bearing upon the subject of history should without previous official sanction be permitted to be used in any school under the Ministry.[25]

At the secondary level there was no requirement that schools submit books for approval, but school inspectors had the right to question the use of books.

The Ministry of Education of Northern Ireland took over the administration of public examinations. History and geography were initially included in the English exam, in accordance with existing custom, but in 1928 a separate history exam was introduced. Corken cites an example of the nature of the public exams at the outset of the Stormont regime: In 1922, the history section of the English exam included a question, "What claims has Cromwell to be a great general?"[26]—a question clearly not designed with sensitivity toward the confusing dilemma it presented to Catholic children.[27]

School History Teaching

After 1925, the nationalist community experienced continued frustration about the limitations on the teaching of Irish culture and history. Nationalist members of Parliament condemned textbooks for being too British in orientation and for not mentioning Irish patriots (e.g., Wolfe Tone, William Orr, William Drennan, and John Mitchel).[28]

In the early years of the Northern Irish state, few state primary schools exercised their right to teach history as an optional subject. A Ministry of Education report of 1936-1937, for example, said that history was rarely found on the timetable of rural grant-aided primary schools. When history *was* taught, it was in the larger schools where there were more teachers on staff; clearly one problem was teachers' lack of knowledge and lack of time to teach history in a "one-room schoolhouse" situation. In secondary schools, history teaching was closely monitored, and annual ministry reports indicated the continued assumption that history classes should teach an approved version of history that would promote citizenship. A Ministry of Education report from 1934-1935 said,

> Some schools continue to give scant consideration to [history]. This is due to some
> extent to a wrong conception of the aims and value of its teaching. . . . In days of
> widespread interest in matters of national and international affairs, the study
> of History thus provides an essential equipment for the citizen.[29]

Occasionally, the teaching of Ulster as distinct from Irish history was referred to positively in inspection reports.[30]

Inspection reports also made clear that teachers were being instructed not to teach exclusively from textbooks. This policy to some degree undermined the state's capacity to control what happened in classrooms and makes it more difficult both to assess what exactly *was* taught and to accuse the government of rigidly pushing its own agenda. In a situation fraught with paradoxes, this policy supplies one more paradox by making it clear that the government was not as controlling as it might have been.

The Junior Certificate and Senior Certificate examinations during this period were focused on the political, social, and economic history of Great Britain and Ireland, and in the case of the Senior Certificate there was an additional paper on modern European history. But Irish history was only likely to arise in these exams when it related to an aspect of the broader syllabus.

In May 1938, the Association of Assistant Mistresses of Secondary Schools in Northern Ireland wrote to the Ministry of Education with recommendations for the syllabus for external exams. These recommendations were the result of a questionnaire that had been sent to members of the association. The recommendations called for more Irish history to be taught at both the Junior and Senior Certificate level and that at least one optional question on Irish history be included in the Senior Certificate Exam. The Ministry of Education sought the views of several Northern Ireland education specialists in response to this memo. One expert suggested that an additional section on Irish history be added to the Senior Certificate exam. But apart from that solo voice, the specialists emphasized in unison (1) that in most papers in recent years one question *had* dealt with Ireland, (2) that usually questions on Irish history get answered badly, and (3) that a problem with regard to including more Irish history is the lack of good textbooks. The irony of these responses seems to have been lost on the ministry. In any event, the issue was dropped.[31]

In the period 1940 to 1943, in the context of a move to introduce more history of the United States into the exam syllabus and make some changes in exam format, four Catholic headmasters' and assistant headmasters' associations called for more emphasis on Irish history in schools. Though certain inspectors were not unsympathetic to this request, the Catholic associations' case was officially rejected. The ministry's given reason was that the standard of Irish history teaching in secondary schools was not good. In June 1943, a letter went out from the ministry outlining the new syllabus for the Senior Certificate where more treatment of the British Commonwealth, along with history of the United States, were to be the principal changes of content. As before, Irish history would only arise when it related to the broad flow of British or American history.

In spite of the limitations to teaching Irish history in schools, during the 1930s, two new Irish history textbooks were written. Ivor Herring's *History of Ireland* was published in 1937. Its narrative was set in the wider British and European context and on the whole avoided partisanship. The foreword acknowledged the support of the two most respected professors of Irish history of that time: Theodore Moody and Robert Dudley Edwards. Randall Clarke's *A Short History of Ireland: From 1485 to the Present Day* came out in 1941. What is unknown is how much these texts were used.

We do know that Methodist College produced its own texts in the 1930s for internal use.[32] Further, evidence in inspectors' reports indicates that at least two other non-Catholic schools, the Royal Belfast Academical Institute and the Friends School, Lisburn, were teaching Irish history in 1951-1952.[33] These three schools all had a reputation for being liberal and were exceptional. Beyond this, anecdotal evidence suggests that some teachers in Protestant schools across the board did make an effort to cover Irish history.

The Ulster History Controversy of the 1950s

In the general elections of June 1945, nationalists gained eleven seats in Stormont. With resultant new self-confidence, one of the new nationalist MPs, M. Conlon, member for South Armagh, raised in a parliamentary session the issue of the lack of Irish history in schools. The minister of education,

Hall-Thompson, instead of responding to Conlon, introduced a case for the teaching of *Ulster* history, as opposed to Irish history, in schools. This response at the very least demonstrates the unionist party's sense of unease in allowing schools to teach about the history of Ireland, and at most suggests that unionists felt threatened by the growing nationalist presence in politics and were taking countermeasures.

In line with Hall-Thompson's new policy, a book was soon disseminated to all schools receiving public money entitled *Northern Ireland, Its History, Resources and People,* written by Dr. Hugh Shearman. The book, and its implicit assimilationist intent, was criticized in the House of Commons by F. Hanna, MP for Central Belfast, who commented on the new policy of teaching Ulster history:

> Coming from the source from which it does come it makes one suspicious that what is being sought is the introduction into schools of a particular form of political propaganda masquerading as history. Anxiety in this matter is increased by the fact that not long ago in this House the Minister of Education publicly acclaimed a publication by Mr. Hugh Shearman (*Northern Ireland, Its History, Resources and People*), a publication which, I understand is almost inspired by his suggestion for a history book for use in schools. If that publication represents his conception of what Ulster history is, then I say it is a very distorted document and one which no person would take seriously. . . . I hope that in future it will not be necessary for any Member to be told in this House that children are being taught some brand of politics under the guise of history.[34]

The issue became a shuttlecock in Stormont in the ensuing weeks. W. M. May, MP for Ards, a man who, eight years later, would himself become minister for education, articulated the unionist viewpoint, calling upon Hall-Thompson to make the study of Ulster history an "obligatory subject in all primary, intermediate and grammar schools which [were] in receipt of any grant from public funds.[35] The minister's reply was to the effect that he could not make the study of history compulsory because of the shortage of reliable textbooks on Ulster history. To a similar question from May in July 1949, Hall-Thompson expressed the hope that the publicity given this issue might encourage the writing of appropriate textbooks; he also stated that it was inappropriate for the government to commission the textbooks.

Demands for Ulster history textbooks were renewed in 1950, 1951, 1952, 1954, and 1956, by a number of Protestant members. Harry Midgley, who in 1950 had succeeded Hall-Thompson as minister of education, responded in 1952 to one of these demands, saying that he would give his support to a history of Ireland that included the history of Ulster and in so doing demonstrated his lack of support for the teaching of an exclusive Ulster history.

In 1956, Midgley, speaking on behalf of the Ministry of Education, disclosed for the first time that a list of recommended texts for Irish history existed. To a request in Parliament for a list of "standard works" on Ulster history currently in use in schools, Midgley gave the names of a few "recommended" Irish history texts: Herring, Clarke, and two of Shearman's books. While the books on the list demonstrated a range of views about Irish history, they were all written by Protestants, in most cases teachers in grammar schools.

The authorities were reluctant to get drawn into a fuller discussion of the matter. To a comment in the House of Commons claiming that there was a substantial difference between history textbooks used in primary and secondary schools managed by the local education authorities and the books used in voluntary (Catholic) schools, the Reverend Moore, responding for the ministry, said that he was "not aware of any substantial difference."[36] A similar set of questioning, with similar responses, occurred in 1959.

Only once did the Ministry of Education openly withhold approval for a textbook. This was in 1956, when it banned an Irish language textbook because it had a photo of a small boy holding an Irish flag, which was objectionable to Protestants.

During the 1950s, various alterations were made to the public examinations, but these did not change the degree of emphasis on Irish history. The curriculum allowed the teaching of Irish history, but students could pass exams without it.

Catholic Schools

What policy did Catholic schools follow under these circumstances? Analysis of official inspection reports in the 1950s shows that some Irish history was taught in many Catholic schools, just as some Irish history was taught in some Protestant schools. Reporting on what he had seen at St. Columb's College, Derry, an inspector in the 1953-1954 school year, writes, "It is satisfactory to find Irish history being given adequate attention throughout the courses."[37] Yet others differed in their definitions of "adequate attention." For example, John Hume, who attended St. Columb's, says that in his days as a student, as well as when he returned there as a teacher in 1960, Irish history was not being taught in the school: the only textbooks he found in 1960 were British history textbooks.[38]

Some Catholic schools clearly taught a very nationalist form of Irish history. Eamonn McCann described his history teacher's approach:

History lessons did not always rigidly follow the curriculum laid down by the Northern Ireland Ministry of Education. One teacher, admittedly regarded as something of an eccentric, was at pains to discredit English propaganda. . . . At the beginning of a new school year he would lead the class through the set text books instructing them to tear out pages of fiction. . . . That done, lessons could begin.[39]

Likewise, Bernadette Devlin describes in *The Price of My Soul* the partisan Irish nationalist history she was taught in her Catholic school.[40]

Christian Brothers' schools have a reputation for teaching a nationalist version of Irish history going back to the nineteenth century when these schools self-consciously aimed to impart an Irish nationalist worldview. As early as 1825, a government report expressed concern over the use of a book, *A Sketch of Irish History*, in Christian Brothers' schools.[41] And in 1870, the Powis Commission report criticized Christian Brothers' texts, which had language critical of the Union and emphasized the cruelty, oppression, and tyranny of England. A "direct training for Fenianism" was the way one of the Powis Commissioners described them.[42]

Some who attended Christian Brothers' schools since 1960 say that they were taught a very nationalist Irish history; others say they were taught no Irish history. This could possibly be explained by the fact that some Catholic schools adopted as their main goal the aim to move their pupils into the mainstream of Northern Ireland life. Anecdotal evidence indicates that in some cases Catholic schools actually discouraged their pupils from answering questions relating to Irish history on exams, for fear it would single out these individuals as Catholics and lead to discriminatory treatment.[43]

Catholic Challenges to History Teaching Policy in the Late 1960s

In 1967, J. O'Reilly, MP for Mourne, asked in Stormont on how the Ministry of Education selected and approved textbooks, asking whether the ministry was persuaded that this duty was being "properly discharged in the public interest."[44] The minister replied predictably: principals submitted a list of selected books to the ministry's District Inspector for approval; prior approval was not required for books used in grammar schools; often books for grammar schools were prescribed by examining bodies. Inspectors saw the books being used during inspections and had the power to prohibit books deemed unsuitable. The minister considered that this duty was being properly discharged.

Several months after the Burntollet confrontation of January 4, 1969,[45] Ivan Cooper, a Protestant civil rights activist representing Mid-Londonderry at Stormont, questioned in Parliament the absence of Irish history in grant-aided schools, saying he himself had only learned a smattering of Irish history. The minister of education's response was that Irish history did appear on the external exams and did appear in the syllabus.[46] Cooper pursued the theme in Parliament in October, arguing that teaching of Irish history would help people know why the conflict was occurring.

In December of that same year, John Hume, now the newly elected MP for Foyle, addressed a question in Stormont to Dr. Robert Simpson, the new minister for community relations, asking if the minister planned to give funds to develop Irish cultural activity. Simpson replied that he had "no statutory power to provide grants for this purpose" and that the Ministry of Education promoted certain parts of Irish culture by teaching Irish language and Irish history.[47] Cooper posed a follow-up question, as did Mr. J. O'Reilly, who said that if the ministry were to promote Irish culture and history as opposed to "Northern Ireland history," "it would make people more broadminded and more tolerant."[48]

Cooper brought up the matter again on February 12, 1970. Segregated education was not, in his view, the cause of the conflict, but as a means to change attitudes he was suggesting that Irish history and Irish traditions should be taught in all schools, "because written into Irish history are several of the divisions of our community."[49] On May 7, 1970, in response to yet another question by Cooper, minister of education William Long declared that history was an optional subject; that it was a matter for the authorities of each school to decide whether to teach it; that the amount of Irish history on exams is determined by the examining body; and that schools would be protective of their academic freedom. To which John Hume replied, "The syllabus is imposed."[50]

In 1970, the *Irish Times* of March 13 reported the remarks of the Reverend P. Livingstone, as he addressed the Clogher Diocesan Society:

> Three-quarters of the pupils over eleven in Northern Ireland attend Intermediate schools where there is permission to teach history but teachers' requests for Irish history textbooks are queried, delayed and frequently refused. By the time the books arrive the year is nearly over and the freedom to teach Irish history, therefore, is in fact taken back by the Ministry's officials.[51]

STRATEGY OF OMISSION

British authorities tried to instill loyalty to the United Kingdom in nineteenth-century schools in Ireland not by teaching British history but by avoiding teaching material that could engender political disagreement or arouse separatist Irish sentiment. Because the British strategy was one of *omission* rather than *commission*, it is not easy to find data where history teaching demonstrates an assertion of British power.

Why was Britain so restrained? British authorities were developing policies to address two relationships in Ireland. They were attempting assimilation for the largely working-class and rural Catholic population. At the same time, they were trying to retain the support of the elite, who were largely Church of Ireland (Anglican). By removing Ireland's parliament in 1801, the British government had removed the only pretext that Ireland was self-governing, and this weakened Britain's relationship with the Ascendancy. Britain was now more reliant than ever on an anti-Catholic ideology to sustain its relationship with the elite. But a divide-and-rule policy based on anti-Catholicism was problematic due to O'Connell's great success in mobilizing Catholics for Catholic emancipation. Therefore, the best the authorities could do in pursuing their goals was to promote a neutered cultural outlook in the national schools by removing religious issues from schools, playing down the Gaelic language, and ignoring history.

Agitation for more Irish history in schools began in the mid-nineteenth century and correlates with the growth of Irish nationalism and growing strength of the Catholic Church. Protest politics did not get far in changing the policy in schools but did frame a nationalist narrative propagated in popular histories in the late 1800s and on into the twentieth century. Nonetheless, given the intensity of support for Irish nationalism, Catholics' campaign for Irish history in schools demonstrates a deficit of passion. Concern about history teaching presumably was weak because other battlegrounds were available: religious education, the Irish language, and financial control.

The same pattern can be seen in the state of Northern Ireland pre-1972. The authorities' belief that history teaching bore a relationship to their task of creating the new Protestant state is clear. Policies to enforce a "British" worldview in Northern Ireland included the near exclusion of Irish history from external exams and the creation of a system for the choice of textbooks in which teachers were encouraged not to step out of line.

Catholics recognized this. Some Catholic schools taught an alternative, Catholic narrative, but this was tempered somewhat by Catholics' concern to help their young people *not* to be marked out and discriminated against. Again, school financing, religious instruction, and the Irish language may have taken some energy away from the issue of Irish history instruction as a battleground where Catholics could push for change. Catholic protest was not uniform in the period 1920-1972, but as time went on, Catholic protest about history teaching increased.

Reforms in history texts began to appear in the 1960s, which means they actually predated the outbreak of the Troubles. Their timing correlates with O'Neill's gestures toward Catholics and suggests that as the authorities began to realize change in Catholic-Protestant relations was needed, history education may have seemed an easier place to begin than some other areas of discrimination. Other reforms in history teaching came in the 1970s. While they happened against the backdrop of the Troubles, it is arguable that broader forces in the West were an important influence. Just as civil rights activists in Northern Ireland were aroused by civil rights movements in other parts of the world, and the business community in Northern Ireland saw the need for economic reform in the context of a changing world economy, education reform was affected by liberalizing influences in Europe and the United States.

Part Four

Cosmopolitan Prescriptions

Chapter Eight

History as Process

The supreme value for the cosmopolitan is universal human potential. In this worldview, human beings have equal dignity and equal rights. Ethnic categories, to the degree that they persist, belong to the private domain. Difference is minimized by focusing on similarities among groups and, necessarily, on *processes* by which groups resolve their disagreements. The cosmopolitan believes that civic institutions of democracy and the rule of law can offer a public space where differences can be discussed, debated, and worked through irrespective of particularist loyalties. Most Western civic institutions reflect the influence of this viewpoint.

As the work of historians evolved during the twentieth century, standards of rigor also became process-based. Historians can never be certain that they are assembling *all* the facts of a given series of events, but they can meet professional requirements by observing the highest standards in gathering their material. This emphasis on the process of investigation is also a way to help young people in schools understand the difference between evidence-based history and received narrative.

Northern Ireland's education reforms focused on four areas that are key to creating a process-based approach to understanding history: academic history, textbooks, curriculum, and teacher training. Northern Ireland was able to launch reforms in these areas fairly quickly as a response to the Troubles because the ground had already been laid before the Troubles broke out. Nonetheless, a series of difficulties arose, demonstrating just how profoundly societal norms—in this case the conflicted nature of the society—insinuate themselves into any effort to bring change.

THE NATURE OF THE PROBLEM

When the Troubles broke out in 1968, many people acknowledged the bifurcation of societal memory along the lines described in Chapter Four. Catholics
saw Irish history as a struggle for freedom. Protestants saw it as an account of
plantation among a hostile people requiring constant vigilance.[1] Neither group
had any sense of the historical basis of the other's point of view.[2]

Chapter Five's account of Northern Ireland's education system during the
first fifty years of the state demonstrates, in addition, that by 1970, people had
long assumed that school history had something to do with the antipathies between the communities. Educators assumed that the dearth of history teaching in nineteenth-century schools had caused people to develop the habit of
absorbing politicized histories as the only available source of information.
Catholics believed that the absence of Irish history from the curriculum was
a deliberate policy of social control by the dominant community. Protestants
believed that Catholic schools encouraged resistance to the state by teaching
Irish nationalist history. The fact that Catholic schools purchased their history
textbooks in Dublin and Protestant schools purchased theirs in London
seemed to corroborate these suspicions. "Experts" from overseas came to inquire into the nature of history teaching, believing they would shed light on
the origins of the conflict.[3]

The degree to which schools were disseminating different histories is hard
to assess, mainly because teachers' freedom in choice of textbooks makes it
difficult to ascertain which texts were used, thus rendering inaccessible the
most useful objective measure. Moreover, teachers often created their own
lessons, teaching materials, and quizzes that departed completely from set
texts. Anecdotal evidence suggests schools diverged considerably in both
communities in what they taught. Among people in Northern Ireland who
completed their secondary education before 1970, one finds Protestants
who learned some Irish history in school and Catholics who learned a lot of
British history in school. One Protestant interviewed for this study said that
his history teacher had advised him and his classmates to avoid the Irish history questions on the public exams, because "the others" always answer them
better. A Catholic interviewed said she and her classmates were advised by
their teachers not to answer Irish history questions on the public exams because it would mark them as Catholics, making them vulnerable to discrimination. History lecturer Jonathan Bardon, who for a time graded the external
exams, maintains that the Irish history questions on exams were rarely answered, and when they were answered, they were answered poorly.[4]

Questions in Parliament in the 1950s, 1960s, and early 1970s on the subject of history textbooks and the teaching of Irish culture demonstrated the

degree to which history teaching had taken on a symbolic, political dimension. The idea, mooted in the late 1940s and early 1950s, of a textbook devoted exclusively to Ulster history was viewed by Catholics as a unionist ploy to erase the larger history of Ireland that was integral to nationalist ideology. To teach the history of the whole of Ireland, linked as that was with nationalism, was considered subversive by unionists. As a matter of public discussion, history teaching clearly had a polarizing effect.

The government of Northern Ireland had operated in a fashion that limited the expression of Gaelic/Catholic culture, but it had avoided measures that eliminated it totally. If accused of controlling history teaching, the Northern Ireland Ministry of Education's first line of denial was the fact that it had fairly limited powers to enforce a syllabus in schools. It had in the past exercised control through public examinations. But by the late 1960s, exams always contained optional questions on Irish history. And by the beginning of the Troubles, exams had been placed in the hands of a quasi-independent body. Moreover, the regime had permitted an environment where an independent historical profession could develop and where radio and TV were used to raise people's awareness of a more objective approach to history.

Yet closer inspection reveals a lack of interest in profound change on the part of the Stormont regime. The Ministry of Education and DENI were populated by individuals for whom "don't rock the boat" was the guiding premise. The newly created "independent" examination body was independent from the inspectorate but not from the Ministry of Education. The Ministry appointed the examiners and these people were unlikely to deviate far from existing norms. A similar situation prevailed with regard to textbook selection. Inspectors could protest the use of certain textbooks in schools but, because they did not need to, they rarely exercised this right. Teachers, a conservative population, selected texts they knew were acceptable to the authorities and concentrated on making sure their pupils did well in public exams. They enjoyed their autonomy and took a cautious view of change. They had developed to an art form the capacity to avoid controversy. As one inspector explained to me, "You could exercise the art of the sidestep." An Australian sociologist who worked in Northern Ireland in the 1970s was more critical, calling teachers "naïve bearers of culture," accusing them of complicity with the system of institutionalized separation.[5]

This tacit agreement to observe social boundaries in order to maintain a veneer of civility is familiar to anyone who has lived in a conflicted society. It is a survival mechanism in places where communal violence is close to the surface. Moreover, educators in Northern Ireland had long believed that schools should provide "oases of calm" for children.[6] In the turbulence of the 1970s, their primary concern was to ensure that violence not spill over into schools. That concern extended to a reluctance to allow sectarian debate or other kinds of disturbance to affect this one place where children could find "normality."

It is sobering for a visitor to absorb on a day-to-day basis the way that everyone who lives in a divided society knows instinctively that they must be careful what they say to people of the other group or to strangers. Though some history teachers interviewed for this study described one of their tasks as "removing myths," no teacher volunteered the notion that they had a role in openly explicating or demonstrating the way historical themes have been used as "myths" by the respective communities. Dubbing some piece of a group narrative "myth" suggests dismissal or moral censure. Recently the task of discussing historical mythologies has been referred to in education circles as "linking past and present," a euphemistic phrase that contains no implied moral judgment. None of this is a surprise to the locals, but it is a healthy reminder to the visitor that any reference to how a group politicizes historical themes is risky because it carries an implied criticism of the community being discussed. This can be equally problematic when speaking of one's own or of the other community.

Similarly, no teacher interviewed said that history teaching should present a common story or common dilemma. Presumably, to do so is again a political statement, as it implies letting go of one political position or another. Social history comes the closest to offering a common story: one teacher, for example, spoke of teaching about the industrial growth of Belfast in the nineteenth century and "how the two separate communities took root in a rapidly growing city." But in the larger narrative of the disputed identity of Ireland, the industrial growth of Belfast is as contested as is any piece of history. Nationalists will argue, as one teacher did to me, that Britain encouraged industrial growth in the North to keep the loyalty of Protestants. Unionists will emphasize the industrial growth of Belfast as a rationale for the northeast to remain closely linked with the other major industrial cities of Great Britain and therefore to reject the unification of the island.

Among those interested in using education to bring greater understanding, views differed, and continue to differ, about how to effect change. Some spent a year or two investigating the role of history teaching in society, concluded that positive shifts were occurring in history teaching in the 1960s and 1970s, and then turned their attention to other concerns such as lack of contact between schools of the two communities and broader social inequities. Others persevered, having concluded that whether or not history teaching had contributed to past enmities, it had a responsibility to contribute constructively to building new relationships.

THE ACADEMIC HISTORY PROFESSION

In the early years of the Stormont regime, professional historians in Northern Ireland were giving Irish history little attention. In the South, by contrast, the writing of Irish history was considered germane to the founding of the state. Irish histories appeared aplenty, usually framed in a "heroic" style, assuming the greatness of individuals who had led the struggle for independence from Britain. This began to change in the mid-1930s when, in both the North and the South, a small number of professional historians began to break free of the limitations politics had placed upon their profession.

Most significant among the historians of the "new history" were Theodore Moody and Robert Dudley Edwards, who together introduced a new historiography to Ireland. In 1936, Moody founded the Ulster Society for Irish Historical Studies in Belfast and Edwards founded the Irish Historical Society in Dublin. These two societies held academic seminars and in due course published papers in a joint publication of both societies, *Irish Historical Studies*, founded in 1938 by Moody and Edwards.

The two societies discouraged old-style disquisitions on familiar historical topics. They emphasized the use of primary research, reinterpretation, and reevaluation. They welcomed articles on research methodology, guides to sources, bibliographies, book reviews, and teaching of Irish history. They had a special category of essays entitled "Historical Revisions," which were designed to refute assumptions and to alert teachers and others to the problematic nature of existing texts. They organized biennial conferences and started a monograph series that could disseminate this new history to a wider academic audience. At the same time, they created ways to make the new approach and new findings available to the public through lecture series and radio talks. In the 1960s, Moody and Professor F. X. Martin did a series for Irish television on "The Course of Irish History."

Moody explained the deeper purpose, or set of views, that lay behind this undertaking in a talk at the Trinity College Dublin Historical Society in 1977, in which he discussed the interrelationship between history and myth as a contrast between "good history, which is a matter of facing the facts, and myth, which is a way of refusing to face them."[7] He highlighted a number of myths in Irish history, including a "separatist sectarian" myth that he attributed to Ulster loyalists and a "unitary nationalist" myth that he attributed to Southern republicans.

Moody was much criticized for the simplistic nature of this comparison of history and myth. Claude Lévi-Strauss's nuanced way of comparing the two[8] was well known in Ireland at the time, and Moody seemed to be ignoring it. But, more significantly for the long term, the Moody speech triggered a raging debate in the South, which carried over to the North, about academic history's relationship to contemporary issues. Up to this point, some historians may have published critiques of traditionally hallowed subjects, but none had spoken publicly on contemporary matters.[9] But in the late 1970s, academic historians began to comment on current affairs and to argue that indeed they and fellow historians had an obligation to alter misconceptions linked with Irish social memory. Many factors contributed to this new development, but the violence in Northern Ireland was undoubtedly significant. And historians in the North supported it.

In his inaugural lecture upon taking the chair in Irish history at Queen's University in Belfast in 1976,[10] Professor David Harkness commented, "Only by understanding their past can the Irish, south of the border, yes, but especially north of it, ask the right questions of their present in order to extract from it a more constructive future."[11] He went on to call for "the utilization of history in the cause of reconciliation"[12] and became involved in a number of projects that attempted to achieve this wider goal.[13]

H. Rex Cathcart, professor of education at Queen's, two years later spoke of the need for more Irish history in the North in order to "promote understanding of difference, the creation of a willing and enthusiastic acceptance of pluralism."[14] F. S. L. Lyons, provost of Trinity College Dublin, in a lecture at Queen's in 1978, entitled "The Burden of Our History," applauded the Irish historiographical revolution in whose context a revisionist history movement had emerged in the South and called for this new trend to shift the focus away from political history to other subject matter and to penetrate the schools.

That the emergence of the revisionist movement was not merely a result of the Troubles is clear from the fact that early signs of the movement predate the onset of the Troubles. The movement in the South drew encouragement from frustration with the deadening, uncreative tone of the Irish state in its first thirty to fifty years and recognition of the history profession's complicity with this. It also was linked with a disillusionment with the Republic and its failure to deliver on promises of economic and cultural attainment in the 1960s. But the Troubles did give the revisionist movement extra steam. Revisionists were said to represent the mind-set of the Fine Gael party in the South, which has tried to distance itself from any suggestion that it promotes the program of the IRA or other violent nationalism in the North. Because the other main political party of the Republic, Fianna Fáil, had a history of IRA connection, Fine Gael may have been using the issue to distinguish itself from its rival. Moreover, in 1973 the Republic had joined the European Economic Community (EEC), and it wanted to be seen on the world stage as rational and trouble free. Revisionism was a way of declaring a disjuncture with the Republic's violent beginnings and of distancing the South from the North.[15]

Without any of these factors, one could still surmise that Irish society in the 1960s would have been affected by trends in universities elsewhere, where cynicism and iconoclasm were the flavor of the month. Young intellectuals of the 1960s were pushing to supplant old ways of thinking, and Ireland was not immune to the trend.

Whatever the reasons for the burst of revisionist writing in the 1970s, this series of new explorations in intellectual life had the effect of changing the focus of many aspects of the nationalist narrative that had been axiomatic for most Irish of nationalist persuasion for over a century. In brief, new historiographic trends tried to steer away from Anglocentric concerns, to demonstrate the complexity of some of the outstanding personalities in Irish history, and to mark out differences in the various phases of nationalism. To antirevisionists, this appeared to whitewash British responsibility for social ills in Ireland and to undercut nationalists' sense of direct continuity with nationalists of earlier times.

Roy F. Foster, professor of Irish history at Oxford and a front-runner in the revisionist movement, argues that revisionism in general is what the historical endeavor is all about.[16] Foster describes revisionism as "an ability to appreciate half-tones, to be skeptical about imputing praise or blame, to separate contemporary intentions from historical effects." He speaks approvingly of the "slightly blasé and skeptical way in which many Irish people view the institutionalized pieties of Irish history."[17]

This presumption of skepticism is one element revisionism's opponents criticize about the movement. Revisionism's most eloquent critic, Oxford professor Fr. Brendan Bradshaw, deplores the clinical approach of modern-day history writing, its removal of "emotion," and the sanitization of trauma that fails to depict the catastrophic nature of Irish history. Bradshaw accuses this historiography of being value-free, denying "the historian recourse to value judgments and, therefore, access to the kind of moral and emotional register necessary to respond to human tragedy."[18] He finds that the movement presumes to be iconoclastic even before it has examined the facts.

The revisionist controversy is somewhat intertwined with the growth and change of the historical profession in the West in the past sixty years. Seeking critical distance has become normal in academic history, as has avoidance of public political rhetoric. Most revisionists feel they have no need to defend themselves: they are observing the most meticulous methodologies of their profession. The nature of the revisionist controversy, which peaked in 1991 at the time of the seventy-fifth anniversary of the Easter Rising, demonstrates the extent of the level of tension between history and politics in a contested society or one that has recently emerged from civil war. The controversy shows how difficult it is to create a "common ground" of intellectual debate in the midst of a protracted political conflict.

The revisionist controversy also draws attention to the direction in which the historical profession is now headed. Following the controversy, historians have moved toward more specialization and differentiation. Their work has become more self-referential and obscure to the ordinary reader. Historians depend, says Ciaran Brady, on the integrity of good practice (in other words, use of primary sources and critical argument), using a purified language and the irony that arises from juxtaposing "new facts" with familiar ones. This latter characteristic inevitably makes history an elitist endeavor because it depends on the reader bringing a body of up-to-date knowledge to the material she reads. Thus the movement begun by Moody and Edwards, and carried forward by the revisionists, contains within it a paradox. Moody and Edwards wanted to remove the influence of those in power to determine the way history was written: every man was to be his own historian. But the outcome has been elitist history.[19]

Nonetheless, the emergence of open debate on salient issues in the historical profession has been healthy. It is better to deal consciously with these matters than to sweep them under the mat. In an effort to promote such a discussion, academic historians have been contributing to public awareness through their writing, by advising on television programming on history subjects,[20] in playing the role of public intellectuals,[21] and in writing school textbooks.[22] And future history teachers enrolling in history classes in Northern Ireland universities from the late 1960s onward have had some exposure to this historiographic debate, which at very least has raised their awareness to the attendant issues.

TEXTBOOKS

Despite the quantity of discussion in Stormont about textbooks, and the general sense in the 1960s that better textbooks needed to be produced, rather little detailed analysis of existing texts was attempted during this period. The main reason for this would seem to be that the problem had been articulated in a particular way—unionist omission of Irish material and Irish ultranationalism—and there was fairly wide agreement about this. People looking at textbooks therefore remarked on these problems but did not explore others. Subtler forms of word use (e.g., military or authoritarian language or gender bias) were not analyzed.[23] Those who believed there was a problem with the textbooks did not think they needed specific analysis of the texts to show what the problem was. The only published research on textbook bias in Northern Ireland was based on a sketchy methodology and summed up the criteria for textbook analysis as "a form of blindness."[24]

This includes an inability to see anything other than good in one's own nation, both in general terms and in relation to individuals. The other side of the coin is an inability to [sic] anything bad in another nation, always greedy, always cruel or always stupid and misguided. The attitude too towards the heroes of another nation is always very revealing, it is a rare form of generosity in text-books that acknowledges those qualities that made those heroes great in their own countries. The other factors that I tried to be aware of were small details that were not in themselves untrue but which diminished the stature of an individual or a government.[25]

The author's single concrete criticism of a Catholic school textbook was the use of mediocre poems about nationalism or martyrdom. The Protestant textbooks, she said, "have a strange blindness towards the rest of Ireland . . . nearly all the events and all the people are taken from Northern Ireland as far as possible."[26]

Nonetheless, the 1960s was a time of considerable concerted action to alleviate the overbearing place of British history in Northern Ireland education through reforms in textbooks and exams. New policies in the South were in part responsible. In 1961, the European Association of Teachers (EAT) formed an Irish board,[27] and the EAT held a conference in 1965, attended by teachers from the North and South, on the subject of bias in history teaching. In 1967, a study group on history teaching in the South issued a report urging teachers to remove the heavy emphasis on politics and war in their teaching at the primary level and emphasize themes of social history instead. At the secondary level, the report called for thorough teaching of the events of 1916-1921, a period often omitted in school history classes in the South up to that point.[28]

Textbook publishing in the 1960s showed a shift away from the rigidity of previous decades. In the North in 1962 and 1964, John Magee published two British history texts[29] containing between them seven chapters on Irish history, and greater emphasis on economic and social history than was usual.[30] These were followed in 1969 by a series of three textbooks, published by Gill and Macmillan in Dublin.[31] The third book of the series included a section, "Ulster 1886-1914," as well as sections on Home Rule, the Orange Order, Carson, Craig, the Larne gunrunning incident, and World War I, all of which are central issues in the unionist history but which had not had much play up to this point in books coming from Dublin. These books had added significance because they came as a series, which meant that they offered comprehensive coverage of the subject. Moreover, the graphics made them appealing, and the content was based on solid research. Though the books were published mainly for schools in the South, Catholic schools in the North also used them.

Editors of these books often mentioned, in their introductory remarks, the problem of bias and the concern that history teaching in the past often perpetuated mythologies and glorified war and violence. Reviewers noted the increased use of photos and other graphics, improved layout, inclusion of recent research, and increased emphasis on social history (though in some cases this could still be better, according to reviewers, and often was not integrated into the rest of the text).[32]

Along with the new energy in the historical profession came a new willingness on the part of historians to participate in textbook writing.[33] Historical scholarship was linking arms with entrepreneurial publishing. At much the same time, the BBC did a series of radio programs on Irish history and published accompanying books. In the mid-1970s, the Public Record Office of Northern Ireland (PRONI) released a large number of documents relating in particular to the early years of the Northern Ireland state. These documents, which had initially been classified for fifty years, were released before their deadline as a result of the social ferment produced by the Troubles. One way these documents were employed was in the production of booklets of original documents for use in schools. PRONI came to be known as "the third university."

One reviewer commented that the previous decades had seen a "radical change" in the teaching of history in Northern Ireland. This was due in part, he said, to concerns about passing on prejudices but more to a questioning about what kinds of history were appropriate to particular age groups, about methods of teaching, and about the "validity and purpose" of history teaching in primary and secondary schools.[34] He pointed out that certain aspects of Irish history that had been previously ignored were included in these new texts, for example, the unionist case from 1880-1920. The reviewer also noted that moralizing and emotional language had been reduced, even if they still crept in occasionally. Overall, he found the textbooks to be fairly evenhanded, sometimes going to great lengths to avoid previously accepted stereotypes.

Yet the reviewer went on to say that the treatment of Northern Ireland remained a problem. Textbooks on British history would relegate Northern Ireland history to a dull chapter; while Irish textbooks gave very little attention to the North after 1920. The practical problem resulting from this was that there was still no text that served the needs of the history teacher in Northern Ireland. While the idea of a school history text written only for Northern Ireland had been derided in the past, people who took the matter seriously saw this as perhaps the only answer.[35]

Early efforts at writing texts for Northern Ireland had proved to be unsuccessful in freeing themselves of bias. Some have already been mentioned in Chapter Seven. G. W. Otway Woodward's *Divided Island*, for example, published in 1976 and 1979, used the history of politics in Ireland to look at the theme of conflict but failed to avoid a tone of national self-justification.[36] Another problem for textbook writers in Northern Ireland was marketing. Unless a publisher could be certain of selling to both communities, there was not a sufficiently large critical mass of buyers to make textbook publishing in Northern Ireland a profitable endeavor.

This problem would persist until the 1990s when the statutory curriculum passed by the Educational Reform (NI) Order of 1989 (ERO)[37] guaranteed a market for history texts that could be used in all schools. Many of the textbooks produced since then have been the product of collaboration of a Catholic and a Protestant author. All of them match precisely the curriculum requirements of the ERO. *Northern Ireland and Its Neighbours since 1920,*[38] published in 1995, was the first satisfactory textbook to present the entire history of the Northern state.

BBC HISTORY BROADCASTING

While the British Broadcasting Corporation (BBC) has been criticized for cooperating with British government censorship in its reporting of the conflict,[39] it has played a significant role in getting discussion about Ireland's history out in the open. BBC programming for schools has been important, and a number of BBC series have produced accompanying texts for schools.

This began in 1954, when the BBC broadcasted and subsequently published twelve talks on the political and economic history of Ulster. Four more radio series and one TV series were to follow in the next decade and a half. Perhaps the most notable of these, "Two Centuries of Irish History," broadcast in 1965, and from which a textbook was published, was designed for the grammar school and secondary intermediate age level. The local producer of the series, James Hawthorne, described the purpose of the programs:

> Northern Ireland is often held to be a history-conscious community, and yet the man-in-the-street—and certainly his teenage son or daughter at the secondary school—knows very little about the origins of that small six-county political unit which was created less than half a century ago. The reasons for this situation are complex, but the one that is most frequently suggested is that the Ulsterman, whether he is descended from the indigenous Celt or the British planter, is willing only to look back selectively at the past. A total view of history might erode that pride in his ancestry which determines his attitude to the community and the members of it who—to use an Ulster phrase—"dig with the other foot." Indeed, for several generations the formal teaching of local history has been largely neglected.[40]

School inspector Vivian McIver has referred to this particular series and its accompanying textbook as a "breakthrough," popularizing teaching of Irish history in government-funded schools.[41] Perhaps more profoundly, these series collectively helped develop a new awareness among adults as well as students that there are objective ways to speak about history and that people could step out of their own group's mind-set and think about the Northern Ireland story in a different way.

John Magee referred specifically to the "Irish History" series in a paper delivered to the Irish Association at Queen's University in November 1970, addressing the concerns that teachers have in teaching political history. The BBC series, Magee said, "tackled this problem 'head-on' with a great deal of success." Magee went on to say that the BBC schools service had rendered "invaluable assistance" to education in Northern Ireland. It was, he said, "the only agency which has seriously and consistently attempted to explain one group or tradition to the other."[42]

PROCESS-ORIENTED HISTORY

Central to history curriculum reform in the 1970s was a shift to studying history through acquiring process skills rather than acquiring a body of knowledge. This took on fairly quickly in Northern Ireland, in part because a lecturer at the Queen's University School of Education had written a number of articles on the pedagogy of history.[43] The Queen's Teachers' Centre developed a plan to replace boring exercises in rote learning of names and dates with social history, which involved using a variety of sources, encouraging pupils to do their own research within their community and emphasizing debate and discussion.

Northern Ireland history inspectors backed these developments fully, showing more inclination for innovation than DENI generally. The same kinds of changes were occurring in history teaching in other parts of the world. Ideas about teaching economic and local history and teaching investigative skills were in the marketplace, available to those in Northern Ireland who wanted to recast history teaching. In the 1970s, the Queen's Teachers' Centre became a hub of innovation in creative teaching methods.

Curriculum Development Projects

Two significant history curriculum experiments were launched in the 1970s. The Schools Cultural Studies Project, though it lasted only five years, was notable because it developed curriculum through an interactive process with teachers of both communities. Teachers from a variety of schools would meet to discuss upcoming class topics and learn from each other about diverse viewpoints. The project tackled controversial local material and explored ways of "increasing levels of mutual understanding among young people in Ireland."[44]

Those interviewed who had taken part in the Schools Cultural Studies Project unanimously lamented its failure to outlast its five-year mandate. Because it wasn't part of a standard classroom subject, it didn't find its niche. Instead, it tended to be pigeonholed as a program for less able pupils. Its assumption was that teachers cannot teach about community relations unless they are learning something about it themselves in a forum with teachers of the other community; this thinking was far ahead of its time.[45]

The other, more successful curriculum project served grammar and secondary school history and came via England: the Schools Council History Project. It had been part of the new history teaching introduced in the United Kingdom in the 1970s and was adopted by the Queen's Teachers' Centre in 1976. One element of the curriculum, even in England, was a close-up look at a particular conflict in the world. The choice was among the Middle East, South Africa, and Northern Ireland.

The Schools Council shifted the emphasis of history teaching in a number of ways. First, its arrangement was discontinuous, based on the argument that any chosen continuity is an assertion of a particular viewpoint. It focused in depth on a few topics and studied continuity and change through the lens of particular subject matter, for example, "Medicine through History." The Schools Council taught children to read primary sources critically, noting the viewpoint and background of the writer, and emphasized the study of history as an investigative process. This introduced what some of its practitioners have described as empathy: "It clarified school history as a humane study concerned with people, their actions and perceptions of events, as opposed to a body of knowledge of largely indisputable fact to be read and regurgitated."[46] The Schools Council demonstrated the relevance of history by teaching history of other societies, discussing why people act as they do, and stressing an understanding of the present as an outcome of past events. In marked departure from previous history teaching policy, the concept of multiple interpretations was emphasized.

The assumptions of this project were later to affect the exams and curriculum when the General Certificate of Secondary Education (GCSE)[47] exam was created in the 1980s and ERO arrived in the 1990s. As a direct result of the Schools Council History Project, exams have ceased to be a recitation of information, and instead focus on the process of extracting information from available evidence. Some GCSE questions now are framed along the lines of, "What would you have felt if . . . ?" This is more popular with some teachers than others. Some teachers I interviewed said the less intelligent pupils have difficulty with this approach and would be more secure with a teaching method where the body of required knowledge was more clearly defined. Because it was rooted in a particular discipline and was a national project backed by the inspectorate, the Schools Council History Project proved to be more successful than the Schools Cultural Studies Project. The Schools Council nourished the morale of teachers, giving them "a renewed belief in the value of history not only as a school subject but as an agent for creating mutual understanding."[48] The Schools Council still exists, and a number of schools in Northern Ireland still use its syllabus and GCSE exam, even though many of its aspects have been incorporated into the mainstream GCSE curriculum.

Primary School History Curriculum

Traditionally, history was not part of the required curriculum of primary schools. In the 1970s, several experimental projects were launched that would challenge this policy. One was a form of social studies that could capture the essentials of history, geography, and current affairs. Another focused on "environmental studies," and in the spring of 1970, Ulster TV did a series on this theme combining geography, history, and economics. DENI's *Primary Education: Teachers' Guide*,[49] published in 1974, included a section on "integrated" or "environmental" studies, bringing together history, geography, and physical sciences and using primary source material to study the environment.

These programs never took hold. They were followed by several programs that grew more directly out of increasing collaboration among the Inspectorate, Education and Library Boards, schools, and seconded teachers. But none of them, it was argued, was an adequate substitute for the teaching of history in primary schools. Richard McMinn, current principal of Stranmillis University and Teachers' College and a former history teacher, became the champion of this cause, suggesting history for primary schools should be a separate subject and that it should be skills based. In 1984, McMinn's work was taken up by the Northern Ireland Council for Educational Development (NICED) when it published "History Guidelines for Primary Schools."[50] His vision reached fruition in the 1990s, when ERO finally made primary school history compulsory.

Reformulating the Examination System[51]

Though more Irish history was included in public examinations in the 1960s, 1970s and 1980s, Irish history remained an optional subject of study until the ERO of 1990 mandated the teaching of twentieth-century Irish history.

Starting in the 1960s, a new General Certificate of Education (GCE) was offered at two levels: Ordinary (O-Level) and Advanced (A-Level). The O-Levels of 1965 included two Irish history questions out of a choice of ten questions on British, Irish, and Imperial history. The A-Level exam also included two Irish history questions on two out of its three papers. The third paper, which examined students on a special subject, now included one Irish subject, "Grattan and His Times, 1777-1801" (dealing with a period when Irish nationalism was civic rather than ethnic in character), as an option. While students could still pass the GCE at both levels without knowing any Irish history, those who preferred to study Irish history could make use of this in the GCE.

The Certificate of Secondary Education (CSE) exam, introduced in 1973 as a slightly lower-level school leaving exam for sixteen-year-olds, went even further: Exams were to be drawn up on the basis of groups of topics, and six out of thirty-two of these were Irish topics. It became possible, in fact, to prepare students for the CSE exam by teaching *only* Irish history, though few schools chose to go this route.

By 1974, 72 percent of schools were teaching Irish history for CSE.[52] If one assumes that all Catholic schools were teaching Irish history, which may not have been the case, one concludes that at least half of all Protestant schools were teaching some Irish history, though how much, and what topics, are crucial questions not covered by the research.

In the 1980s, further reforms in the exams led to the introduction of more Irish history questions. The A-Level history exam was reduced from three to two papers. Paper I was "British and Irish History, 1485-1964" or "European History, 1494-1964"; paper II was a special subject which could be chosen by the school. Three of these special subjects were on Ireland: "Home Rule 1912-1923"; "Grattan and His World, 1789-98"; and "Victorian and Edwardian Belfast." It was still possible to get through the exam without studying Irish history, but for those who preferred Irish history, more options were available.

In 1988, the GCE O-Level and CSE were amalgamated to create the General Certificate of Education (GCSE), and the new GCSE held its first history exams. For paper I, "Modern World Study," one of several options was "Ireland 1905-1972"; for paper II, the choice was between "Medicine" and "Energy through Time." It was possible to do the exam with no knowledge of *British* history at all. Unionists were incensed and went as far as organizing protests at Omagh High School, coinciding with a visit of Minister of Education Brian Mawhinney. The Anglo-Irish Agreement had been signed not long before, and unionists were already feeling betrayed. But in the first GCSE exam, 60 percent of the candidates responded to questions in the Ireland 1905-1972 section,[53] again indicating that some Protestant schools did opt to teach Irish history.

TEACHER TRAINING

In the 1970s, the Queen's Teachers' Centre was a focal point of in-service training for history teachers. It offered inspiration and vitality because it was also the hub of new curriculum experiments. The high point of the school year for history teachers was their annual conference, the Wiles History Week, financed by the Wiles History Trust. Teachers were given a week off school on paid time in the spring to attend, with travel and other expenses paid. For a more select group of teachers, the Combined Education Departments of England, Ireland, and Northern Ireland have organized a series of seminars every two years dealing with topics relating to history teaching, with their venue rotating among England, the Republic, and the North.

Nowadays, shortage of funding for the Wiles Weeks has reduced the gatherings to one or two days, and all but travel funding has been cut. Smaller in-service teacher training events make up for this to some degree, as does the availability of a history officer on each Education and Library Board. Conferences organized by the Council of Europe have provided a forum for new ideas in history teaching in Northern Ireland to be discussed, though these are not accessible to large numbers of teachers in Northern Ireland.

There is a general feeling among history teachers and policy advisers in Northern Ireland that teacher training is inadequate for the nature of responsibility required of teachers. As changes are instituted in the history curriculum, teachers have to learn to teach materials that they have never taught before. Teachers remain uneasy about the overlap of their subject matter with politics and still prefer to avoid discussing controversial issues.

Another concern that relates to all teachers, not just history teachers, is that three-quarters of teacher trainees attend the two traditional teacher training colleges, Stranmillis and St. Mary's; these teacher trainees will receive their training in environments with a minimum of diversity, and most will eventually get jobs in schools that are linked with one community or the other. While the occasional conferences have been good, their limited duration does not allow teachers time to interact over an extended period. This problem is more serious for history teachers because they are, supposedly, the ones who can use their subject matter to make their pupils more cognizant of the mind-set of the other community. It is unfortunate that history teaching trainees have little opportunity to test their own ideas with members of the other community.

Teacher trainees need training in how to relate to the other community, and beyond this basic training they need a means to maintain ongoing interaction with the other community. Without this, the vision of education for diversity is almost bound to produce disappointing results.

Another question policymakers ask themselves is whether those recruited to be future teachers are the right type of people for the task. People who go into teaching in a society of this kind need to have excellent relational skills, a capacity for intercultural understanding, and a capacity for change. Currently, the numbers applying to receive teacher training are far higher than places available, which means admissions are based on academic learning. This may need to be examined afresh.[54]

PIONEERING WORK

Northern Ireland was better placed than many divided societies to attempt the kinds of reforms required for a cosmopolitan polity. Reforms moved ahead in developing an academic history profession dedicated to debate and objectivity, in revising textbooks, in creating a new pedagogy of investigation rather than received learning, and in giving history teacher trainees more in-service training in history. Nonetheless, challenges and pitfalls developed, underlining just how resistant the society was to change of any kind.

Academic history demonstrated considerable freedom of debate from the 1930s onward. Yet Irish academic history is accused by antirevisionists of promoting clinical, value-free, and emotionally distant historical accounts that tend to be elitist and thus rob ordinary people of the joy of following historical debates as they did in the past. New textbooks eradicated old biases, old-fashioned formats, and moralistic language, but the first adequate textbook on the history of Northern Ireland appeared only in 1995. High stakes exams did incorporate Irish history, but not on a compulsory basis until 1990. Before 1990, they left considerable room for the two communities to instill or reinforce different mind-sets in their pupils. And teacher training still does not offer trainees the experience of interacting with people of the other community because teachers still are trained in segregated teachers' colleges. To this day, student teachers gain extraordinarily little experience exchanging ideas with those of the other community.

Nonetheless, even if they were slow in coming, the reforms instituted by the ERO show Northern Ireland moving solidly in the direction of a more cosmopolitan, rational approach to teaching history. Investigative forms of teaching, and curricula that emphasized primary sources and a variety of interpretations, were pioneered in schools with considerable success.

Chapter Nine

The Common History
Curriculum and Its Discontents

A key aspect to the cosmopolitanization of education in a deeply divided society is to ensure that a common history curriculum is offered in all schools. At a perceptual level, this should dispel the notion, always rife in the mindset of groups in conflict, that the "others" are teaching the next generation negative material about "us." At a substantive level, this approach addresses the culture hypothesis (see Chapter Six), the idea that schools promote different mind-sets by teaching different material.

Efforts to create a common curriculum in Northern Ireland focused principally on including Irish history in the curriculum. This was a gesture of fairness toward nationalists. The new curriculum met little protest from unionists and created no province-wide debate. The enforcement of the new curriculum demonstrated in several ways, however, just where the tensions actually lie in efforts to create a common sense of belonging in a society deeply divided by ethnonationalist contentions. The biggest challenge to enforcing a common Irish history curriculum proved to be that teachers feared addressing contentious issues in the classroom and were chary about making critical moral judgments concerning the other group. More generally, teachers doubt the capacity of their teaching to displace narratives students have picked up in home and community settings, and this has an effect on the way they teach. Now education researchers are looking for new ways to make history teaching relevant to the conflicted nature of the society, taking these concerns into consideration.

THE EDUCATION REFORM (NI) ORDER 1989 (ERO)

As discussed in Chapter Six, ERO, passed in 1988 for England and Wales and in 1989 for Northern Ireland, was the product of Prime Minister Margaret

Thatcher's desire for education in the United Kingdom to reverse the "liberal-izing" tendencies of the previous three decades, to make education more rigorous, and to reestablish national cohesion in the face of considerable immi-gration and resultant new diversity in the British population.[1] It called for a common curriculum, which had never existed before, and for the reintroduction of market economics in schools. Schools' examination results would be pub-lished, which would be a way for the public to judge the quality of each insti-tution. The common curriculum would ensure a baseline of comparison among schools. The new curriculum was greeted with much suspicion in England and its announcement was followed by considerable discussion about how British identity was being reconfigured in the process.[2] The "imposition" of a particu-lar concept of Britishness was seen by some as a slap in the face toward those in the population whose sense of belonging had different salient characteristics.

That a similar, intense public debate did not take place in Northern Ireland seems curious. The absence of controversy is probably best attributed to the bifurcation of the school system. Because Northern Ireland's schools do not function as a single body, schools tend to focus on how issues affect their par-ticular school much more than they focus on the broader implications of pol-icy. Another reason for the lack of debate about the new history curriculum was that in the minds of history teachers, a bigger and more significant sea change had come just a few years earlier when evidence-based methodologies were introduced with the new GCSE of 1988. Teachers who might have op-posed the introduction of Irish history to the detriment of British history were less concerned because they knew that the enquiry approach would not re-quire them to teach the other community's story.

Teachers did object to having to adjust to teaching new material, to the fact that their schools lacked the resources, such as books, needed to teach this material, and to the way the new curriculum overloaded the timetable. More profoundly, teachers felt their professionalism was being questioned, since traditionally they had been granted broad autonomy in what they taught.

On the other hand, many teachers interviewed for this research took pride in these reforms, believing there was a connection between history teaching and the conflict and that they were in some sense on the frontline in trying to address the conflict. More than three-quarters of those interviewed (twenty-nine out of thirty-six) said they believed they had a positive role to play as a history teacher vis à vis the conflict. The research is biased in this regard, given that those willing to be interviewed were more likely to be the ones who supported reform, or at least would be aware of what DENI would wish them to say. And teachers may think their work should help address the conflict without believing they should explicitly discuss anything to do with the con-flict. But at the very least among this body of teachers, their belief that teachers have a positive role to play in helping students understand the conflict helped them overcome reservations about the new curriculum. The requirement to teach about the Troubles since 1968 posed a more pointed challenge to teachers, and we will examine this later in the chapter.

Another factor in the ease of passage of the ERO curriculum is that by 1990, a team of pioneering people had come into being, both in DENI and among teachers more generally, representing both communities. These people now had a track record of working together to bring educational reform. Their work with the Schools Council History project had led to enquiry-based history and to the new GCSE. ERO seemed one more step forward in their long-term commitment. As one of those spearheading reforms commented, "We were working together to bring change. Those who didn't want more Irish history were the same ones who stayed in the woodwork."[3]

Many agree that much credit should go to history inspector Vivian McIver, whose own cosmopolitan outlook, in part resulting from travel to the Middle East and the United States, ensured that a cadre of history teachers developed who supported reform. On the policy side, the role of Minister of Education Brian Mawhinney, appointed by the Thatcher government, but a person born in Northern Ireland who was determined to get some change in education, should not be overlooked. Whereas the minister for education in England and Wales did not make history a required subject for fourteen- to sixteen-year-olds, Mawhinney did. He also pushed hard for the two cross-curricular themes of Education for Mutual Understanding and Cultural Heritage (see Chapter Six), even insisting that they would be addressed in the curriculum design process before the traditional subjects. Mawhinney's successors, particularly Lord Belsted, kept the torch alight.

Some would say that most of the reforms came from a liberal educational agenda that existed quite apart from the need to respond to the conflict.[4] The energy for reform in DENI was reinforced by a desire to introduce cutting-edge ideas into education.

HISTORY AS A SUBJECT IN THE ERO

ERO made history a compulsory subject in primary schools. Classes were to focus on social history through the topics of early times in Ireland, the Vikings, and the Victorians. Classes were also required to introduce children to the notion of history as an investigative endeavor, leading to various interpretations. Political and national histories were to be avoided.

Four key goals guided ERO at the postprimary level. In the first five years of postprimary education (leading to the General Certificate of Education exam for sixteen-year-olds), history classes were to deal with Irish, British, and European history in equal parts. Second, history was to be a compulsory subject through to age sixteen. Third, for the eleven to fourteen age group, Irish history would focus on a core topic each year: "The Normans" (the Normans' arrival in Ireland); "Conquest and Colonization" (British colonization in the seventeenth century); and "The Act of Union to Partition." Fourth, fourteen- to sixteen-year-olds would be required to learn the history of Northern Ireland, through to 1985, in preparation for taking the GCSE.

Key to making the new curriculum take hold was the creation of new textbooks. Perhaps DENI's most significant achievement in this regard was to create a textbook on the history of Northern Ireland, 1920-1993, which could be used in schools of either community. *Northern Ireland and Its Neighbours since 1920* was written jointly by a Catholic and a Protestant secondary school history teacher and edited by a member of the Council for the Curriculum, Examinations and Assessment (CCEA). The challenge was to present the differing interpretations of events without feeding the rigid mind-set of one community or the other but also without demonstrating prejudice. The book achieves this by making as clear as possible a distinction between fact and interpretation. Within every subsection, it lays out basic facts and then uses sidebars and colored boxes to introduce quotations by a variety of observers and commentators of the time, who demonstrate a range of viewpoints. While the text is not perfect—critics have pointed out the very small space given to Bloody Sunday—it was a leap forward compared to what had gone before.

Textbooks were also produced for the eleven to fourteen age group and for primary schools, again based on collaboration of a Catholic and a Protestant. Textbook publishers now had more incentive to be involved because the required curriculum meant that they would have buyers from both communities in large numbers. Among the most popular textbooks in Northern Ireland for use with the Northern Ireland curriculum now are those produced by Colourpoint and Focus.

At the same time, it is important to remember that the enquiry-based nature of the history curriculum meant that teachers were not as reliant on textbooks as they had been in the past.

REVERSION TO NARRATIVES

While much of the discussion on reforming history teaching in Northern Ireland focused on incorporating *Irish* history into the timetable, this discussion sometimes obscures the particular concerns related to teaching the history of

Northern Ireland. This in fact proved to be the area of greatest tension with regard to the substance of the new curriculum. If history teaching provides a measure of political and social realities, then this is where we should be applying our yardstick.

The ERO curriculum reforms were introduced one year at a time, so that it was four years after the passing of ERO that the spotlight fell with some concentration upon the new syllabus for fourteen- to sixteen-year-olds, which was to be introduced in 1995. By that time, teachers had experienced some years of tackling new material, and they were weary. They strongly resisted the new GCSE syllabus, complaining that the new syllabus expected them to cover too much ground, that their past experience left them unprepared to teach the history of Northern Ireland, and that their schools lacked the necessary resources to teach it.

Two members of the CCEA told me that despite the reasons given, teachers had dug their heels in with regard to the GCSE course because they were frightened to teach about Northern Ireland since 1968. CCEA was itself divided in how to respond to that reluctance. Some felt the requirement to teach the entire history of Northern Ireland was the very heart of ERO and should not be abandoned. Others felt that if teachers were not ready for it, there was no point in coercing them. The latter group won the day.

In response to these complaints and accompanying concerns about the overloaded timetable, the requirement that all fourteen- to sixteen-year-olds take history was abandoned.[5] History became an optional subject after the third year of postprimary school. Perhaps more interestingly for the purposes of this study, the course on Northern Ireland from 1920 to 1985, designed for fifteen- and sixteen-year-olds preparing for GCSE, was curtailed. Teachers were now to choose between teaching about "Northern Ireland in World War II" or "Northern Ireland, 1965-85."

While the choice offered, between World War II and the Troubles, might seem to be a choice between innocuous history and controversial history, it could also be seen as a choice that plays to the differing narratives of the two communities. Certainly nationalists see the history of the Troubles as *their* history. They see it as a story of their revolt against the status quo in the North. The topic "Northern Ireland in World War II" resonates well with unionists, who view the war as a period when the North met the test of loyalty to Britain while the South remained neutral. The choice of these two topics left out the need to teach about the founding of the state and early prejudicial treatment of Catholics.

In interviews of history teachers for this project, half of those teaching at Protestant schools said at least one teacher in their school had chosen to teach about the Troubles. This compared with two-thirds of those teaching at

Catholic schools who said someone in their school teaches about the Troubles. All history teachers at integrated schools interviewed said someone at
the school teaches about the Troubles.

These statistics are not sufficient to build a case that Catholics are more
willing to teach about the Troubles than Protestants, though they signal a tilt
in that direction. Catholics' particular interest in the post-1968 period was underlined when three of the Catholic teachers interviewed for this study raised
the particular issue of the Bloody Sunday incident in 1972 without it having
been previously introduced, citing it as a crime against Catholics that had
gone unpunished.[6] For them this was an elaboration of the idea that the Troubles tell a story in which the Catholics suffered unfair treatment but pursued
a liberation struggle. Said one:

> Bloody Sunday was a terrible chapter in British history. I personally believe [that
> the British said to themselves] we will take a few of these boys out. The over-
> whelming evidence indicates there was a breakdown of the command structure in
> the army. But you will never get the British establishment to admit that that hap-
> pened. To me it is not the English nature. The British establishment—that high
> level of command structure in the army—is not going to turn around and say they
> were wrong, that they lost control. The British Army never loses control.

When I raised the question of Bloody Sunday with one Protestant former
history teacher, he in turn raised the matter of a bombing by the IRA in
Belfast city center not long after Bloody Sunday, where many Protestants
died, for which Gerry Adams is reputed to have responsibility. Catholics believe that Protestants will avoid discussing the history of the past thirty-five
years and that they will explain this by saying they consider it of less relevance than other parts of history. Protestants feel that Catholics are not willing to see that Protestants have been under attack and have suffered too.

The larger point here is that of the two choices offered for the study of the
history of Northern Ireland, one choice resonated with the Protestant/unionist
narrative, and the other resonated more with the Catholic/nationalist narrative. This is confirmed by research of Barton and McCully, elaborated upon
later in this chapter, that students who attend controlled schools, who are
mainly Protestant, find Northern Ireland's history from plantation to World
War II to be the history they most closely identify with, whereas Catholics
find history of Northern Ireland after 1960 closer to their sense of identity.[7]
The choice offered to teachers for their GCSE curriculum played into this tendency, allowing teachers from each community to teach only that portion of
the history which is salient or important to their own group's history.

Nonetheless, even if the Troubles are a story of Catholic liberation, several
Catholic teachers expressed their *caution* about teaching this subject matter.

One teacher in a maintained (Catholic) school said that while he has no difficulty explaining to his pupils the mentality of the unionists during the Home Rule debate (1885-1920), he finds it much harder to speak about Bloody Sunday or, for that matter, "the reasons why Padraig Pearse was willing to sacrifice his life."[8] In these cases he was obliged to highlight what he regarded as clear injustices of the British, and he feared he was giving his pupils additional reasons to be involved in paramilitary activity.

Teachers interviewed who chose not to teach about the Troubles often gave as their first reason that the school did not have the money to purchase the new teaching resources needed to teach that subject. Very often they would go on to say something like, "In any case, I think the subject matter is too controversial." One or two said they hoped they were not being disingenuous by saying resources were the main concern, demonstrating, in other words, some measure of self-reflection in the matter. Other reasons for not teaching it were that there would be complaints from parents, that the pupils were tired of politics, or that the teacher was tired of politics. A (female) teacher at a Protestant girls' school said that the subject was too political for the girls—there were too many concepts to learn and the girls got confused. Another teacher said that teaching about the Troubles may trigger off in the children the notion that you must take one side or the other.

Teachers' concern that they were being asked to teach material that was not history but rather contemporary politics could not be easily dismissed, particularly in a seriously contested political environment. Be that as it may, the fundamental point is that the "common" curriculum deviated from being "common" in precisely the area that was likely to be most fraught with contention.

THE SMOKESCREEN PROBLEM

Can improved history teaching actually change the views about politicized history that young people absorb elsewhere? Many teachers describe a "smokescreen problem," where pupils separate the facts they learn in the classroom and the political uses of history outside. Several cited the historical example that the Pope sided with the Protestant protagonist, King William of Orange, at the time of the Battle of the Boyne in 1690 because of their mutual opposition to Louis XIV. The students, however, do not make the leap from this to considering that Catholics and Protestants do not always have to take opposing sides in a conflict. The experience of a teacher attempting to make an analogy between republicans' responses to the executions following the Easter Rising and republicans' responses to Britain's treatment of the hunger strikers was that the students (mostly Protestant), who had been very open to discussion about the first topic, completely closed down and refused to engage when it came to the second.[9]

In general, when asked whether history teaching can alter ideas pupils have acquired at home, more than three-quarters of the responses in interviews for this research were that it could not. This is not only a discouraging statistic with regard to what students can gain from education but a signal of a sad reality among teachers. Teachers believe they *should* be having an impact to change things for the better, but in reality they have little hope that they *can*. Such cognitive dissonance makes their work disheartening, removes incentive, and ends up functioning as a self-fulfilling belief.

The teachers had varied rationales for their views. One teacher said that history teaching will never alter the ideas of young people who have extreme political views. Another said that history teaching will never alter the ideas of the highly intelligent pupil who comes to school with ideas firmly in place, while others said it was the less intelligent pupils who take up rigid positions. A few teachers insisted that it is not the role of history teaching to change children's political views: "We talk about interpretations and bias, but not to change their opinion. I have no right to speak in any way that will influence behavior."

Recent research has attempted to shed more light on this issue. A study in the Netherlands finds that young people have absorbed, transgenerationally, considerable information about the family's experience in World War II well before they study the war in school. Subsequently, these same young people will interpret this knowledge according to the aspects of collective memory they pick up at school as well as through the "prevailing zeitgeist."[10] Extrapolated to Northern Ireland, this research suggests that children come to school with a personalized account of family trauma, but only later match this up with the societal collective memory. This is corroborated by research by Cairns et al.[11]

Conway tells us that in the minds of students ages eleven to fourteen in Northern Ireland, history classes are definitely the most important resource for their knowledge of history, with history books coming second and relatives third.[12] The level of this influence drops as the students get older and, presumably, are susceptible to other social sources. Barton and McCully also tell us that age thirteen to fourteen is the stage when students begin to identify more strongly with the tradition of their own community.[13] Therefore, they argue, eleven to thirteen is the period when students are perhaps most receptive to history they learn in school and have not yet come to see ideas about history as central to their community identification.[14] They propose that history teaching has the potential to address the problem of sectarian histories to form competing national identities if this intervention is made at the eleven to thirteen age range. They argue that schools should make more of this possibility[15] and that teachers do not have the grounds to be as pessimistic as they are on this score.

The authors of the above research go so far as to raise the question whether current history instruction is in fact still *assisting* young people's identification with their own community. They speculate that school history teaching, despite its intentions, may, in some cases, facilitate students relating more to politically charged historical symbols as they get older. They point out that those in the thirteen to fourteen age group, who are studying "The Act of Union to Partition," undergo a hardening of their political views. They suggest that by focusing on these particular topics, the school curriculum may be encouraging students' community identifications.

The authors of the research do not consider, however, how this hardening of political views correlates with students' maturing process and a felt need to demonstrate their maturity by declaring political opinions. But they underline that students absorb what they are taught in class selectively, hence, as a young person becomes more interested in community politics, the curriculum makes available ideas that the student can make use of in the political sphere. Research has shown that this tendency toward selective learning is most seen, in the eleven to fourteen age group, in boys who attend controlled (Protestant) schools.[16]

CRITICAL MORAL JUDGMENTS AND CONTROVERSY

In a society that rewards reticence about religion and politics in any environment where you do not know the background of all present, the notion of discussing anything political in the classroom goes against one of the operating assumptions of the culture. Inevitably, teachers are going to feel uneasy about teaching about the Troubles. But in addition, in teaching about earlier Irish history, teachers feel uneasy about making a link between the past and the present, such as, for example, the gunrunning of the Ulster Volunteer Force in 1912 and the activities of the current paramilitary group of the same name. Teachers take umbrage in the thought that once students are introduced to investigative methods and the notion of several interpretations in history, they will make inferences with regard to the present conflict situation. Teachers do not like to make these links explicit.

Moreover, even in their teaching about the past, teachers are hesitant about making value judgments concerning the behavior of the other community. This was demonstrated in interviews with teachers on how they teach about the famine.

The famine, which, for Catholics symbolizes British gross discrimination against the Catholic, nonlandowning class in Ireland, has been central to the nationalist narrative of British brutality and irresponsibility, and it has provided the basis for archetypes of hunger and separation that have lived on in subsequent generations. On the British side, conventional wisdom for many decades was that by repealing the grain tariff (the Corn Laws) and relying on free trade principles, Britain had handled the crisis in an enlightened fashion.

Recent research rejects the notion of the famine as genocide, even if that is what is being taught in some U.S. public schools.[17] Revisionist historians are now finding many new ways to study the period, most significantly by trying to understand British neglect in the context of the mind-set of that particular era. In addition, the famine has provided comparative material for the study of other famines. Another point being made these days is that while the northeast suffered less, this is not to say that the northeast was unaffected or that Protestants did not die.

According to anecdotal evidence, in the more distant past, Catholic schools devoted months to studying the famine, but even before ERO, use of the famine as an instrument for passing on nationalist propaganda had fallen off. Now teachers see their task as dispelling myths by emphasizing social history and complexity.

In responding to the question "How do you teach about the famine?" teachers' responses clustered in two areas. Five out of the twenty teachers interviewed brought up the question of the British causing the famine, saying that belief is a myth. Four out of the five saying this were Catholics: they were questioning the conventional wisdom of their own group. Four out of the twenty teachers interviewed, in this case all Protestant, made the point that the famine had contributed to the strong feelings of nationalists. Taken together, these responses demonstrate that teachers of both communities have some capacity to recognize and acknowledge how an event in history has affected the mind-set of the other group and to distance themselves from the conventional narrative of their own group.

At the same time, only three out of the twenty teachers made the obvious point that the famine was "not handled right," that there was a "selfish, economic aspect" to the story, or that the British were negligent. The question whether British authorities could have handled it better, and if so why they chose not to, seems to get little consideration. If that question is not engaged, then introducing complexity and focusing on local issues obfuscate rather than enlighten.

Teachers are anxious about discussing contentious issues in the classroom because they are frightened of losing their appearance of neutrality and demonstrating biases of which they are unaware. They believe reticence is the most effective way to demonstrate fairness and do not recognize that to remain silent is, in fact, a form of avoidance that is really partisan. Teachers in a divided society cannot, in fact, be neutral.

The easiest approach to teaching controversial issues is to teach about conflicts in other parts of the world. This can familiarize pupils with the dynamics of conflict without creating the discomfort involved in subject matter closer to home. According to several teachers interviewed, one of the difficulties with this approach as far as the Middle East is concerned is that Protestant students tend to take the Israeli side and Catholics the Arab side. This may not be the case in all schools that attempt to teach this subject matter, but certainly the presence of Zionist and Palestinian flags and slogans in the graffiti of the respective communities holds out this possibility. Nonetheless, the vast majority of teachers interviewed saw this as a valuable exercise, because it allows discussion of conflict.

CONTEMPORARY ISSUES

One of the most successful efforts to enable students to discuss controversy was a project in the mid-1990s, *Speak Your Piece*, which made videos of interschool discussions of political topics in a joint project with Channel Four Schools Television. Adding to its spirit of relevance, the *Speak Your Piece* project was presented at an International Seminar on "Education for Peace and Tolerance" in Jerusalem, in June 1996. The curriculum materials that accompanied the videos laid down structures and ground rules to train young people to facilitate difficult discussions.[18] The key to its success was dedicated teachers who were not afraid of discussing politics in the classroom. One teacher who participated in this program was convinced that her ability to handle controversy derived from her own willingness to say where she stands. She added that she could not hold a debate on current issues in the classroom were it not for the fact that the pupils feel a high level of trust in her. How has she created that trust? She believes it is because she has been available to pupils as a counselor and also informally by staying in at lunch hour, and because she has shown a willingness to participate in discussions herself.

Another approach to teaching controversial issues is computer conferencing between schools in Northern Ireland and continental Europe.[19] Northern Ireland students who participate often find themselves explaining Northern Ireland to students in distant places.

At the end of the day, teachers and policymakers are still seeking ways to grapple with critical, politicized issues. What is needed is an investigative approach where the teacher does not impose an "answer" but, nonetheless, the teacher facilitates an interaction where students can discuss contentious issues themselves.

LINKING PAST AND PRESENT

Recently some teachers have been experimenting with deliberately making connections between history and uses of memory in the classroom. This allows young people to gain some objectivity about current politicized narratives.

An example of how teaching of history might link past with present was attempted in a unit focusing on the Easter Rising of 1916 for a group of young people at a mainly Protestant school.[20] The exercise was to compare two movies that treat this subject—*Rebel Heart*, which had recently been aired by the BBC, and *Michael Collins*. The class studied newspaper reactions to *Rebel Heart* as a way of discussing the strong feelings people in the present have about the past. They created a comparative chart, judging each of the movies according to various criteria—handling of the surrender, depiction of British soldiers, depiction of the executions, and so on. And they discussed which of the movies rendered a portrayal that came closer to the primary evidence. A series of questions at the end of the exercise helped students summarize their learning by examining the results of the Rising, asking why the Rising is remembered and how we should view the Rising today.

Students evaluated this exercise positively, saying that it helped them gain understanding about present issues. At the same time, an exercise of this kind takes on extra teaching challenges when the subject matter is part of the students' *own* group mythology. The teachers who tried this experimental unit made the point that in this approach, teaching a group predominantly from one community may look different from teaching a group from another community, depending on the subject matter discussed.[21]

The idea that students' social and cultural background should be a determinant of how material about history is taught in schools is a valid one. Given that the preexisting mind-set of young people from the two communities is different, ways of helping to make that mind-set less rigid will inevitably look a bit different in each community. A teacher who is helping young people of the Protestant/unionist/loyalist community to understand the Battle of the Somme, and ways this history resonates in the present, would approach this somewhat differently from a teacher doing this in a Catholic school. Fundamental to the exercise will be teachers who are willing to bring their own personal story and outlook into the light of day[22] and who are able to help the students feel comfortable in this kind of discussion.

CHALLENGING GROUP NARRATIVES

In deeply divided societies, an official decision to rationalize history teaching by imposing a common curriculum is only the beginning of the story. Teachers and students alike have a developed sense of how to mentally insulate any subject under discussion from its current political implications, even in the homogeneous environment of segregated schools. Critical thinking, evidence-based arguments, and multiple interpretations are considered "best practice" in history study, but teachers shy away from explicitly connecting these with present-day politicized expressions of history. Teachers have to overcome their fear and depart from long-established procedures in order to discuss current politics and expose their own views.

Discussions linking "past and present" are a way to address the mythic power of narratives. In order to do this, teachers must find creative ways to discuss current uses of history, bearing in mind that challenges to their own group's narrative will be harder for younger people to absorb than challenges to the narrative of the other group.

Chapter Ten

Fragmenting Rigid Identifications

The same person who in Texas describes herself as a Houstonian, in Buffalo describes herself as a Texan, in Stockholm as an American, and in Jakarta as a Westerner. Could emphasizing the multilayered nature of identity be a means of destabilizing the solid identifications of the two communities in Northern Ireland?

The chapter explores three available alternative identities in Northern Ireland and the question whether history teaching can encourage these as a way to diminish other rigid emotional bonds. The locality, Ulster, and Europe supply aspects of people's sense of self that could be given more emphasis. Of these three, one has been co-opted by one of the two communities. The other two have received attention in school history, though in terms of having an impact on young people's self-understanding, their influence is currently small.

LOCAL CONNECTIONS

In the final paragraphs of his comprehensive work on the conflict in Northern Ireland, John Whyte suggests that future research on the conflict needs to take into consideration the great contrasts between one part of Northern Ireland and another.[1] Whyte proposes that a workable settlement would have to take account of local differences, but, in addition, this argument seems to suggest that recognition of local distinctions might help people to focus more on their sense of local identity in contrast to other identities that are more contested.

Interest in local and social history is pervasive in Northern Ireland. Several sources outside of the region have influenced it. These include the Annales school of historiography, which moved the historical profession toward social history;[2] the influence of the left in British political life, whose followers undertook various means of giving history back to the ordinary person; and the British Public Records Act of 1958, which decreed that records would become available fifty years after their writing and was followed in 1966 by an even broader provision. From within Northern Ireland, some of the most notable influences were the pioneering work in social history of E. Estyn Evans; the creation of the journal *Ulster Folklife* in 1956; the proactive policies of PRONI; and a new willingness of publishers to publish on local history subjects. [3]

For all of these reasons and in addition, perhaps, for reasons relating to the current conflict itself,[4] local history societies in Northern Ireland have risen in number from twenty in 1975 to seventy-five in 1995.[5] In 1995, the Federation of Ulster Local Studies reported eighty-five such societies in the nine counties of traditional Ulster.

Local history's ideology of inclusion and empowerment of ordinary people, both as subjects for study and as participants in the process of history writing, is a means of drawing people into discussions of history. This is a good way to learn how to talk about subjects many find threatening.

Interest in local history has never been absent in Ireland. The Belfast Natural History and Philosophical Society was founded in 1821. Similar societies sprang up during the 1920s. Notable after the Second World War was the founding of a number of Catholic diocesan historical societies, as well as the Ulster Scots Historical Society, which later became the Ulster Historical Foundation. This disparate group of associations is now held together by the Federation of Ulster Local Studies, founded in 1975. The society publishes a biannual journal and organizes conferences, smaller gatherings, and projects on many subjects. It has, predictably, a good deal of interaction with museums, and professionals move among jobs at museums, school history departments, and work with the Federation.

A recent increase in interest in local history correlates with the activities of PRONI, which came into possession of a huge quantity of new material in the 1960s. In response to the Troubles, PRONI declassified many documents on an accelerated schedule. Newly released archives were made readily accessible for use in schools and elsewhere when volumes of documents on specific topics were assembled.

Taking the longer view, the contribution to this movement of E. Estyn Evans, who came to Queen's University as a lecturer in geography in 1928 and became the first crusader on behalf of social history in Ireland, is highly significant. Though isolated by his colleagues and eclipsed since his death,[6] Evans pioneered a form of history writing that focused on the landscape and mentalities of ordinary people and took an interdisciplinary approach that made use of anthropology, oral tradition, archaeology, geography, and ethnology. His unconventional methods contributed to his nonacceptance by his peers, but in addition he was criticized for attempting to introduce local history into Queen's University, a policy deemed to imply a political agenda in an institution that was supposedly committed to neutrality. Ironically, Evans was more often accused subsequently of avoiding controversial political issues. This latter "lacuna" was in fact an essential part of his purpose: to show the common heritage lying beneath the diversity of the people of Ireland. He chose as subjects for study universal aspects of rural life, and he stressed diversity, the multifaceted nature of the past, and the many sources that have nourished Irish culture. Writing about Ulster, Evans said:

> We have to live with variety and exploit it rather than let it disturb our peace; because it is precious in that it stands in contrast to the almost universal monotony of modern culture, its dullness, its commercial exploitation and material values, its mass production. This variety is potentially a great source of strength for the future. It reflects differences, not only in landscape, but in dialect and attitudes of mind, but there is common ground in the emotions which bind people to this bit of country or to that.[7]

Evans was instrumental in the founding of the Institute of Irish Studies in 1965 and thus left an institution that has operated as a nonpartisan think tank, generating research on all manner of cultural issues in both the North and the South.[8]

If Evans was not able to have as much influence as he hoped, the victory of the Labour Party in 1964 did help to bring a new focus on "people's history." In the late 1960s, English universities' extramural departments got more funding to send staff out to work with people to develop projects on their own local history. The Open University also encouraged local history and met with particular success with its urban projects.[9]

Somewhat overlapping with the Federation of Ulster Local Studies in its activities, and also growing out of the British left's concern to empower the working man and woman, is the Workers' Educational Association (WEA), which came into existence in the late nineteenth century through the Fabians.[10] The WEA has continued to provide a framework in which broad educational opportunities are offered to the working class. Traditionally it has worked more in urban areas, and among its many programs it offers assertiveness and capacity building training for women, supports women's interest in politics, and has worked closely with the Women's Coalition. It teaches creative writing as a form of "therapeutic reminiscence," gives instruction in personal health and empowerment, and offers a "Prejudice Awareness Interface" where contemporary issues are discussed. It has also developed a series of classes in history, "Pathways Through the Past — A Structured Look at Irish History."

In 1991, the WEA got three years of funding from the Cultural Traditions Group (and later received funding for the next three years from DENI) for a People's History Project that has served not only to produce people's history but to organize volunteer projects where people of the two communities could work together. Directed by Jack Johnston, a former history teacher based in Clogher, Co. Fermanagh, the project ran 270 courses on 70 locations over a six-year period and issued in several books.

In order to find a neutral venue in which to hold the meetings for these projects, Johnston was sometimes forced to go outside the community where he was working or to meet alternately in Catholic and Protestant schools. "At the beginning they would have gone to sit with their own. After a year or two they would sit anywhere. I deliberately structured it so this would happen. In dividing up the research I made sure they weren't just doing it with their pals, but with someone from the other side — for example, looking at gravestone inscriptions."[11] Johnston, nonetheless, had to tread carefully when conflicting accounts of the same event cropped up. Often he would use newspapers, showing how the nationalist and unionist paper in the same town respectively reported a single incident. "Every town has two newspapers, so you have two accounts of every event. You see differences in the choice of words — one might use the word 'volunteer' and the other 'terrorist.' We were able to demonstrate to people that these words were emotive. [We told them] if we can ferret out the facts here we have done something."[12]

The final meeting of the six-year project took place at the PRONI office in Belfast and ran all day on Saturday, May 3, 1997. Its tone was somewhat reminiscent of a gospel meeting as the groups from various regions got up to tell the story of their project. Willie Carlin, a railway worker from Strabane whose group project, *Railway Days in Strabane*, was to be published later in 1997, told the group, "Strabane is known as republican, but that is completely different from what you find when you get to know it. . . . Whenever I had seen books about Strabane they seemed to be written by someone from the outside. Jack was telling me not to sit back and let people from Belfast do this for us."[13]

As far as the teaching of local history in schools is concerned, a number of teachers interviewed for this study complained that the ERO reforms have left them fewer opportunities to teach local history. This is ironic because local history is an ideal vehicle for introducing complexity about rigid notions of group identity. It demonstrates how the communities have intermingled and cooperated and how traditionally Protestant names like Adams have ended up in Catholic families and vice versa. Moreover, process-based history teaching in schools has a natural affinity with the teaching of local history. If pupils need to learn how to gather information, then they are most able to do this in their own locality. Local history teaching, therefore, has a fourfold value in a postconflict situation. First, it helps people develop a stronger identification with their locality; second, it brings social history, as distinct from political history, to the forefront and thus tones down the politicizing capacities of history study; third, it offers the possibility of projects that people can pursue with others from the other community; and fourth, it allows hands-on experience in the gathering of empirical evidence.

Many of the curriculum development projects of the 1970s emphasized local history, both for primary and secondary schoolchildren.[14] According to interviews conducted for this research project, teachers believe in the importance of local history: when teachers were asked if history should teach a sense of belonging, the most popular answer of those who replied in the affirmative was that history should inculcate a sense of belonging to their own locality.[15]

This seems to indicate a level of idealism on the part of teachers that is not replicated in the society at large. In the surveys of 1978 and 1986 cited by Whyte, those questioned about their identity could choose among Irish, British, Ulster, Northern Irish, Don't Know, Sometimes British/Sometimes Irish, Anglo-Irish, and Other. In 1978, only 0.2 percent of Protestants and 0.5 percent of Catholics chose Other (which would include identification with one's immediate locality or Europe). In 1986, 2 percent of Protestants and 2 percent of Catholics chose Other.[16]

ULSTER IDENTITY

One of the questions the outsider is bound to ask as he wrestles with the complexities of Northern Ireland is, Why not a Northern Ireland, or Ulster, identity? Catholics would say that Ulster identity has no resonance for them and that a truly Ulster identification would have to include the three Ulster counties that have remained part of the South. On the other hand, unionists demonstrate a burgeoning interest in Ulster Scots customs and dialect, describing the latter as a language deserving equal recognition with Gaelic. The political agenda of greater recognition for unionism through cultural assertion is unmistakable in celebrations of "Ulsterness."

The historical argument for an Ulster identity has been treated in considerable detail by medical doctor and amateur historian Ian Adamson, a longtime

Belfast city councillor and former Lord Mayor of Belfast. Adamson's work develops the argument that the people of Ulster are descended from the Cruthin, a people who came to Ireland during the Neolithic period from Galloway in southern Scotland, or from Cumbria, and who were referred to in those regions as Picts. He proposes that the Celtic invasion of the early Middle Ages brought fairly small numbers of Celts to Ireland, but that these Celts, or Gaels as they came to be called, quickly took positions of power and employed genealogists to recast the history of Ireland so that the Cruthin were removed from Irish history.

According to Adamson, one Cruthin grouping, the Dál Riata, crossed over from Ulster to settle Argyle and the islands of the western seaboard of Scotland. Another Cruthin migration went to Galloway, which is verified by similarities in archaeological finds in Galloway and Ulster. He argues, therefore, that the Scots who came to settle the Ulster plantations in the seventeenth century, "particularly those who came from areas in Scotland which in previous centuries had been populated by immigrants from Ulster, may be justly considered as returning to the home of their ancestors."[17]

Adamson's argument that the Scots who arrived in Ulster in 1609 were returning home implies at a minimum that the Ulster Scots have as good a claim to belong in the island of Ireland as anyone else. But by emphasizing that the Cruthin predate the Celts, he is arguing that the Cruthin have a *prior* claim to Ireland. Moreover, in redefining the Protestant plantations of the seventeenth century as a return of the Cruthin to their native soil, he is undermining a principal icon of Irish nationalism—the Protestant as invader and oppressor.

Adamson thus puts a knife into the heart of Irish nationalist ideology and then twists it by co-opting a series of other nationalist symbols along the way. First, he argues that not all Irish culture is descended from Gaelic culture. Because the Celts came in rather small numbers to Ireland, he suggests, they could not have immediately subsumed or absorbed the Cruthin. He backs up this argument by appropriating for his own narrative the warrior Cúchulainn, hero of the Irish epic "The Cattle Raid of Cooley." Irish republican leader Padraig Pearse used the story of Cúchulainn to impart to the young people in his educational experiment at St. Enda's a vision of the heroic ideal. Pearse, inspired by the image of Cúchulainn meeting his death by fighting off his enemies single-handedly against impossible odds, made Cúchulainn an idol of his own struggle. He saw in both Cúchulainn's death and in Christ's passion models of blood sacrifice that matched well with the struggles of republicanism. His leadership of the Easter Rising of 1916 and subsequent execution is commemorated by a statue, in the General Post Office in Dublin, of the dying Cúchulainn. Adamson, by contrast, has reclaimed Cúchulainn for Ulster, recasting the tale as a narrative of salvation for the Cruthin people.

Second, Adamson's work questions the Gaelic/nationalist claim of responsibility for the spreading of Christianity[18] by arguing that when St. Patrick returned to Ireland on a mission to Christianize the island, a number of his most significant early converts were Cruthin people in Ulster. One of these, St. Comgall, founded a monastery at Bangor which became the most important Christian settlement in Ireland. Music, literature, and religious writings originated there and had considerable influence on Irish civilization. Another saint whom Adamson claims to have been a Cruthin is Columbanus, the monk trained at Comgall's monastery who led twelve companions on a missionary journey through northern France, Austria, and Italy, and who was referred to by Robert Schuman, the Catholic postwar foreign minister of France, as the "patron saint of those who seek to construct a united Europe."[19]

Adamson's books did not initially attract much response from professional scholars in Ulster. Jonathan Bardon's *A History of Ulster* only indirectly engages Adamson's arguments, saying, in relation to the Celtic invasion of Ireland:

> It is too simple to see the conquerors as Gaelic Celts and those in retreat as Ulster's original inhabitants, as some have done. Certainly the Cruthin seem to have been an ancient people. . . . They retained an ancient identity for many centuries to come, but they do not seem to have had a language, social structure, or archeological heritage separate from the rest of the Irish. It is likely that there was a constant blending with descendants of the earliest inhabitants and later arrivals. Indeed it could be said that in the early Middle Ages Ireland had a remarkable cultural unity.[20]

Bardon describes the Dál Riata's move to Scotland as *Gaelic,* that is, not Cruthin, colonization.

A series of other reviewers have been more forthright in raising questions about the legitimacy of Adamson's work. "This theory is nonsense and Adamson has a brass neck in expounding it," commented one reviewer;[21] "spurious authenticity" said another;[22] "disputed theories" was the comment of a third.[23] Adamson was referred to in *The Irish News* as an "academic eccentric."[24]

Michael Hall has been one of Adamson's principal defenders. Hall, who is well known for his cross-community activities in the Falls and Shankill Roads in Belfast, has published a series of pamphlets, "Island Pamphlets," that intertwine his own vision for Northern Ireland with conversations he has had with people in both communities. He aims for grassroots unity, harmony, and empowerment where the working class develops its own political strategies. He speaks of Ulster going it alone, not as a "Protestant homeland" but rather as a "new society to which both communities could give allegiance.[25] He calls upon loyalists to recognize the Irish elements in their heritage and the nationalists to recognize the British elements in their heritage and asks that both groups "see how the 'Irish' and 'British' aspirations can be harmonized to our mutual benefit."[26] Pluralism, Hall argues, must transcend zero-sum thinking and be discovered in an intercommunity dialogue that gives legitimate expression to both traditions.

Hall reasons that the two communities have a lot in common both because of their working-class character and because both have experienced some form of distancing from the community they formerly regarded as their own: from Dublin in the case of the nationalists, and from London in the case of the loyalists.

Hall uses Ulster history to demonstrate the elements held in common between the cultures of the two communities. He mentions the prehistoric links between Scotland and Ireland seen in the identical Stone Age burial monuments; the implied shared kinship that follows from this; the Irish Sea as a focus of social interaction between Scotland and Ireland; the Ulster settlers who named Scotland and also brought the Gaelic language to Scotland; and, more generally, quoting another author, "the North Channel culture-province within which obtained a free currency of ideas, literary, intellectual and artistic."[27] He devotes one of his "Island Pamphlets" to the Cruthin story and the controversy surrounding it, enumerating, and then refuting one by one, the detractors' concerns.[28] Hall is somewhat better than Adamson at discussing his use of sources, and after picking apart the illogicality and inconsistency of his critics, Hall delivers himself and Adamson onto fairly solid ground in terms of the viability of their historical work. Indeed, Adamson's argument that early Irish history was an "invented tradition" created by Gaelic chroniclers is acknowledged by Roy Foster.[29]

The idea of an independent Ulster was in the past easily dismissed on the grounds it was not viable economically. But this criticism is less salient in the era of the European Union.

At best, the problem with Adamson's vision is that it is unlikely to be unifying for Northern Ireland. His comprehensive concept of Ulster identity leaves nationalists unenthusiastic.[30] Traditional Ulster was split in 1920, so that the present state of Northern Ireland has only six of the original nine counties. The reason was to ensure a Protestant majority in Northern Ireland. Adamson's version of Ulster seems to be a six-county version. Catholics regard an independent Ulster as a consolidation of Protestant hegemony. Surveys of 1968, 1978, and 1986 demonstrate that the "Ulster" identity has never been popular with Catholics and its popularity has diminished with the Troubles.[31]

Hall argues, nonetheless, that there is a basis for these two groups to find common cause. "For Belfast's Catholic working class in particular," he says, "it is what they have actually gone through, rather than any supposedly inborn attitudes, which determines how they perceive [that] reality" and he quotes one of those involved in his discussions:

The Unionists were always obsessed with the threat from Irish nationalism, but if they had offered Catholics a genuine equality I am convinced Republicanism as an ideology would be near dead. People around here aren't Republican because of something coming through their mothers' milk—they're Republican because of their experiences.[32]

Critics of Adamson concede that even if the Cruthin story fails as a unifying narrative for Catholics and Protestants, it could offer Ulster Protestants elements of a more satisfactory group narrative than presently exists. Ulster Protestants have been denied ownership of their Gaelic heritage because it was appropriated by the cause of Irish nationalism. The independent Irish state, with its "one nation" thesis, made it impossible for Protestants to develop their own sense of Irish heritage. In addition, the Northern Ireland state, by neglecting history teaching in primary schools, made it more difficult for Protestants to develop a knowledge of their local heritage. Adamson gives the Protestant community a claim to be native to the soil of Ireland, removing the stigma of being "colonists."[33]

But a further problem with the vision of Ulster identity is that Adamson does not even speak for all unionists. The secular nature of Adamson's message makes it unattractive to the Reverend Ian Paisley.[34] More generally among Protestants, the notion of an Ulster identity has diminished in the last thirty years as Protestants show an increased preference to be designated "British."[35]

Adamson is criticized on more serious grounds for making his philosophy available for the use of the Ulster Defense Association (UDA), a loyalist paramilitary organization. To this accusation he responds that he cannot control how his ideas will be used, though Adamson did, presumably by choice, lecture on his first book to various groups including members of the UDA. The second printing of *The Cruthin* has an introductory preface by Glen Barr, who was then a UDA officer and who later became leader of the Ulster Workers' Council, the body that coordinated the loyalist general strike in 1974 that brought down the Sunningdale power-sharing agreement. In addition, Adamson's articles have appeared in *Ulster*, the UDA organ, under the pseudonym Sam Sloan.

In spite of his claim to articulate a common Ulster identity, Adamson is generally viewed as the creator of a partisan narrative.

TILTING TO EUROPE

The significance of Europe for the Northern Ireland conflict has been understood in a variety of ways.

Catholics in Ireland have looked to their fellow Catholics in Europe for support since the period of the Penal Laws, and to this day their links with European Catholicism are strong. More directly, nationalists made use of the European Convention on Human Rights, under the Council of Europe, as a means to challenge the British policy of internment.[36] Both factors have encouraged the Catholic/nationalist predisposition to view the European Union (EU) as a positive resource in the conflict. But even without that predisposition, the many advantages the South has gained from the EU's investment argue strongly for the notion that Ireland's interests lie with Europe.

John Hume, who attended seminary in France, exemplifies this affinity. Hume was for many years a member of the European Parliament from Northern Ireland while serving simultaneously as a member of the House of Commons in Westminster[37] and, latterly, in Stormont. His sense of the importance of Europe goes well beyond his personal love of the French language and his belief in the usefulness of European institutions for Ireland. He often cites the reconciliation between France and Germany that has developed since World War II as a sign of hope for Northern Ireland, and he holds up the European Union as a model of the kind of pluralism and coexistence that he hopes for in his "Agreed Ireland."[38] Hume has lent his support to the vision of a Europe of the Regions, in hopes that a special status for Ireland as a "region" might help to remove the constitutional impasse in the North.[39]

Traditionally, unionists have been suspicious of the European Union or, at best, reluctant to place much importance in it. The logic of this stance is fairly obvious—if unionists are using their British identity as a rationale for their political aim of remaining within the United Kingdom, then any process that might dissipate Britain's own sense of identity could disadvantage the unionists. One Protestant grammar school teacher said to me, "The pupils see the EU skeptically—it would mean the House of Commons would be reduced to a county council. It is the liberal intellectual elite that supports the EU."

Ian Paisley and other Protestant fundamentalists like to characterize Europe as synonymous with Catholicism, and thus deserving of unequivocal opposition. The *Protestant Telegraph*, which articulates Paisley's worldview, has described the European Union as a plot by the Pope to Catholicize Britain and Northern Ireland.[40]

For some in Northern Ireland, the EU supplies a vision of an alternative identity which might manage to dissipate either unionist or nationalist allegiances. But if assessing the subject matter of school history classes provides a measure of a societal swing toward a new European self-concept, then the evidence would suggest that no such shift is occurring. If anything, the requirement to teach more Irish history has reduced the amount of European history taught in schools. More than one-third of teachers interviewed in this study said they are now teaching less European history than before ERO, and the same number said they are now teaching about the same amount as before. One said that European history, in the terms in which it used to be understood, has disappeared from the timetable: now European history means the Normans, the Reformation, World War I, and the Holocaust. Less than half of the history teachers interviewed for this study said they make a point of talking about the EU in class. When they were asked whether they would like to see the proportion of Irish-British-European-world history changed, over half believed that the mix is fine as it is, but about a quarter said they would like to see more European or world history taught. When teachers who said they believed history should teach a sense of belonging were asked how they would describe that sense of belonging, many gave more than one answer, but "European" and "belonging to one's own locality" were the most popular answers. Catholics outnumbered Protestants in the groups who proposed each of these categories, but this may have been because Protestants were more reluctant than Catholics to say that history classes should build any sense of belonging at all.

Outside of history classes, a variety of school projects are attempting to shift school pupils' focus in a European direction.[41] When asked if their school offered other courses relating to Europe apart from history courses, two-thirds of teachers interviewed responded in the affirmative. Often the European Union is studied in political science classes. In addition, some schools offer a Certificate of European Studies. A European Studies Project, instituted in 1986 in the wake of the signing of the Anglo-Irish Agreement, linked schools in the Republic of Ireland, Great Britain, and Northern Ireland for projects with Belgian schools. The project has gone on to use e-mail, video conferencing, TV and radio, and residential periods at Leuven to bring children into working contact with pupils from France, Spain, Belgium, and Germany.[42] Though some Protestant schools in Northern Ireland were unwilling to take part, it was unclear whether this was because of political concerns or caution about overloading the timetable. After the agreed six years of the program, London dropped out for lack of funding. Belfast and Dublin have continued—Belfast's funding now comes from sources designated for EMU activities. The person who headed the project, Roger Austin, has moved on to developing computer conferencing between Northern Ireland schools and European schools, allowing discussion of history and politics while developing children's computer skills.

Another aspect of Northern Ireland school involvement with Europe has been Northern Ireland's representation in the Council of Europe's history conferences, many of which are geared to the particular challenges of history teaching in postcommunist countries. Here, the experience of revising history teaching in Northern Ireland has become an exportable commodity. The Council of Europe's Central Bureau for Educational Visits and Exchanges has held several conferences in Northern Ireland, bringing delegates from other Council of Europe countries to discuss topics of particular importance to Northern Ireland teachers. In 1994 the theme was "Education for Mutual Understanding," and in 1998, "The Teaching of History in a Divided Community."

Revisionists are also making use of the European connection to challenge the idea of Ireland's past as uniquely painful, an idea that gives Ireland's mythic history extra power. When compared with the history of other European countries, they argue, Ireland's history is not as unusually traumatic as many have made out. Liam Kennedy has coined the term MOPE—Most Oppressed People on Earth—as part of his campaign to challenge the intense ways that historical myths are used in Ireland. Kennedy pinpoints the various bases upon which the MOPE worldview stands—numbers of deaths in war, statistics on ownership of land, lack of religious freedom, and loss of language—and compares these statistics with other European countries. He demonstrates some ways in which the unique circumstances of Ireland's situation indeed contributed to its sense of suffering, but argues that there is no basis for the MOPE view.[43] Brian Walker takes a similar tack, citing the European wars of religion to argue Ireland was not unique in its focus on religious difference.[44] Frank Wright's *Northern Ireland: A Comparative Analysis* compares Northern Ireland with what Wright calls "ethnic frontiers" in former Yugoslavia and Poland as well as the South in the United States.[45]

Placing Ireland in the context of Europe produces useful comparative points, but it is not clear where this is leading in terms of shifting identities. Attacking the "uniqueness" of Ireland's concerns could destabilize the two main communities' narratives, but far from reducing the conflict, this might be experienced as threatening to both groups.

THE INTERCULTURAL COSMOPOLITAN

If one definition of the cosmopolitan is the person who moves easily among cultural settings and treats all as valuable but none as superior, then Northern Ireland possesses the raw materials to develop this mind-set. Increasing numbers of immigrants from Asia and Eastern Europe are bringing a variety that used not to be part of the scene.

Increasingly people speak about "racism" as the problem of Northern Ireland, which is a way to say that the problem of dealing with difference goes beyond the problem between the two main communities. Multicultural awareness is coming to Northern Ireland.

One aspect of this multiculturalism is the recognition of the multilayered nature of all identifications. Connections with the locality and with Europe seem viable ways to break down people's narrow sense of communal identification.

This research found little evidence that, in the short term, alternative identifications are gaining salience for those connected with the two principle groupings. But perhaps that is not the point. The value of recognizing various alternative identifications is not in supplying an alternative agreed narrative but in reducing the intensity of the either/or dynamic that feeds antagonism.

A special feature of European influence in Northern Ireland is the growing European focus on "citizenship" in schools and elsewhere. Citizenship is a valuable concept for Northern Ireland because it offers a way to embrace common values without requiring loyalty to a particular state. This will be addressed in the next chapter.

Chapter Eleven

Education for Citizenship

At the end of the 1990s, a number of converging factors led educators in Northern Ireland to reconsider and overhaul the statutory curriculum. Developments in the area of citizenship education in Europe and worldwide, as well as input from students and teachers, helped steer this change of direction. The new curriculum that is now proposed outlines the entire educational experience for young people from ages five to sixteen, making education for society and citizenship a central goal.

RESPONDING TO THE CONFLICT

In the preceding chapters, we have examined a number of ways that education attempted to respond to the conflict. Among the most significant were encouraging integrated schools, funding cross-community activities for schools, creating a common history and religious instruction curriculum, requiring the themes of Education for Mutual Understanding and Cultural Heritage to be made part of all classes, and addressing social inequities.

The integrated schools movement and the common curriculum instituted by the ERO have been discussed in previous chapters.

Cross-community contact schemes began to be funded by DENI in 1987. The requirements placed on schools in order to get funding were few beyond organizing an event with a school of the other community. These cross-community events were never made mandatory by DENI. To the degree that they existed, the projects depended upon the initiative of individual teachers and did not require buy-in from the school itself. Museums became a destination of choice, and several museums, such as the Ulster American Folk Park and the Ulster Folk and Transport Museum, began to devote considerable energy to preparing school events, some of them residential and lasting as long as three or four days. Money for these projects is still available, though the projects now involve no more than 10 percent of pupils.[1] Currently, DENI is trying to encourage schools to adopt three-year plans with community relations goals that are appropriate to the environment where the school is located. Staff development activities are being included in this new venture. The hope is to get schools to commit to cross-community contact for the long term, rather than have individual teachers carry the load.

EMU and Cultural Heritage as cross-curricular themes to be used by all teachers became a requirement with ERO. They aimed to enable pupils "to learn to respect and value themselves and others; to appreciate the interdependence of people within society; to know about and understand what is shared, as well as what is different, about their cultural traditions; and to appreciate how conflict may be handled in non-violent ways."[2]

Over time it has become clear that the themes have not had a significant impact. The requirement that teachers incorporate the themes in their classes met obstacles because teachers had inadequate training and lacked ideas about how to do this. The plan failed to take into full consideration that teachers generally avoid teaching about anything touching on the controversial matters of sectarianism, politics, or violence. Another criticism leveled at EMU was its deficit of intellectual rigor. Schools lacked conviction about the themes and therefore did not push the teachers hard enough. Many schools persuaded themselves that they had fulfilled their EMU requirement when they had organized a contact program.[3]

RECONSIDERATIONS

In the late 1990s, a convergence of considerations caused DENI to take stock. The signing of the Belfast Agreement of 1998 was obviously a landmark. The Agreement commits signatories to develop integrated education and to give support for Irish language education. It also speaks of the need to develop a "culture of tolerance" in the society. DENI set up two working groups as a direct response to these stipulations. The first recommended a more systematic approach to the development of integrated schools, sufficient and effective guidance for schools wishing to transform to integrated status, and funding to help all schools meet the challenge of pluralism.[4] The second working group's report examined education's contribution to the promotion of community relations, including the contact schemes described above, and highlighted areas where more could be done.[5]

At much the same time, the Education Reform (NI) Order 1989 reached its ten-year anniversary. With a decade of experience behind them, education policy advisors were assessing the effects of the ERO-required curriculum. A seminal study published in 1995 highlighted a range of reasons why EMU had failed to be effective. Research on attitudes of Northern Ireland teachers toward the teaching of values conducted two years later revealed that many teachers were favorably disposed toward the idea of imparting values in the classroom but felt that support and guidance were lacking.[6] Five years later, a social attitudes survey of 2002 indicated that most respondents believed schools should be involved in addressing difficult issues of politics and human rights (though more Catholics than Protestants were enthusiastic about this).[7]

Simultaneously, interest was growing in possibilities for citizenship education, and a survey of employers undertaken by the Confederation of British Industry (CBI) supported the value of citizenship education for the needs of the workplace.

From 1996 to 2003, a longitudinal study was undertaken that revealed that young people in general were frustrated with education's apparent lack of relevance to their lives at present or in the future.[8] Taken along with the other research, this confirmed the need to rethink the curriculum. Students under sixteen said most education seemed only to be geared to passing exams, and they were bored by the repetition that seemed to be necessary to this end. Students over sixteen said that with hindsight they could see more relevance in what they had learned, but they emphasized that if teachers drew more parallels with real life while they were teaching, this would enhance students' motivation. Students also suggested that making connections among the various subjects they study would be more interesting, and pointed out that they are better learners if they are able to learn skills in some progressive fashion.

The Council for the Curriculum, Examinations and Assessment linked these findings with other relevant research. Recent investigations in neuroscience underline that thought is filtered through the emotional part of the brain first, and meaning is made by perceiving patterns and connections. Therefore, connections will be made better if emotions are engaged. In addition, we learn best when we can apply what we learn and can transfer learning from one situation to another.

INTEREST IN CITIZENSHIP EDUCATION

Meantime, an increasing body of curriculum materials on citizenship was becoming available from European sources. Interest in teaching for citizenship has grown in Europe in the 1990s, linked with the collapse of communism and attendant democratization in postcommunist countries, a rising awareness of pluralism in all countries, and the European Union and Council of Europe's interest in developing ideas of what it is to be a citizen of Europe.

In addition to the universal values promoted in citizenship education, the new Europe of the EU calls upon people to be aware of the complex, many-layered nature of their identity. European citizenship allows people freedom of movement within the EU while retaining privileges of EU citizenship in all locations. This makes it possible to think about citizenship in ways that are not tied to national affiliations. The 1997 Treaty of Amsterdam (Article A) affirmed the EU's determination to develop a sense of European citizenship in the wider social framework, with the intention of encouraging citizens to participate in all areas of the democratic process.[9] The EU has published resources for schools, including *Education for Active Citizenship in the European Union* (1998), which says European citizenship is "based on the shared values of interdependence, democracy, equality of opportunity and mutual respect."[10]

Equally, the Council of Europe through the Council for Cultural Co-operation (CDCC) promotes public awareness of European citizenship, encouraging curriculum development and the gathering of ideas for projects from teachers and school heads. European identity is considered to be related to citizenship;[11] therefore, education for democracy is viewed as a core element of teaching about European citizenship.

By the mid-1990s, many involved in these initiatives believed a new program was needed, and the CDCC responded with a project on Education for Democratic Citizenship (EDC). EDC consisted of activities to better equip young people and adults to participate in democracy by exercising their rights and responsibilities.[12] It focused on four areas: political and legal, social (how individuals relate to each other and to their social and civic institutions), economic (the world of work and functioning of the economy), and cultural (expressions of shared values and traditions within and between groups). EDC recognized that controversial issues would arise and should be addressed and encouraged the necessary teacher preparation for this.

The International Association for the Evaluation of Educational Achievement initiated an international project, carried out between 1995 and 2001, to study citizenship education in as many countries as possible. Among other findings, the study emphasized that citizenship education is closely linked to the historical and political context of each country; that schools adapt slowly to the transitions that are required to introduce this kind of education; and that civic education should cut across disciplines, be participative and interactive, and be conducted in a nonauthoritarian environment that demonstrates awareness of social diversity. Another finding was that curriculum usually includes an aspiration to develop critical thinking or education about values, but these often do not make it into the classrooms, which are usually dominated by knowledge transmission. The study also found that, across the board, fourteen-year-olds believed that free elections and availability of organizations for people to join strengthen democracy; however, this age group is only moderately interested in politics and sees television as a key source of political information.

Another prod in the direction of citizenship curriculum for Northern Ireland came from the UN, which named the decade 1995-2004 the "United Nations Decade for Human Rights Education." The UN General Assembly produced a Plan of Action for the Decade and created guidelines for governments to use in developing national plans of action for human rights education. These national plans were then compiled so that countries could share information. The national plans show a strong awareness of the need to integrate human rights education into other teaching subjects, to introduce human rights education into community and youth programs as well as schools, and to ensure that human rights principles are demonstrated in school culture as well as in classrooms. One of the biggest challenges proved to be shifting the human rights language to be more user-friendly for young people and making it clear how these ideas play out practically in their lives. Citizenship education offers an obvious place to educate citizens about their rights and responsibilities.

A pilot project in the Republic of Ireland from 1993 to 1996 led to the South's introduction of a new program in second level schools: Civil, Social, and Political Education (CSPE). As a course in citizenship based on human rights and social responsibility, it incorporates seven key concepts: democracy, rights and responsibilities, human dignity, interdependence, development, law, and stewardship. The course is taught through four units of study: The Individual and Citizenship, The Community, The State, and Ireland and the World. In England, an advisory group on citizenship issued its final report in 1998, *Education for Citizenship and the Teaching of Democracy in Schools,* which was to be the basis of citizenship education in English schools.

CITIZENSHIP PILOT PROGRAM AND CURRICULUM REVIEW

Acting in response to all these factors, CCEA, in partnership with the University of Ulster, began to explore how EMU might be strengthened or replaced by a more conceptually rigorous focus on citizenship education. With the assistance of the Citizenship Foundation in England, funding was acquired from the Nuffield Foundation and an anonymous American philanthropist to establish a pilot project at the University of Ulster; this project would explore the conceptual basis and methodological approaches to supporting the teaching of citizenship in Northern Ireland. A pilot CSPE project was established in twenty-five schools. It drew much of its inspiration from the expertise of colleagues in the Republic of Ireland, while simultaneously seeking to address the very specific challenges posed by sectarianism in Northern Ireland.

At the same time, the CCEA was considering the adequacy of the whole of the Northern Ireland curriculum to meet the needs of young people in the new century. They advised DENI in January of 1999 to embark on a total curriculum review in order to more explicitly define aims, objectives, skills, and values. Among the issues identified for review, though by no means the only issue, was the need for explicit emphasis on citizenship for all young people aged four to sixteen.

The review process began in late 1999 and was scheduled for completion by 2001. For a number of reasons, not least the challenge of winning support for this fundamental overhaul, the review lasted three years longer than expected. Funding had already been set aside to support implementation from 2001, and when the review's completion was delayed, DENI sought advice on ways to put the funding to good use.

This led to a strategic decision to support the expansion of the CSPE project into an official pilot scheme. Experienced staff from the pilot project joined the CCEA to develop a plan to train up to five teachers from every postprimary school by 2006 to teach this material.

THE REVISED NORTHERN IRELAND CURRICULUM

The review of the Northern Ireland curriculum sought to strengthen and make more explicit the values that should inform young people's entire educational experience up to age sixteen. The new curriculum that has emerged aims to "empower young people to develop their potential and to make informed and responsible choices and decisions throughout their lives as individuals, contributors to society, and contributors to the economy and environment."[13] Central to the curriculum is the determination to make learning applicable to life and work; students are given skills and capabilities as core elements of learning, rather than as matters that students are expected to somehow pick up in the interstices of traditional class subjects.

The main practical change is that modules on Education for Employability, Local and Global Citizenship, and Personal Development will now be required for eleven- to fourteen-year-olds, along with the "general learning areas" that contain conventional subjects. Part of the impetus for this decision was a recognition that if the vision that underpinned Education for Mutual Understanding and Cultural Heritage were to be effective, they needed to be made explicit within every subject, and that aspects of the themes not addressed within traditional subjects needed to be allocated actual space on the timetable so that teachers could not ignore the requirement.

The statutory requirement for Local and Global Citizenship means that every pupil in Northern Ireland will engage in an appropriate way with the four concepts of Diversity and Inclusion, Human Rights and Social Responsibility, Equality and Social Justice, and Democracy and Active Participation. Comprehensive guidance has been developed to support teachers in delivering Local and Global Citizenship as an active and enjoyable experience in the classroom. The support materials include concept outlines and activities in relation to the topics, as well as background information for teachers on race relations, sectarianism, and international human rights protection.

HISTORY IN THE REVISED
NORTHERN IRELAND CURRICULUM

In line with the overall policy to create flexibility in the new curriculum, history no longer has a detailed outline requiring the study of specific periods. Rather, students are required to, for example:

- Explore how history has affected their personal identity, culture, and lifestyle;
- Investigate how history has been used by individuals and groups to create stereotypical perceptions and to justify views and actions (e.g., explore different attitudes to the same historical event); and
- Investigate the causes and consequences of the partition of Ireland and how it has influenced their own notions of nationality, citizenship, and democracy (e.g., compare a range of viewpoints on allegiance and how it has been shaped by history).[14]

The decision to lay down minimum requirements that might be interpreted by teachers in different ways is a radical departure from the detailed specifications of the previous decade, when a selection of periods from European history, world history, and Irish history were required study.

A chief reason for the change is to restore trust in both teachers' professionalism and their ability to interpret the curriculum in ways that best suit the interests and abilities of their pupils. The hope is that greater flexibility will enhance teachers' enthusiasm and creativity.

The changes in the history curriculum have also been informed by research mentioned in Chapter Nine that suggests that even though current textbooks seek to offer Irish history from a range of perspectives, pupils, nonetheless, often succeed in subverting both the aim and the methodology by selecting to absorb and retain only those interpretations that fit with their community perception. Other insights suggest that the detail of the historical periods studied are too complex for perhaps all but the most able pupils in the eleven to fourteen age group, leaving many with a confused and unhelpful smattering of knowledge that fails to have any impact on their community-derived folklore.

Discussions with teachers have also revealed continued concern about teaching more recent Irish history and a sustained reluctance to engage with the challenge of confronting stereotypical viewpoints. Many history teachers continue to hold the view that their role is to address historical understanding only, not to probe how history informs pupils' understanding of society today.

The revised history curriculum seeks to address a number of these concerns in a subtle way. It tries to relate historical issues directly to pupils' lives, requiring teachers to help pupils explore history's impact on their personal identity, culture, and lifestyle; to confront the misuse of history for political purposes, by teaching about uses of history by individuals and groups to create stereotypes; and to explore not just the causes but also the consequences of the partition of Ireland and its impact on pupils' notions of nationality, citizenship, and democracy. In all these ways, the revised curriculum examines how historical ideas remain alive in current society.

While the increased flexibility heightens the risk of teachers gravitating toward teaching only those elements of history that are easiest, least controversial, or best known to them, a number of mitigating strategies will be put in place to ensure that this will not happen in practice. Detailed guidance will accompany the curriculum, illustrating how teachers might (and by implication should) interpret the minimum requirements. This will contain challenging examples of what is expected. Accompanying this will be new textbooks and materials that will illustrate in much greater detail how these challenging issues can be addressed within the classroom. These will be linked more strongly and explicitly to the values and citizenship messages that underpin the whole curricular philosophy. Custom and practice suggest that a good textbook will go a long way to influencing the content addressed and the methodological approaches adopted by a teacher. Textbooks tend to be authored by people associated with the Curriculum Advice and Support Service, who can then back up these messages using in-service training programs.

Implementation will be monitored by the Education and Training Inspectorate, which is likely to enquire about the extent to which schools have responded to the recommendations. What, therefore, is flexible and allows room for interpretation and creativity, is also subtly geared toward the goal of making history explicitly relevant to young people's lives today, supported by well-thought-through materials that seek to ensure challenge, motivation, and engagement.

The hope is that history classes of this kind, aligned with specific provision for citizenship, will help to break down tendencies toward rigid, stereotypical thinking and that, in the long run, this will be more important to students for their future lives than learning the details of historical periods that seem to have little relationship to the present.

IMPLICATIONS FOR TEACHER EDUCATION

All those involved in the creation of the new curriculum recognize that teacher education is going to be crucial to its success. As indicated earlier, DENI has instituted in-service training for postprimary teachers from fifty schools per year, with up to five teachers per school. Provision will also be made, in the implementation phase, for the training of primary teachers in those aspects of the revised curriculum that relate to citizenship and, given that research indicates that children acquire their views about sectarianism at a very young age, it would seem that primary teachers should be the "front line" in the teaching of citizenship.

In this respect, a number of innovative approaches have been developed in Northern Ireland, engaging the power of the moving image, of multimedia, and of effective storytelling, which deserve international attention. The BBC in Northern Ireland has, since the mid-1960s, illustrated how responsible and thoughtful educational programming can support and motivate teachers to address challenging issues, particularly in relation to controversial aspects of Irish history. From the early 1990s, Channel Four Education also joined in this endeavor, focusing almost all of their programming on issues related to history teaching and citizenship in Northern Ireland. The work of both companies has helped to develop the talents of indigenous media companies who have provided a number of films, CD-ROMS, websites, and materials which afford both the stimulus and safety to address difficult issues.

MEMBERSHIP IN THE GLOBAL COMMUNITY

The new curriculum design responds to a new sense of membership in the global economy and to the European vision of citizenship. As far as history teaching is concerned, it might appear to be a backward step, removing the hard-won common history curriculum instituted in 1990. At the same time, it tries to be realistic about the difficulties encountered with the themes of EMU and Cultural Heritage and to address the ways those themes failed to gain traction in schools.

At the end of the day, citizenship, like EMU and Cultural Heritage, and like the most forward-looking approaches to teaching history, depends for its effectiveness on the way the teachers deliver it. The experience with EMU has shown how easily teachers take the line of least resistance in delivering pioneering programs. If citizenship education is to succeed, it will need considerable support and monitoring from DENI and CCEA.

Part Five

Neopluralist Prescriptions

Chapter Twelve

Parity of Esteem

In the last four chapters we have studied several different strands of the cosmopolitan vision for a multiethnic society as expressed in history education. These approaches differ in emphasis, but they share common underlying assumptions: that group designations are not permanent categories; that identity is malleable and many-layered; that the way to handle difference is to make sure that processes are instituted that give maximum voice to all in decision making; that all individuals have the right to be treated equally by virtue of being human; and that ethnic group loyalties, to the degree that they persist, are matters for the private sphere.

If there is a problem with this vision of the world, it is that it tends to have a deficit of emotional content. Societies founded on such universals need empathetic frames of reference for cohesion and bonding. Even civic nationalisms require a culturally defined national mind-set. They try to achieve this by assimilation, presuming minority groups will adopt the dominant culture. In a contested society, assimilation is, by definition, not acceptable: the conflict represents a rejection of assimilation.

The common history curriculum in Northern Ireland, described in Chapter Nine, was greeted without demurral in Northern Ireland because, based as it was on an enquiry approach to history teaching, each community saw it as a way to ensure that the other group would not co-opt the societal mind-set. It was an effort to give reassurance to both communities that neither was trying to assimilate or subvert the other and to begin to develop some common ground. But the goal to ensure a common history curriculum was pursued at a certain cost. Teachers felt their professionalism was not honored when they were given minute instructions about what to teach, and their creative energy dwindled. In the end, teaching a common curriculum has come to seem so artificial that Northern Ireland is modifying this policy.

Now educators in Northern Ireland are focusing on teaching about citizenship as a way to overcome differences. In the past, citizenship denoted a complex interrelationship between the "nation"—both in the functional sense of the people participating in democratic institutions, and in the emotional sense of awareness of being a common group—and the state. But in our twenty-first-century, pluralistic world, people are raising questions about whether citizenship must be linked with a particular country or state. The emergence of European citizenship suggests that it need not. Likewise, the language of human rights provides us a means to think about citizenship as a matter of rights and responsibilities rather than national allegiance.

And yet, in spite of current European interest in the unifying capacities of citizenship, we live in a world where local, ethnic affiliations are not only not diminishing, they are increasing. This tendency to define oneself on the basis of group identity has grown at the same time that support for cosmopolitanism has grown. This is a curious fact. One reason for it is that changes begun by the Enlightenment have removed long-standing social hierarchies; and whereas, several centuries ago, people would have defined themselves according to their position on the social ladder, the world of greater nominal equality requires that people find new ways to identify themselves. They naturally turn to ethnicity.

As people define themselves increasingly according to their ethnic affiliations, the universalist call to respect equal human dignity leads us to give more recognition to cultural groups. The paradox, or irony, of this is that cosmopolitanism has within it a dynamic that leads it to support that which it originally denied, namely the validity or salience of cultural difference in public life. Human rights have helped this process along by asserting rights based on group affiliation, along with other rights. Cosmopolitanism leads to neopluralism. Rather than understanding these two visions as alternatives, we see that they have a connection.

A situation like that of Northern Ireland underlines this. Because the two groups have such enormous reluctance to give up their attachment to their own identifications, those trying to resolve the conflict recognize that they cannot simply ignore ethnic affiliation: they must seek processes of mutual acknowledgment. In so doing, they implicitly question a key assumption of cosmopolitanism. And yet, this approach seems the only sensible way to defuse the conflict, since both groups are so determined to gain recognition. As Roe and Cairns succinctly put it, "Peacemaking processes which acknowledge, even value, [such] distinctives, rather than mask or attempt to eliminate them, ultimately may be more effective, since groups in conflict rarely desire to deny their group allegiance."[1]

This chapter explores possible historical discourses that push people of the two communities toward greater mutual acknowledgment. Both groups start from an assumption that the two parties in the conflict are not comparable actors. Each party sees its own sense of identity as the legitimate identity and the other group's sense of identity as instrumental or bogus.

Understanding history in terms of *multiple interpretations* is one way to inch the two communities toward greater acknowledgment of the other without feeling undercut. This is now accepted practice in the history classroom in Northern Ireland. A second approach, demonstrating *parallel cultural patterns*, highlights the similar types of symbols used in the two groups' narratives. A third, *complementarity*, demonstrates instances where the experiences, narratives, or folk histories of both communities, when juxtaposed, deliver a rounded account of past events. A fourth, recognizing the *multiperspectival* nature of history, involves the realization that different groups actually experience the same event differently.

All of these approaches assist understanding of the other community, but only up to a point. This chapter considers the limitations of these four approaches and goes on to demonstrate how neopluralism, or parity of esteem, which is the common phrase for neopluralism in Northern Ireland these days, can simply increase the sense of entitlement of the two groups, without requiring them to acquire new learning about the other group. At worst, parity of esteem reifies difference and leads back to a partisan mindset.

Another drawback to the notion of parity of esteem is that in accepting different realities, it can promote a relativistic understanding of history, where moral accountability is finessed because each group is allowed to cast its narrative in ways that serve its interests. Parity of esteem, even in its best sense, thus turns us back to search for overarching standards by which to hold groups accountable as they tell their story. Human rights norms, legal mechanisms, and democratic institutions are the cosmopolitan's response to this need. But the neopluralist looks for benchmarks that connect more effectively to people's emotional life.

DIVERGENT INTERPRETATIONS

Our starting point for this research was the zero-sum mind-set that plagues the discourse of both groups in the conflict. Each community considers the other to be an illegitimate actor in the story. Hence, people are quickly dismissive of the other's articulation of the past.

The assumption that the same set of facts forms the core of the two groups' histories, but that each group has a different *interpretation* of the events, provides a means of sidestepping the "not comparable actor" thesis. This is now the standard way of teaching history in Northern Ireland. Teachers interviewed tended to assume that they should demonstrate different interpretations of history. When asked what subject matter they use to do this, three-quarters of those asked cited the Home Rule debate of the 1880s. Five, all Protestant, cited partition. One cited history of sports.

The divergent interpretations approach is the most politically cautious way to approach mutual legitimation because it is based on sound principles of critical argument and, as such, seems apolitical. One reason it feels non-threatening in schools is that for most pupils in Northern Ireland, divergent interpretations of history are discussed in a homogeneous setting. It is rare that school history classes have students from both communities present. Even when they do, as in integrated schools, teachers refrain from making a personal connection between members of a class and the subject matter being discussed; they also avoid lingering over matters that seem awkward. A teacher in a Protestant grammar school with a high Catholic enrollment described a moment during a class on the English Civil War when the word "Papist" had arisen in the text they were reading. (This word is a contemporary pejorative used by Protestants to describe Catholics.) There was an undercurrent of giggling. The teacher asked the students to suggest pejoratives for Protestants, which they did. But even though he had created some reciprocity in the situation, the teacher said, "I pass over something like that pretty quickly."

Exposing students to a discussion between people from the two communities who perceive a historical event differently is relatively unexplored terrain. The Schools Cultural Studies Project started down this path by offering teachers of both communities the chance to talk with each other on a regular basis in preparation for their social studies classes and by organizing joint work between postprimary schools. The *Speak Your Piece* program, which used video debates between students holding different points of view to provoke classroom discussion of controversial issues, emulated this approach. By using a video, the discussion could be held at a "safe" distance, and individual teachers could develop the discussion in their own classes at whatever level they chose.[2]

Discussing multiple interpretations of history helps pupils articulate, albeit indirectly, the mind-set of the other community. But within this characterization of reality, it is perfectly possible for a pupil still to think her or his own group is right: "my interpretation" and "their interpretation" are simply substituted as terms for "right" and "wrong."

PARALLEL CULTURAL PATTERNS

Museum displays in Northern Ireland have shown considerable creativity in presenting material that can draw the two communities together. A factor that has energized this process is the money that has been available for joint school expeditions through the cross-community contact scheme. Many of these outings are museum trips. Today, a substantial part of Northern Ireland's museum revenue comes from schools, and in some cases school children visit museums for a residential experience of several days.

Education officers in museums have tended to avoid discussing controversial material with joint school groups. Usually they understand the purpose of the visit as commingling in a nonthreatening atmosphere and showing what people from both communities share in terms of heritage. They have a cosmopolitan view of the exercise, based on the contact hypothesis.

But several recent displays have found new ways to depict the intertwined story of the two communities. One is to explore cultural elements that the groups have in common. A case in point was an exhibition at the Ulster Folk and Transport Museum on "Brotherhoods" focusing on Orangemen,[3] the IRA, trade unions, and freemasons, which showed how the ritual actions, regalia, lists, charts, and so on of these different brotherhoods demonstrate that the two communities, as well as other groupings in Northern Ireland society, make use of similar cultural categories.

Likewise, an exhibition on wall murals[4] followed how this medium has been developed by both communities to support their political position. In 1994, the Cultural Traditions Group sponsored an exhibition on symbols. Here, the point was made in a number of ways that even if certain symbols have been appropriated by political groups, the patterns governing the kinds of symbols that are adopted indicate a larger culture that all groups share. Hats, banners, wall murals, flags, and personalities are common categories of symbols for all groups. The exhibition was therefore operating on two levels: at one level it was demonstrating a common culture; at another level, it was giving recognition to cultural elements that have been appropriated by various groups.[5] Such displays help people to develop cognitive categories in which both communities have an equally valid place.

COMPLEMENTARITY

Traditionally, cosmopolitan efforts to recast history have disparaged popular narratives, suggesting that they are not based on fact and are used to exaggerate and exacerbate divisions. But another approach is to respect and make use of these histories by presenting the two folk narratives of both communities side by side. A comparison between the commemorations of the three hundredth anniversary of the Battle of the Boyne at the Ulster Museum in Belfast and at the Ulster Folk and Transport Museum in Cultra highlights the possibilities of this approach.

The Battle of the Boyne of 1690 is central to the Protestant narrative. It is remembered as a victory of Protestants over Catholics, and it is personalized as a victory of King William over King James. The "Kings in Conflict" exhibition at the Ulster Museum in Belfast tried to make the story more complex by placing the event in the context of the wars of the European mainland, where the Boyne was a brief sideshow in a contest over Louis XIV's supremacy in Europe. As has been mentioned in an earlier chapter, the Pope in fact sided with the Protestant King William, because the Pope was more interested in reining in Louis XIV, who was supporting King James, than in re-Catholicizing England. The exhibition included King Louis XIV along with King James II and King William III, so that the Battle of the Boyne no longer was presented as a neat contest between Catholic and Protestant contenders for the English throne and instead became part of the "War of the Three Kings." Traditional Protestant accounts of the Boyne were shifted in another sense by giving considerable attention to the Treaty of Limerick, which marked the end of this war. The treaty guaranteed various rights to Catholics but was soon after betrayed by the Protestant elite who, through the Penal Laws, imposed severe restrictions on the lives of Catholics. The implied message of the exhibition was that popular histories have failed to capture for us what actually happened during this important time, and the real events are quite different from those appropriated in the present to support identities.

The Ulster Folk and Transport Museum's exhibition to commemorate the Boyne was based, by contrast, on popular histories of the period. It focused on banners, bonfires, narratives, and songs. It showed how organizations had appropriated particular events of the war. The purpose of this exhibition was to say that folk histories are incomplete, not incorrect. Their incompleteness can be remedied by placing the unionist and nationalist folk traditions side by side. In this case, the museum was not saying "the professionals know best" or "ethnic histories are wrong." Instead, it confirmed each group's experience by demonstrating how it contributes to a complete picture.[6]

Another example of complementarity is Derry's Tower Museum. Opened in 1994 in a tower that forms part of the city walls, it is the only museum in Northern Ireland that tracks the whole story of the conflict. The permanent exhibition, which has been assisted by a generous benefactor and the most up-to-date display techniques, focuses on the history of Londonderry and follows the separate stories of the two communities from preplantation times to the present. At one point, the viewer walks down a narrow corridor where memorabilia from the nationalist side of the Troubles are displayed on one side and those from the unionist side are displayed on the other. Near the end, a ten-minute video draws the two stories together, focusing on the struggle to bring peace.

MULTIPLE PERSPECTIVES

A further form of historical discourse with a neopluralist goal is to say that participants in a historical event actually experienced that event differently. The idea is controversial because it suggests more than one reality and seems to promote relativist, postmodern history. But the key to this discourse is to accept that historical events can be seen from many perspectives and none of these is mutually exclusive. Each perspective must pass tests with regard to accuracy of observation. Objectivity need not be jettisoned. One strength of multiple perspectives over divergent interpretations is that students are called upon to have more empathy for how others experienced history. While divergent interpretations can be mutually exclusive, multiple perspectives are not.[7]

The Georg Eckert Institute for International Textbook Research has developed this view of history instruction in recent years. In the 1950s, 1960s, and 1970s, Eckert's textbook revision was based on a harmonization principle, the belief in the possibility of a common history being reached in textbooks by smoothing over or eliminating different viewpoints. When disagreements arose between textbook writers from two different countries, these matters were often left out altogether. In the early days, those working on Eckert projects had no intention of presenting different angles or interpretations.[8] But in the 1970s, the Eckert Institute broke away from the harmonization principle.

The new approach, according to Falk Pingel,[9] arose in the context of the German debate over its national-socialist past. Citing as an example *Kristallnacht*, the night of November 9, 1938, when the Jewish synagogues were destroyed, Pingel argues that focusing on the experience of the victims is "not enough to explain or make comprehensible why [the Nazis had] so many active supporters." Two different experiences of the event need to be accounted for: "The history teacher's task can no longer be just to present history 'the way it was.' His task is to incorporate the motivation and real-life experience of historical subjects and use the contradictions for discussion purposes. Controversy becomes the object of the lesson."[10]

Historical experiences of the same historical event are different, says Pingel. This proposition goes beyond the idea that there can be multiple interpretations of an event. "Different interpretations" suggests that it is the historians, writing about past events, who perceive them differently. "Different historical experiences" suggests that the people living through a particular time in history experienced that time differently. Pingel cites the work of South Africans to develop a new history and new textbooks as an example. In South Africa, old history books propounding Afrikaner nationalism are being thrown out and new textbooks written where neither side is portrayed as heroic. "It's not about goodies and baddies. It's about understanding people's motives for what they did."[11] Pingel comments on this attempt at understanding:

> We cannot offer such an experience of unity or such certainty for the future in history lessons. It would otherwise only serve to legitimate present interests and possibly future hopes. International textbook research is not the art of finding answers acceptable to everyone; this is sometimes only possible by leaving out aspects of central importance. It aims more than anything at activating a process of communication which will lead to an agreement over contents which offer conflicting points of perception.[12]

Does the "two historical consciousnesses" approach lead back to historical partisanship? Pingel believes this need not be so: "A process of communication concerning history can be undertaken where it is clear from the outset that each side has the right to his own history and none can claim that his history alone holds the key to the future," he says.[13] But he goes on to describe a drawback in the conception. In the South Africa of the future, says Pingel, whites will on the whole turn away from a history that legitimizes their superiority but will not find it easy or attractive to adopt a history that gives more legitimation to blacks or pushes whites to the margins. Whites will prefer history lessons focused on global matters and oriented toward the future. It is black South Africans who have expectations for real change in history lessons, because they will interpret that change as a sign of their enhanced power.

If the multiperspectival approach allows groups to pass over those areas of the past that reflect badly on the group, then it is, surely, a reversion to partisanship. One key test of a legitimate multiperspectival approach, therefore, is whether the separate accounts of the two communities include the other group's perspective on the story.

PARITY OF ESTEEM

In Northern Ireland, the phrase *parity of esteem*, first articulated by the Opsahl Commission of 1992-1993[14] and subsequently encouraged by the British and Irish governments, is a key theme of the Belfast Agreement. By establishing this principle, the Agreement recognizes that mutual acknowledgment is necessary in order to create a greater sense of security on all sides. The Agreement sets up a consociational political structure that recognizes and relies upon group affiliation. Voting in the Assembly cannot pass without at least 40 percent of support from members of each community.[15]

Parity of esteem requires a mental juggling act, because we generally assume that a political entity represents a single consciousness or mind-set among the citizenry. In a neopluralist world, we accept the postmodern notion that more than one consciousness can coexist within a polity. The literature of multiculturalism encourages us to accept the validity of this. Canadian philosopher Charles Taylor argues that multiculturalism derives from principles of universal equality and equal human dignity. These are cosmopolitan values. But in a world where identity has replaced other hierarchical social categories, recognizing different group identities is part of the conferring of dignity. This quickly ushers in a politics that presumes the equal value of different cultures.[16]

According equal value to both cultures in Northern Ireland is an attractive vision. It is understood as a path toward increased individual self-esteem. The presumption is that people's sense of personal identity is fragile because their group identity is contested. This causes people to react defensively against anything that questions the validity of their group. Neopluralists argue that if people are permitted measures that support group difference, this will give them needed psychological space, free from a sense of threat, where they can develop individual self-confidence.

This view, sometimes less explicitly articulated, is prevalent in many areas of Northern Ireland society today. It has been taken up by those in community relations work, who are now devoting considerable energy to "single identity" projects. This view can also be seen in burgeoning cultural programs, such as those of the Ulster Scots.

The literature of intercultural communication elucidates what actually goes on here. One way of understanding the partisan mind-set is to say that it lacks mental categories in which the "other" can be given some legitimacy. This state of "denial" would be described as the least advanced stage of intercultural competency.[17] The first key to unlocking the tight gates of the partisan mind-set and making possible a cognitive venture down the path of intercultural competency, is one that moves a person out of habits of denial.

Once a person has taken that initial step, he will try to find the least cognitively challenging ways to handle the new information. He will set up mental defense mechanisms or else seek ways to minimize difference by appealing to areas of common ground or overarching visions. He is then called upon to make a further transition—this time to recognize the existence of more than one cultural frame of reference. This is the transition into cultural relativism.

According to Milton Bennett, as a person becomes comfortable with this cognitive state, he accepts that cultural difference is a necessary, possibly even preferable human condition. Acceptance of cultural relativism, argues Bennett, drives people to behavioral changes because of their increased recognition of the importance of intercultural communication skills. Bennett sees the first stage in the acceptance of cultural relativism as respect for behavioral difference, including respect for a different language, communication style, and nonverbal behavior. But more crucial for accepting cultural relativism, he says, is the stage that follows, when one begins to develop a respect for value differences.[18]

For Bennett, "values" are the worth attached to various phenomena that exist in reality. He underlines that values are not something we *have* but rather something we choose to espouse. Assigning value is a result of the way we mentally organize the world. But, in addition, our choice of values helps to perpetuate the pattern by which we organize the world. Thus there is some circularity to this process. Giving merit to something arises from our patterns of thinking but also solidifies them. The intercultural breakthrough, Bennett argues, comes when we can enter the mind of the other sufficiently enough to recognize and accept *her* values and assumptions and temporarily sideline our own.

Both Taylor and Bennett envisage a multiculturalism where the mere acceptance of two realities will, of itself, cause people to offer more respect toward the other. But in the Northern Ireland situation, the conferring of respect has so far proven to be a rare outcome of the strategy. More often, neopluralist approaches seem to be reinforcing each group's sense of entitlement. The reason for this is that the leap toward respecting the "values" of the other is stymied because of the zero-sum nature of the value system in Northern Ireland. Anything esteemed by one group is intrinsically unacceptable to the other group.

While parity of esteem's capacity to help people broaden their mental categories suggests it has validity as an approach, it also has deficiencies:

> [Parity of esteem may] make (some) people in those areas feel better about themselves, but it does not necessarily make them feel better about each other. Or, more to the point, the better republicans feel about themselves, the worse they are regarded by unionists/loyalists, who are decidedly unnerved by shows of republican self-confidence, and (perhaps vice versa). At any rate, not too many Protestants/unionists are keen to participate in the West Belfast festival, even when invited. And republicans need not even expect to be invited to comparable events in East Belfast.[19]

Prioritization of difference is looking increasingly like reification of difference. In the post-1998 Assembly, consociationalism has fed oppositional politics and done little to support cooperation. Political disengagement in Northern Ireland is getting worse and sectarianism is becoming more entrenched than ever. Neopluralism is reverting to partisanship.

INTERACTIVE PLURALISM

This brings us to a paradox at the heart of peacemaking in a contested society that has interesting implications both for long-term societal goals and for uses of history and memory. Cosmopolitans' quest to reach a shared identity, by means of a common history and reliance on democratic social institutions, asks too much of those in Northern Ireland who feel threatened by the thought of releasing their communitarian attachments without endeavors being introduced to respect difference. However, we find that *respect* for difference soon becomes *reification* of difference. This hardening of diverse mind-sets seems to undercut the gains achieved by the establishment of a common public space.

How can neopluralism lead to a form of mutual acknowledgment that truly accepts difference? The missing element seems to be a discourse that appreciates the other or values difference for its own sake. This discourse, what I call "interactive pluralism," has been difficult to achieve in a number of areas.

Among professional historians, where one might look first, the revisionist controversy demonstrates how easily historical debate can be politicized and become the victim of profound acrimony. Integrated schools have been greeted with considerable skepticism by both communities. Teachers shy away from discussion of controversial issues in classrooms and fear allowing a critical debate of a historical topic to go to the point where it could support an existing politicized narrative. And at the end of the day, studying the complete history of this contested statelet, founded in 1920 as a compromise that ran against the wishes of all concerned, is not a required element at any point in the curriculum.

The culture of reticence that pervades a deeply divided society is antithetical to discussion of contentious issues. But changing the culture of reticence is hardly likely to occur if schools offer no opportunities for the young people of one community to meet those of the other community or to interact with them on normal terms, let alone discuss areas of difference. School integration does not in itself guarantee that interactive pluralism will be modeled: interactive pluralism requires an act of courage and confrontation to change forms of silent avoidance. Nonetheless, it is hard to avoid concluding that integrated schools are the only hope for overcoming the profound social and cognitive divisions.

Yet, while the number of integrated schools continues to grow, and the movement acquired new energy when the ERO of 1990 increased government commitment to full funding, the rate of increase of integrated schools is likely to slow in coming years. The reason for this is that the number of children entering schools in Northern Ireland is falling, so there is not an overall need to create new schools. DENI is therefore unwilling to put money into creating this particular kind of school, just as it is unwilling to create any other kind of new school. DENI is now exploring ways to create official links between existing schools as an alternative to integrated schools. Such measures could be more realistic on a number of counts, given the enormous conceptual and social hurdle integrated schools have presented. And these measures may be assisted by the fact that the eleven plus exam is to be abolished in 2008, instigating a rethinking of many considerations in the relationships among schools. But modeling interactive pluralism through these school linkages has not yet been specifically planned.

Interactive pluralism in the history classroom is still a matter of experiment and exploration. The proposal that teachers engage students in discussions of current uses of memory and connect them with study of written history is an important signal of a willingness to explore this. On the unionist side, this process could be a means to helping young people understand processes of domination that their community created and legitimized based on its own sense of victimhood. On the republican side, the process could be a means of understanding that violence reinforced unionist ideas of victimhood and thus entrenched unionists in their positions. But linking past and present will be particularly hard when it is adopted as a means of challenging students' own group narratives, and so far the research tells us little about how well this works.

ONE STEP ON THE ROAD

Parity of esteem, not as an end in itself but as a way station on the path to a cosmopolitan society, is a compelling strategy, and indeed this is the vision of those in community relations who support neopluralism. But this raises a question. What additional ingredient is needed in the neopluralist approach to overcome its centrifugal tendencies? And what kind of society will be the outcome?

In a setting where societal memory[20] has supreme power over peoples' mind-sets,[21] all members of the society must be participants in an interactive process to acknowledge the group memory of the other. This interactive pluralism is hard work, and most people resist the idea that "normal" life should require such self-conscious effort. Crucial to understanding what is required is the realization that interpersonal interaction has a different dynamic from intergroup interaction. On a personal level, people can usually find ways to cooperate with reasonable civility. When they are forced to see each other in the context of their group loyalties, they behave differently. Interactive pluralism requires an awareness of how the particular groups interact in order to counter that dynamic and truly make a difference.

Afterword

Frontier of Discovery

Societal memory has been one locus of the conflict in Northern Ireland. Historical narratives have become part of the group identity of the two communities involved. Contested histories continue to be articulated on the streets in wall murals and other graffiti, in partisan newspapers, in theatre and other art forms, and in popular historical accounts. They undergird the mind-set of paramilitary groups. They support the mental constructs of politicians in their view of themselves, their group, and the other group. They provide discourses that are used by all members of the population as they try to make sense of their situation.

Efforts to break out of the clutches of overdetermined societal memory, and to examine historical legacies in less partisan ways, are by no means absent. Sadly, they are sometimes accused of political motivation by those who see their own partisan viewpoint threatened by such endeavors.

During the nineteenth century, the British government aimed to use the national education system to instill loyalty to Britain in the population. As far as their way of teaching history was concerned, this policy was executed by minimizing the teaching of any history in schools. Some Catholics complained about the lack of Irish history instruction. But the Catholic Church was mainly preoccupied with retaining as much independence as possible from the state authorities while retaining maximum legitimacy and funding assistance. To the degree that the Catholic Church authorities were interested in matters of curriculum, their main concern was to retain control over religious instruction in Catholic schools. In the late nineteenth century, Catholics who saw education as a place to further their nationalist vision made use of Gaelic language classes more than history classes.

Under the Stormont unionists, history teaching was regarded as important in enforcing a unionist mind-set. State schools emphasized British history, and Irish history was an optional subject in schools right up to 1990. A number of Catholic schools nonetheless used history lessons to impart an Irish nationalist history. At the same time, Catholics, as the lower power group, found political leverage in the cause of promoting more Irish history in schools. It is therefore fair to say that in the late 1960s, at the time of the outbreak of the Troubles, two histories were acrimoniously cohabiting in the province of Northern Ireland in public life, in the minds of the general population, and in schools.

Northern Ireland has been fortunate to have an academic history profession committed to genuine research and criticism who, to a considerable degree, have refused to be drawn into a politicized battle over histories. Since the 1930s, academics have been dedicated to rigorous standards of modern scholarship and debate. A number of history teachers trained by these academics in the 1960s and 1970s became committed to a new kind of teaching that would help undermine partisan narratives. These teachers also had available to them the most forward-looking teaching practices of the time. Revision of textbooks was underway before the Troubles broke out in 1969. If we want to test the hypothesis that history teaching is an indicator of political and social realities, the very fact that efforts were being made *during* the Northern Ireland conflict to revise the teaching of history correlates with the fact that in spite of the seriousness of the conflict, Northern Ireland did not experience total societal breakdown.

Reformers who tried to bring change were, nonetheless, hemmed in by a conservative outlook that slowed the process. School authorities initially resisted any initiatives responding to the conflict: they wanted schools to provide a womb of normality in the midst of the mayhem. It was after the talks of the 1970s had broken down, and the deaths in 1981 due to the hunger strikes cast a pall over the society, that the Department of Education in 1982 instructed teachers that their work needed to have an impact on community relations. By that time, twenty-five hundred people had been killed and thirteen years of violence endured.

The next five years were spent in developing a curriculum in Education for Mutual Understanding that teachers could use voluntarily and in introducing enquiry-oriented history teaching. The 1989 decision to create a common, statutory curriculum, which had never before existed, came in the context of a much larger policy change, originating with the Thatcher government, that was in no way trying to respond to Northern Ireland's needs. Thus the opportunity to create a required history curriculum arose by coincidence. A decade after introducing the common curriculum, education advisers are now recommending requirements that give teachers more room for initiative in responding to the needs of their students. If teachers take the line of least resistance in following the new directives, falling back on what they know best or feel most comfortable with, then this new policy risks a reversion to teaching partisan narratives. It will require considerable monitoring and in-service training to ensure otherwise.

Despite the enormous energy, not to mention money, that has been expended in educational reforms, very few young people in postprimary school in Northern Ireland can expect to have a discussion with their peers of the other community about their differences in background and political outlook. Moreover, at no point in their school career are young people required to learn the history of the Northern Ireland province from its inception to the present. Although for some time history teachers have used a process-based approach to history teaching and emphasized multiple interpretations, only now are teachers beginning to experiment with teaching approaches that link the study of history with an open discussion of politicized uses of history.

Policy makers are now introducing a mandatory citizenship education that teaches about human rights, democratic values, and tolerance. Citizenship education will have a slot in the timetable, making this type of training much harder to sidestep than it has been in the past.

LESSONS FOR OTHER CONFLICT REGIONS

Textbooks, curriculum, and teacher training are at the heart of the project to reform the teaching of history in any situation. All depend on the prior existence of an academic history profession that will model a critical approach to the historical endeavor and will also ensure that texts and curriculum cover a broad enough range of topics and opinions.

As far as textbook writing is concerned, teams representing the contending communities must work together to ensure balance and accuracy. This must also be the case in creating new curriculum. But in addition, getting teachers' commitment to a new curriculum is a matter of central concern. An ongoing process of interaction between education authorities and teachers is critical.

Crucial to reforming education of any sort is teacher training. History classes can raise students' level of awareness about the uses of history in society and about the point of view of the other group, *if* teachers are trained how to do this. In order to do it well, teachers must be willing to frontally discuss current uses of history or ways the past informs the present. But teachers can have an impact on their students in ways that go beyond the substantive material taught in class, and the extent of their own experience in interacting with the "other" will give them the grounding to help the next

generation to have fewer inhibitions in this regard. This relates to all teachers, not just history teachers. Indeed, given that historical discourses suffuse
so many aspects of popular culture in a divided society, it is arguable that all
teacher trainees should have some minimum opportunity to think about, or
talk about, uses of history in the society.

Introducing a specific citizenship curriculum opens up an opportunity to
give training to teachers on how to teach about diversity issues. Teachers, and
indeed all people working on community relations, need to understand
and impart the concept that diversity recognition is a matter of gaining understanding about the other more than it is a matter of asserting entitlement.
This is a difficult notion to get across in the midst of the normal myopia of
conflict. In the language of human rights, it means underlining the responsibilities that go along with rights.

While few societies are free of minority-majority issues, and some like the
United States carry the additional baggage of excruciating exploitation of one
group by another, the contested society is one with very few common assumptions. Distrust is so deep that any proposal for change is assumed to be designed
to advance the position of the other group or at least to be available for co-
optation by the other group. Proposals for change usually attract an automatic
negative response; alternatively, the culture of reticence takes over and people
recoil from suggestions that call upon them to break habits of a lifetime.

In this context, it is curious why "Education for Mutual Understanding,"
the common history curriculum, and citizenship education policies created so
little public controversy in Northern Ireland. This might suggest a general
cynicism about whether any school curriculum can change mind-sets, or it
might hint at a more particular judgment about the unchallenging nature of
these approaches. Perhaps, in recent years, the debate over academic selection through the eleven plus exam has absorbed the quota of passion available
for educational concerns.

INTERACTIVE PLURALISM

History's role in contested societies is a complex one, introducing questions
of anthropology, religion, politics, and group psychology. This book has attempted to isolate a single issue, that of school history teaching, in order to
shed light on a number of related issues and to understand what is involved
in carrying out reform. It assumes that, in spite of our recognition that all history is in some sense invented and has the potential to be distorted and used,
history classes in schools are an accepted and important part of education and
will, at some level, remain so.

Studying history teaching reform leads inevitably to a discussion about visions of the future and, in particular, the place that particular group identifications will be given in that future. Traditionally, the Enlightenment vision was one of a universal culture based on rationality and procedural concerns that would respect diversity by allowing people to worship and observe their own cultural practices in private. The increasing importance of human rights in the past sixty years has added a further set of universal values and contributed to a growing vision of "citizenship" separated from national allegiance.

At the same time our rising awareness of diversity, the growing salience of ethnic identity as an ingredient of personal status, and the growing observance of group rights create an imperative to place considerable emphasis on difference. Cosmopolitanism has within it a dynamic that leads to its antithesis. Because it is premised on equality and human dignity, it leads to greater group recognition. But, as we find in Northern Ireland, greater group recognition does not necessarily usher in greater intergroup understanding or sensitivity. The acceptance, and indeed honoring, of pluralism does not automatically lead to an interactive form of pluralism. The decision to study history teaching in Northern Ireland leads to a discussion about what we mean by a plural society.

Clearly a plural society asks us to define common ground and social cohesion differently than we have in the past. Instead of searching for some workable form of homogeneity, the society is called back to ideals of the common good and to processes of cooperation.

Some in Northern Ireland are calling for "intercultural" approaches to engaging with difference. They make the point that "multiculturalism," at least in the way it is understood in the United States, suggests that groups see themselves as autonomous and separate from the wider dominant culture. But in Northern Ireland, where the Troubles have themselves created social apartheid, multiculturalism doesn't introduce sufficient change of view. "Interculturalism" underlines the interactive aspects of culture and presents identity as fluid.[1] Others speak of the "multicontextual" approach to engaging difference.[2] Here we imagine people learning to move from one context to another, being comfortable wherever they are.

Interactive pluralism, by whatever name we choose to call it, is the frontier of discovery in places of diversity right now. We are only at the very beginning of the road in exploring it. Those designing history curricula can take their part in this exploration, or they can choose not to do so. What is certain is that the exploration is imperative and that history teaching supplies a potential forum in which to conduct it.

Northern Ireland shows us through the segregated school system, the culture of reticence, and the pluralism of entitlement that the sticking point in education, and in postconflict rebuilding more generally, is in the matter of interaction of those of the two communities. The society has in the past handled interaction by a canny refraining from dialogue over the things that matter most.

Some signs of interactive pluralism are beginning to be seen in Northern Ireland. Cognitive interaction is just beginning to be seen in schools. First steps taken to create discussion about contentious issues occurred in the brief life of the Schools Cultural Studies Project and the *Speak Your Piece* program, as described in Chapter Seven; teaching history in terms of multiple interpretations and ventures into connecting the present with the past were described in Chapters Eight and Nine; and other creative approaches to cognitive interaction, through museum displays and multiperspectival history, were described in Chapter Twelve.

Functional interaction can be seen in the work of some of the Peace and Reconciliation Partnership Boards, created in the mid-1990s as cross-community entities in each of the twenty-six local government districts in Northern Ireland, in order to make decisions how to divvy up a large "peace grant" from the EU.

Interaction must also happen at the emotional level. Education reformers are keen to introduce a greater emphasis on emotion into teaching for reasons that go far beyond the exigencies of the conflict. But engaging in a discussion of the conflict on an emotional level with someone of the other group is the most psychologically challenging experience many can imagine.

GRAPPLING WITH THE PLIGHT OF THE VICTIMS

If any model of emotional interaction exists it is probably best seen in some of the victims groups in Northern Ireland. Most victims groups are ostensibly, or unostensibly, partisan. But a few have succeeded in creating a safe place where victims from all sides of the conflict have been able to come.

The situation of the victims in Northern Ireland is a complex one and has been deliberately separated from the subject matter of this book. All recognize that one key aspect to dealing with the past, and drawing a line under the past, is to acknowledge the victims in the conflict. But even defining who the victims are becomes a contentious matter. So far, acknowledging victims has been addressed only in a limited way,[3] and no reparations have been given.

At the end of the day, the matter of victimhood is central to the ongoing question of how history is understood and treated and how the two communities can see a linkage in their respective pasts. Addressing victimhood is the bridge between intellectualism, functionalism, and reticence on the one hand and a genuine emotional encounter on the other.

The sense of victimhood that is felt by both communities sets up the possibility for ongoing cycles of revenge and counter-revenge that at worst can perpetuate the conflict endlessly. Even if this victimhood is corralled in a ceasefire so that it no longer instigates violence, it holds the society in a stalemate of noninteraction that blunts creative possibilities. It leaves people with the idea that separation or noninteraction are the best to be hoped for, and interactions, to the degree they occur, happen under the shadow of unhealed hurts and mutual distrust.

Legal mechanisms offer a possible way out of the perpetual trap of an ongoing sense of victimhood. Legal action sometimes can satisfy the need for revenge, thereby allowing the victim to shed this burden.[4] The most obvious example of the legal approach to overcoming victimhood in Northern Ireland is the Saville Inquiry into Bloody Sunday. Prime Minister Tony Blair's decision to reopen this inquiry has had enormous symbolic importance for the nationalist population. The costs, both in terms of money and time, have been great and, according to some, might have been put to better use in social programs or paying reparations to victims. More recently, the Corry Report has called for four more such inquiries relating to the notorious deaths of four individuals. Whatever their outcome, they will only make the smallest dent in the fact that 1,800 unsolved murders remain on the books in Northern Ireland. Moreover, they may end up being perceived as only a partial reckoning, reinforcing some people's sense of injustice and frustration that their voice is not being heard.

This history of violence and victimhood is the real "common history" in Northern Ireland. Legal procedures will take decades to address it. They may afford some redress to those who were wronged, but they may supply less satisfaction than hoped. They will probably polarize the society more in the meantime.

Many turn to ideas about forgiveness as a way out of the stalemate. But apology and forgiveness in a situation of this kind can seem to be acts of weakness, where the harmful deeds of the other are excused, possibly without repentance, penalty, or reparation. Where apology is concerned, nobody wants to take the first step.

Perhaps a more genuine basis of commonality for the future lies in personal and societal contrition. Notions of parity of esteem and equal recognition of cultures can obfuscate rather than elucidate the matter of fault. Chapter Twelve describes how parity of esteem allows two societal narratives to stand unchallenged, where neither expresses criticism of its own group. This partisanship in pluralist clothing must be overcome, and only a quantum leap into a new reality will make that happen.

The quantum leap goes beyond accountability, although it includes accountability. The accountability it requires is a personal accountability, where individuals search their hearts about the things they did or failed to do that allowed the conflict to proceed as it did. Contrition is not about equal sharing of the blame. It is not legalistic. It operates irrespective of comparison. It recognizes that outside of legal mechanisms of accountability, individuals are in the end accountable to their own hearts and that a new spirit of truth only arises out of this very personal experience of true humility.

Where does this leave history education?

Some argue that the best we can expect from history teaching is a refusal to propagate lies: to expect more is to place a burden on teachers and the education system that is too great to bear. Moreover, a society must absorb its past by other means before that past can be adequately expressed didactically. But none can deny that rigid mind-sets are a part of the ongoing cycle of conflict in Northern Ireland, creating a fertile ground where ideas about good and evil take root. The teaching of history surely has the capacity to disturb them. In Northern Ireland we see that this does not happen by inference alone. Creative and courageous teachers must engage this need frontally.

In the long term, the trend of reducing the amount of history taught in schools in favor of other subjects deemed more important to the contemporary timetable is a matter for concern. The next generation needs a knowledge of historical events and debates in order to respond critically to politicized narratives. History classes can teach how to participate with integrity in a world of heightened possibilities for communication by imparting skills for research and critical thinking. And the best history teachers will lead their students toward an understanding of history that demands the fullest attention and consideration given to the mind-set of the "other." In the end, history's value for students is that it helps them understand the present, and history education will be culpable of failing in its task if it stands back from that assignment.

Notes

PREFACE

1. See Boutros Boutros-Ghali, *An Agenda for Peace: Preventive Diplomacy, Peacemaking and Peace-keeping*, Report of the Secretary General pursuant to the statement adopted by the Summit Meeting of the Security Council on 31 January, 1992 (New York: United Nations, 1992); Stephen John Stedman, "Alchemy for a New World Order: Overselling 'Preventive Diplomacy,'" *Foreign Affairs* (May/June 1995): 14-20; and Michael S. Lund, "Underrating Preventive Diplomacy," *Foreign Affairs* (July/August 1995): 160-63.

2. Boutros Boutros-Ghali, *An Agenda for Peace*.

3. Under Prime Minister Margaret Thatcher, a major overhaul of British education not only reintroduced a market structure but for the first time imposed curriculum standards aimed to assert a more conservative, "nationalist" mentality. Textbooks in the new states of former Yugoslavia have rapidly emerged, reflecting a reformulated understanding of these states' identities and interpreting the history of "enemy" states negatively.

NOTES TO CHAPTER 1

1. Merle Curti, *Peace or War: The American Struggle, 1636-1936* (New York: W. W. Norton, 1936).

2. Paul Kennedy, "The Decline of Nationalistic History in the West," *Journal of Contemporary History* 8 (1973) 1: 92.

3. Carnegie Endowment for International Peace, "History Teaching and School Textbooks in Relation to International Understanding," Reading List No. 29, March 4, 1931: 2.

4. Ibid., 7.

5. Garnet McDiarmid and David Pratt, *Teaching Prejudice: A Content Analysis of Social Studies Textbooks Authorized for Use in Ontario,* Curriculum Series 12, The

Ontario Institute for Studies in Education, 1971. The first chapter of this book contains an exceptionally good synopsis of history textbook revision work worldwide up to 1970.

6. Ibid.

7. UNESCO and the Eckert Institute have developed institutional links, including joint production of a newsletter, "UNESCO International Textbook Research Network Newsletter" published at the Eckert Institute in Braunschweig.

8. See, for example, Wayne Ivor, *Can History Textbooks be Analyzed Systematically? A Methodological Inquiry,* unpublished doctoral thesis, Department of Sociology, American University, Washington, D.C., 1971.

9. Hilary Bourdillon, ed., *History and Social Studies—Methodologies of Textbook Analysis,* Report of the Educational Research Workshop held in Braunschweig (Germany), September 11-14, 1990 (Amsterdam: Swets & Zeitlinger, 1992); Falk Pingel, *UNESCO Guidebook on Textbook Research and Textbook Revision.* Paris: UNESCO, 1999.

10. Stephen Van Evera, "The Cult of the Offensive and the Origins of the First World War," in Steven Miller et al., eds., *Military Strategy and the Origins of the First World War* (Princeton: Princeton University Press, 1991); Jack Snyder, "Nationalism and the Crisis of the Post-Soviet State," in Michael E. Brown, ed., *Ethnic Conflict and International Security* (Princeton: Princeton University Press, 1993).

11. See Paul Kennedy, "The Decline of Nationalistic History in the West," *Journal of Contemporary History* 8 (1973) 1: 92; Boyd Shafer, *Nationalism: Myth and Reality* (New York: Harcourt, Brace, 1955), 183-86; Stephen Van Evera, "Primed for Peace: Europe After the Cold War," *International Security* 15 (Winter 1990/91) 3: 23; Stephen Van Evera, "Hypotheses on Nationalism and War," *International Security* 18 (Spring 1994) 4: 26-33; Charles Kupchan, "Introduction, Nationalism Resurgent," in Charles Kupchan, ed., *Nationalism and Nationalities in the New Europe* (Ithaca: Cornell University Press, 1995), 14.

12. A 1992 conference in Bruges, Belgium, organized by the Council of Europe, provided a forum for teachers from thirty countries to discuss a charter for history teachers that would include not only a listing of essential skills to be taught but possibly a set of criteria for the selection of topics, or even a list of essential content. A symposium in October 1994 in Sofia, Bulgaria, organized by the Council of Europe's Council for Cultural Co-operation (CDCC) was entitled "History, Democratic Values and Tolerance in Europe: the Experience of Countries in Democratic Transition." A May 1995 conference in Prague was funded by USIA. The Slovak Republic has supplied the venue for an ongoing project among Austria, Hungary, the Czech Republic, and Slovakia to develop a reader for teaching history in secondary schools, according to UNESCO International Textbook Research Network Newsletter No. 2. Northern Ireland has hosted several conferences.

13. Luis Maris De Puig, Rapporteur, "History and the Learning of History in Europe: Report of the Committee on Culture Education" (Strasbourg: Council of Europe, 1996).

14. Carmel Gallagher, "History Teaching and the Promotion of Democratic Values and Tolerance: A Handbook for Teachers" (Strasbourg: Council for Cultural Co-operation, Council of Europe, 1996).

15. Falk Pingel, "Plural societies: history teaching and the dilemma of a national curriculum," *Yesterday and Today* 25 (May 1993): 16-21.

16. Ibid.

17. Hanna Schissler, "Perceptions of the Other and the Discovery of the Self," in Volker Berghan and Hanna Schissler, eds., *Perceptions of History: International Textbook Research on Britain, Germany and the United States* (Oxford: Berg Publishers, 1987), 27-28.

18. The Eckert Institute considers its most significant project to have been the process of reaching an agreed history between German and Polish historians. The project was undertaken and completed in the 1970s.

19. The term comes from Kupchan, 6-11.

20. Donald Horowitz, *Ethnic Groups in Conflict* (Berkeley: University of California Press, 1985).

21. Mats Friberg, "The Need for Unofficial Diplomacy in Identity Conflicts," in Tonci Kuzmanic and Arno Truger, eds., *Yugoslavia Wars* (Lubljana, Slovenia: Peace Institute, 1992), 62; quoted in Jean Paul Lederach, *Building Peace: Sustainable Reconciliation in Divided Societies* (Washington, D.C.: United States Institute of Peace, 1997), 8. Jay Rothman, *Resolving Identity Based Conflict in Nations, Organizations and Communities* (San Francisco: Jossey Bass, 1997), 11.

22. Ted Robert Gurr, *Minorities at Risk* (Washington, D.C.: The United States Institute of Peace, 1993), 20.

23. For the use of the term *intractable* to describe these conflicts, see Louis Kriesberg, Terrell A. Northrup, and Stuart J. Thorson, eds., *Intractable Conflicts and Their Transformation* (Syracuse: Syracuse University Press, 1989). Edward E. Azar uses the term *protracted social conflict*. See "The Theory of Protracted Social Conflict and the Challenge of Transforming Conflict Situations," *Monograph Series in World Affairs* 20 (M2 1983): 81-99; "Protracted International Conflicts: Ten Propositions," *International Interactions* 12 (1985) 1: 59-70; *The Management of Protracted Social Conflict* (Hampshire, England: Dartmouth, 1990). John Burton uses the term *deeply-rooted conflict*. See *Resolving Deeply-Rooted Conflict: A Handbook* (Lanham, Md.: University Press of America, 1987); *Conflict: Resolution and Provention* (New York: St. Martin's Press, 1990).

24. See summary of a speech by Professor Wolfgang Höpken, laying down general principles which should underpin history textbooks: "First we must recognize the selective process involved in constructing a textbook and ensure that here multi-perspectivity is central in order that proper critical discussion can proceed in the classroom." *Preliminary Observations and Conclusions,* from a Symposium on History, Democratic Values and Tolerance in Europe: The Experience of Countries in Democratic Transition, Sofia, Bulgaria, October 19-22, 1994, prepared by the General Rapporteur Professor David Harkness, Queen's University of Belfast. See also Sandra Gillespie and Gerry Jones, *Northern Ireland and Its Neighbours Since 1920* (Belfast: Hodder and Stoughton, 1995), a history textbook for fourteen- to sixteen-year-olds which briefly lays out the facts of each event and then follows that with original source material showing a variety of responses and interpretations of the event.

25. An example is Frances Fitzgerald's analysis of U.S. school textbooks in the wake of the Vietnam War in Frances Fitzgerald, *America Revised: History Schoolbooks in the Twentieth Century* (Boston, Little, Brown, 1979).

26. See, for example, Ayesha Jalal's analysis of Pakistan's textbooks to show how the current regime has made the national narrative a Muslim narrative. Ayesha Jalal, "Conjuring Pakistan: History as Official Imagining," *International Journal of Middle East Studies* 27 (1995): 73-89.

27. Here "civil society" is defined, according to Ignatieff's definition, as the institutions that order society according to the rule of law, economic competition, and open debate and discussion, where negative checks and balances prevent the unjust accumulation of influence. In other words it means more than grassroots volunteerism, though it requires engagement of the population in supporting and upholding the institutions. See Michael Ignatieff, "On Civil Society: Why Eastern Europe's Revolutions Could Succeed," *Foreign Affairs* (March/April 1995): 128-136.

28. Ibid.

29. Jonathan Friedman, "The Past in the Future: History and the Politics of Identity," *American Anthropologist* 94 (1992) 4: 855.

NOTES TO CHAPTER 2

1. See Antonio Gramsci, *Collected Works, L'Opere di Antonio Gramsci* (Turin: Einaud, 1947), Vol. III — *Intellettuali e L'organizzazione della cultural*, 1949. Hegemony, for Gramsci, is "an order in which a certain way of life and thought is dominant in which one concept of reality is diffused throughout society in all its institutional and private manifestations, informing with its spirit all taste, morality, customs, religious and political principles, and all social relations, particularly in their intellectual and moral connotations." Gwynn A. Williams, "Gramsci's concept of *Egemonia,*" *Journal of the History of Ideas* XXI (Oct-Dec 1960) 4: 587, quoted in John Cammett, *Antonio Gramsci and the Origins of Italian Communism* (Stanford, Calif.: Stanford University Press, 1967), 204. Cammett elaborates: "Hegemony refers to the 'spontaneous' loyalty that any dominant social group obtains from the masses by virtue of its social and intellectual prestige and its supposedly superior function in the world of production." Cammett, 204.

2. Robert Graves and Raphael Pataki, *Hebrew Myths: The Book of Genesis* (Garden City, N.Y.: Doubleday, 1969), 11.

3. David Carr, *Time, Narrative and History* (Bloomington, Indiana: Indiana University Press, 1986), 149-50.

4. Walter F. Otto, *Die Gestalt und das Sein: Gesammelte Abhandlungen über den Mythos und seine Bedeutung für die Menschheit* [Image and Existence: Collected Essays on Myth and Its Meaning for Mankind] (Dusseldorf-Koln: Eugen Diedrichs Verlag, 1955), 73-78. Quoted and translated by Raphael Patai, *Myth and Modern Man* (Englewood Cliffs, N.J.: Prentice Hall, 1972), 38.

5. Patai, 72.

6. Bronislaw Malinowski, "The Foundations of Faith and Morals," in his book *Sex, Culture, and Myth* (New York: Harcourt, Brace, 1962), 299.

7. Bronislaw Malinowski, "Myth in Primitive Psychology," in his book *Magic, Science and Religion and Other Essays* (Glencoe, Ill.: The Free Press, 1948), 85.

8. Ibid., 79.

9. Ibid., 93. Malinowski elaborates on this idea, particularly in relation to religious dogma, in "The Foundations of Faith and Morals."

10. Bronislaw Malinowski, "Myth in Primitive Psychology," 103.

11. All the states issuing from the former Yugoslavia have engaged in this practice. Quebec separatists, Scottish nationalists, Palestinians, and Greek and Turkish Cypriots would be other examples.

12. See Ayesha Jalal, "Conjuring Pakistan: History as Official Imagining," *International Journal of Middle East Studies* 27 (1995): 73-79; Edward Said, *Cultural Imperialism* (New York: Knopf, 1993).

13. Joyce Appleby, Lynn Hunt, and Margaret Jacob, *Telling the Truth about History* (New York: W. W. Norton, 1994), 233.

14. For a discussion of leadership as storytelling, see Howard Gardner, in collaboration with Emma Laskin, *Leading Minds: An Anatomy of Leadership* (New York: Basic Books, 1995).

15. Henry Tudor, *Political Mythology* (London: Pall Mall Press, 1972), 9-38. See especially p. 16 for a discussion of the nature of political myth and the assertion of *purpose* as a defining feature. Tudor rejects, therefore, any account of the myth apart from the context in which it is used. Tudor, 47. Another useful definitional discussion can be found in Leonard Thompson, *The Political Mythology of Apartheid* (New Haven: Yale University Press, 1985), chapter 1.

16. Tudor, 48.

17. For elaboration of this and subsequent points, see Stephen Van Evera, "Hypotheses on Nationalism and the Causes of War," in Charles Kupchan, ed., *Nationalism and Nationalities in the New Europe* (Ithaca: Cornell University Press), 151-53. Van Evera highlights three types of chauvinist myths: "self-glorifying," "other maligning," and "self-whitewashing."

18. This function is closest to the one described by Malinowski above.

19. See Clifford Geertz, "The Integrative Revolution—Primordial Sentiments and Civil Politics in the New States," in Clifford Geertz, ed., *Old Societies and New States: The Quest for Modernity in Asia and Africa* (New York: The Free Press, 1965), 109. A primordialist view would be the following: "Basic group identity consists of the ready-made set of endowments and identifications that every individual shares with others from the moment of birth by the chance of the family into which he is born at that given time in that given place." Harold Isaacs, *Idols of the Tribe* (Cambridge, Mass.: Harvard University Press, 1975), 38. Primordial elements, for Isaacs, would include physical characteristics shared with family members, birthplace, name, history and origins, religion, and "condition of national, regional, or tribal affiliation." Isaacs, 39. At its most extreme, nowadays, primordialism proposes that ethnicity is an innate aspect of human identity, a given, that requires description, not explanation, and has no purpose beyond the psychological one of supplying a sense of identity. Such a definition suggests that ethnic groups have always been part of the human experience. The essentials of this definition come from Marcus Banks, *Ethnicity: Anthropological Constructions* (London: Routledge, 1996), 39.

20. Situational ethnicity sees context as crucial in the expression of ethnicity. An extreme version of this argument suggests that there is no one single homogeneous expression of an ethnic identity, but rather a number of different identities are manifested depending on the situation. Banks, 27.

21. Frederik Barth, "Introduction," in his book *Ethnic Groups and Boundaries* (Boston: Little, Brown, 1969). Barth was developing arguments of Edmund Leach,

Political Systems of Highland Burma (London: Athlone, 1954), but Barth's articulation of these ideas proved to be so elegant and succinct that his 1969 "Introduction" is the work usually cited in this connection.

22. See, for example, Anthony D. Buckley and Mary Catherine Kenney, *Negotiating Identity: Rhetoric, Metaphor and Social Drama in Northern Ireland* (Washington, D.C.: Smithsonian Institution Press, 1995).

23. Ibid, 92-95.

24. Max Weber, *Economy and Society: An Outline of Interpretive Sociology*, Gunther Roth and Claus Wittich, eds. (Berkeley, Calif: University of California Press, 1978); cited in Walker Connor, "Terminological Chaos," in his book *Ethnonationalism: The Quest for Understanding* (Princeton: Princeton University Press, 1994), 102.

25. Ernest Gellner, *Nations and Nationalism* (Ithaca: Cornell University Press, 1983).

26. Benedict Anderson, *Imagined Communities* (London: Verso, 1983).

27. See Eric Hobsbawn and Thomas Ranger, eds., *The Invention of Tradition* (Cambridge: Cambridge University Press, 1983).

28. Ernest Renan, "Qu'est-ce qu'une nation?" in *Oeuvres Completes* 1, 892. Cited in Anderson, 6. Renan's lecture, delivered in Paris in 1886, is considered the seminal lecture that launched the study of nationalism. See also Friedrich Nietzsche's essay on historical consciousness, where he speaks of "creative forgetfulness" and describes how memory of some part of the past depends on forgetting other aspects; cited in Eric Foner, *Who Owns History? Rethinking the Past in a Changing World* (New York: Hill and Ware, 2002), xiii.

29. Anderson, 205.

30. "As numerous studies have shown, history from inside, including 'emic' ethnohistory . . . is written in the present and expresses present concerns. . . . Thus the work of historians, lay or professional, may ultimately be equaled with informants' statements by this kind of anthropological perspective." Thomas Hylland Eriksen, *Ethnicity and Nationalism: Anthropological Perspectives* (London: Pluto Press, 1993), 92.

31. Buckley and Kenney, chapters 1 and 2. These authors discuss the pervasive presence of particular metaphors in the two communities of Northern Ireland. When metaphors get used as operational frames to guide actions and values, they argue, they tend toward objectivity. But when metaphors are used rhetorically, they are more likely to stray from the truth.

32. Henri Tajfel, *Human Groups and Social Categories.* (Cambridge: Cambridge University Press, 1981); Henri Tajfel, ed., *Social Identity* (Cambridge: Cambridge University Press, 1982).

33. Sites posits eight basic needs: "a need for response, a need for security, a need for recognition, a need for stimulation, a need for distributive justice, a need for meaning, a need to be seen as rational (and for rationality itself), and a need to control." Paul Sites, *Control: The Basis of Social Order* (New York: Dunellen Publishers, 1973), 43. John Burton, who examines the matter from the standpoint of ethnopolitical conflict, posits the needs for identity, security, and recognition. John Burton, *Conflict: Resolution and Provention* (New York: St. Martin's Press, 1990).

34. Stanley Allen Renshon, "The Role of Personality Development in Political Socialization," in David C. Schwartz and Sandra Kenyon Schwartz, eds., *New Directions in Political Socialization* (New York: Free Press, 1975).

35. Burton, 92. Burton argues that the idea of basic needs is a long-standing one. He cites James MacGregor Burns, "Wellsprings of Political Leadership," *The American Political Science Review* LXXI (March 1977). Burns's research led him to assert the "vast pools of human energy known as wants, needs, aspiration and expectation." Barrington Moore, in his search for a definition for the notion of justice said, "It is obvious that human beings have something that can be called innate needs," and cited needs for respect and recognition, for "distinction" (which Burton suggests means the same as identity), for the absence of boredom or for stimulus, and for control (which implies the freedom to take aggressive action against a source of danger). "As a working hypothesis, I propose a conception of innate human nature, innate in the sense of being prior to any social influences but not necessarily immune to them, for which not only physical deprivations are noxious but also psychic ones; specifically, the absence of favorable human responses, boredom, and the inhibition of aggressions. Barrington Moore, *Injustice: The Social Bases of Obedience and Revolt* (New York: Pantheon Books, 1978).

36. William Bloom, *Personal Identity, National Identity and International Relations* (Cambridge: Cambridge University Press, 1990), 50.

37. Ibid.

38. Herbert Kelman, "Negotiating National Identity," *Negotiation Journal* (October 1997): 336.

39. Bloom, 52.

40. Ibid.

41. J. E. Mack, "Cultural Amplifiers," working paper presented to the Committee on International Affairs at the Fall Meeting of the Group for the Advancement of Psychiatry, White Plains, New York, November 10-12, 1984; cited in Vamik Volkan, "Psychoanalytic Aspects of Ethnic Conflicts," in Joseph Montville, ed., *Conflict and Peacemaking in Multiethnic Societies* (New York: Lexington Books, 1991), 84.

42. Volkan, "Psychoanalytic Aspects of Ethnic Conflicts," 84. See also V. D. Volkan, *Cyprus: War and Adaptation* (Charlottesville: University Press of Virginia, 1979).

43. Volkan, "Psychoanalytic Aspects of Ethnic Conflicts," 84.

44. George Kelly, *A Theory of Personality: The Psychology of Personal Constructs* (W. W. Norton, 1955, 1963), 43.

45. Terrell Northrup, "The Dynamic of Identity in Personal and Social Conflict," chapter 4 of Louis Kriesberg, Terrell Northrup, and Stuart Thorson, eds., *Intractable Conflicts and Their Transformation* (Syracuse: Syracuse University Press, 1989), 65. The reference in the quotation is to George Kelly, *A Theory of Personality: The Psychology of Personal Constructs* (New York: W. W. Norton, 1955, 1963).

46. Vamik Volkan, "Bosnia–Herzegovina: Ancient Fuel of Modern Inferno," *Mind and Human Interaction 7* (August 1996) 3: 110. Volkan uses the term *enveloping* for this process of bundling and externalizing.

47. Vamik Volkan, *Bloodlines* (New York: Farrar, Straus and Giroux, 1997), 43.

48. Volkan, "Bosnia-Herzegovina," 112.

49. Ibid. The term *chosen trauma* is Volkan's.

50. Volkan, *Bloodlines,* 48.

51. John Mack, "The Psychodynamics of Victimization," in Vamik Volkan, Demetrios Julius, and Joseph Montville, eds., *The Psychodynamics of International Relationships,* Vol. I (Lexington, Mass.: Lexington Books, 1991), 125.

52. Van Evera, "Hypotheses." One way to achieve a more accurate history in a post-war context, Van Evera argues, is for each side to subject its history-writing to the criticism of the other. Van Evera concedes that this is not a foolproof approach when he admits that agreement can occur on untruth. This situation, he says, is better than no agreement and can have a peaceful outcome. See also Leonard Thompson, who says that acceptable myths need to pass three tests: Is the myth compatible with the evidence? Does the myth conform to scientific probability? Are the myth's effects good or bad? *The Political Mythology of Apartheid* (New Haven: Yale University Press, 1985), 2.

53. "The very effect of historical change, the ending of wars, for example, and the influence that such external changes have upon thinking give the lie to the notion that words are arbitrarily connected to things. . . . Practical realism thwarts the relativists by reminding them that some words and conventions, however socially constructed, reach out to the world and give a reasonable true description of its contents." Appleby, Hunt, and Jacob, 249-50. "There are commonly accepted professional standards that enable us to distinguish good history from falsehoods like the denial of the Holocaust. Historical truth does exist, not in the scientific sense but as a reasonable approximation of the past." Foner, xvii.

54. This was a matter of central consideration in the creation of South Africa's Truth and Reconciliation Commission. By offering amnesty to those who came forward and voluntarily confessed their crimes, the TRC hoped to maximize the amount of reliable information that came out in the process.

55. For a discussion of the way reminders of traumatic experience may bring back the traumatization, see M. J. Horowitz, *Stress Response Syndromes* (New York: Jason Aronson, 1976).

56. Mack, 126.

57. Volkan, "Psychoanalytic Aspects of Ethnic Conflicts," 89.

58. Ibid., 89-90.

59. Joseph Montville, "Epilogue: The Human Factor Revisited," in Joseph Montville, ed., *Conflict and Peacemaking in Multiethnic Societies* (New York: Lexington Books, 1991), 538-40.

60. Though Barth's thinking on boundaries has been developed by constructivists, it can be argued that Barth is a primordialist in two respects. Barth argues that the boundaries of the group may change *form*, but they persist, even if the group's content and distinctive characteristics change. The implication of this is that ethnic groups, once formed, are in a certain respect unchanging, that the idea of the group remains despite changes in its markers and content. He also argues that ethnicity itself is a permanent, essential condition. These points are made by Banks, 13.

61. Donald Harman Akenson, *Small Differences: Irish Catholics and Irish Protestants, 1815-1922, An International Perspective* (Kingston: McGill-Queen's University Press, 1988), 143-44.

NOTES TO CHAPTER 3

1. Jonathan Bardon, *A History of Ulster* (Belfast: The Blackstaff Press, 1992), 125.

2. Historians continue to argue over the facts of this rebellion. James Anthony Froude (1818-1894) told the story in terms of the evils committed by the Irish; W. E.

H. Lecky (1838-1903) tried to refute Froude. Roy Foster accuses Lecky of nonetheless giving too high an estimate of the numbers of settlers killed. The figure of 2,000 settler casualties given here comes from Roy Foster, *Modern Ireland 1600-1972* (London: Penguin Books, 1989), 85. Bardon, 138, says the figure was 4,000.

3. For a rich account of the building of British identity on the basis of anti-Catholicism, see Linda Colley, *Britons: Forging the Nation 1707-1837* (London: Pimlico, 1992). Colley does not discuss the implications of this for Ireland but the inference is easily made.

4. P. J. Helm, *History of Europe, 1450-1660* (London: G. Bell and Sons Ltd., 1961), 220.

5. In Ireland, the Anglican church was, and still is, called the Church of Ireland, despite the fact that the vast majority of people in Ireland are not Anglican.

6. These statistics come from Bardon, 300.

7. Northern Ireland, as part of the United Kingdom, was mobilized in the war effort even if military service was not made compulsory; Belfast was severely bombed several times by the Nazis. In spite of the Republic's neutrality, it conferred overflight rights to the Allies.

8. These statistics come from Bardon, 492.

9. Bardon, 614.

10. See Bew, Gibbon, and Patterson for the argument that O'Neill's policies were a response to changes in policy in London vis à vis Northern Ireland with the coming of Harold Wilson's Labour government in 1964. Wilson, they argue, though not his Cabinet, was leaning toward the South and possible unification. Though Wilson's ideas were overruled by his Cabinet, Catholic expectations were raised by the election of a Labour government. O'Neill was therefore pressured to make more gestures to Catholics. Paul Bew, Peter Gibbon, and Harry Patterson, *Northern Ireland 1921-1996* (London: Serif, 1996), chapter 5.

11. Bardon, 638-39.

12. This was replaced in 1989 by the Fair Employment Commission, which was tightened in several respects.

13. The official Inquiry of 1972 was headed by Lord Widgery, Lord Chief Justice of England. On the twenty-eighth anniversary of Bloody Sunday, Prime Minister Tony Blair announced the opening of a new inquiry to be headed by Lord Saville of Newdigate. This inquiry is still in progress.

14. Paul Arthur and Keith Jeffery, *Northern Ireland since 1968* (Oxford: Blackwell, 1996), 68.

15. Ibid., 80.

16. Arthur and Jeffery, 28, 99.

17. This was part of the "Downing Street Declaration" of August 19, 1969, made in part to assert the ultimate sovereignty of the parliament at Westminster at a moment when it was not entirely clear who was finally in charge and in part to reassure unionists at a moment when the British government was recognizing the need for changes to respond to legitimate civil rights grievances of Catholics.

18. Gerry Fitt and John Hume were responsible for the founding of this party in 1970.

19. Arthur and Jeffery, 12.

20. Sir David Goodall, one of those responsible for the 1985 Agreement, called the Joint Declaration "a political statement of attitude and intent directed primarily at the IRA. The two heads of government have carefully shelved all the difficult longer term issues in order to make a bid for an IRA ceasefire." Sir David Goodall, "Terrorists on the Spot," *The Tablet,* 25 December 1993/1 January 1994: 1676; quoted in Arthur and Jeffery, 118.

21. Quoted in Arthur and Jeffery, 119.

22. Ibid.

NOTES TO CHAPTER 4

1. John McGarry and Brendan O'Leary, *Explaining Northern Ireland* (Oxford: Blackwell, 1995), 363.

2. "There is the conflict itself, and there is the meta-conflict—the conflict about the conflict." Donald Horowitz, *A Democratic South Africa?* (Berkeley, Calif.: University of California Press, 1991), 2; cited in René Lemarchand, *Burundi: Ethnic Conflict and Genocide* (Cambridge and New York: Woodrow Wilson Center Press and Cambridge University Press, 1994), 17.

3. In 1968, 39 percent of Protestants described themselves as British, 32 percent as people of Ulster, and 20 percent as Irish. In 1989, 68 percent described themselves as British, 10 percent as people of Ulster, and 3 percent as Irish. The numbers of Catholics who described themselves as British dropped in the same period from 20 percent to 6 percent. Edward Moxon Browne, "National Identity in Northern Ireland," in Peter Stringer and Gillian Robinson, eds., *Social Attitudes in Northern Ireland: The First Report, 1990-1991* (Belfast: Blackstaff Press, 1991).

4. http://users.tibus.com/the-great-war/sommewww.htm

5. According to Professor David Harkness, who, until 1996 had the chair of Irish history at Queen's University Belfast, the fears of Protestants in the North were heavily affected by Pope Pius X's *Ne temere* decree of 1907, which decreed that Catholics who marry Protestants must bring up their children as Catholics. Interview with David Harkness, June 6, 1996.

6. John Whyte, *Interpreting Northern Ireland* (Oxford: Clarendon Press, 1990). Whyte was the first to summarize the various views on the causes of the conflict, and the distinction between external and internal sources is his. Whyte concluded that since the late 1960s the internal thesis has become more plausible and accepted.

7. John McGarry and Brendan O'Leary, *Explaining Northern Ireland* (Oxford: Blackwell, 1995).

8. Joseph Ruane and Jennifer Todd, *The Dynamics of Conflict in Northern Ireland: Power, Conflict, and Emancipation* (Cambridge: Cambridge University Press, 1996), 7-14.

9. David Miller, *Queen's Rebels: Ulster Loyalism in Historical Perspective* (Dublin: Gill and Macmillan, 1978); cited in McGarry and O'Leary, 356.

10. McGarry and O'Leary, 229.

11. See Donald Harman Akenson, *Small Differences: Irish Catholics and Irish Protestants, 1815-1922, An International Perspective* (Montreal: McGill-Queen's University Press, 1988) for a full account of this process of group formation.

12. The use of intellectual property in group definition is described in Anthony Buckley and Mary Kenney, *Negotiating Identity: Rhetoric, Metaphor and Social Drama in Northern Ireland* (Washington: Smithsonian Institution Press, 1995).

13. McGarry and O'Leary, 253.

14. Ibid., 214-64.

15. The term was coined by Arend Lijphart. See, for example, Arend Lijphart, *Democracy in Plural Societies* (New Haven: Yale University Press, 1977); *Patterns of Democracy: Government Forms and Performance in Thirty-Six Countries* (New Haven: Yale University Press, 1999). Lijphart originally advocated consociationalism for Northern Ireland, but in recent years has acknowledged the drawbacks.

16. Frank Wright, *Northern Ireland: A Comparative Analysis* (Dublin: Gill and Macmillan, 1987).

17. Ruane and Todd, 7-14.

18. McGarry and O'Leary, 357.

19. Paul Arthur expressed his disagreement with this view in an interview in Washington, D.C., July 6, 1998. Clearly crosscutting loyalties, leading eventually to a politics of class rather than nationalism, would be a desirable long-term outcome for Northern Ireland, and Arthur and others believe it is only a matter of time before this will occur.

20. McGarry and O'Leary, 363.

21. Porter characterizes cosmopolitanism and neopluralism as Assimilation and Prioritizing Difference. Norman Porter, *The Elusive Quest: Reconciliation in Northern Ireland* (Belfast: The Blackstaff Press, 2003), 46-63. Kincheloe and Steinberg have five categories: conservative multiculturalism, liberal multiculturalism, pluralist multiculturalism, left-essentialist multiculturalism, and critical multiculturalism. Liberal multiculturalism and pluralist multiculturalism closely approximate the categories of cosmopolitanism and neopluralism. Joe L. Kincheloe and Shirley R. Steinberg, *Changing Multiculturalism* (Buckingham: Open University Press, 1997), chapter 1. Parekh has five models for the interrelationship among cohesion, equality and difference: procedural, nationalist, liberal, plural, and separatist. My use of cosmopolitanism combines his procedural and liberal categories; my use of neopluralism approximates his plural category. Bhikhu Parekh, *The Future of Multi-Ethnic Britain* (London: Profile Books, 2000), 42.

22. Porter, 50, attributes this phrase to Ernest Gellner.

23. Ignatieff makes the point that the eighteenth-century philosophers who first articulated the idea of civil society did not assume democracy was a necessary part of civil society. Michael Ignatieff, "On Civil Society: Why Eastern Europe's Revolutions Could Succeed," *Foreign Affairs* 74 (March/April 1995) 2: 130.

24. Marxism, of course, can be used to support partisan programs in the conflict in Northern Ireland. See McGarry and O'Leary for the differentiation among "green," "orange," and "red" Marxism.

25. In his remarks on civil society, Ignatieff implies that the cosmopolitan vision may only work in a strong state. Ignatieff, "On Civil Society."

26. Tom Hennessey and Robin Wilson, *With All Due Respect: Pluralism and Parity of Esteem,* Democratic Dialogue No. 7 (Belfast: Democratic Dialogue, 1997), 6.

NOTES TO CHAPTER 5

1. Donald Harman Akenson, *The Irish Education Experiment: The National System of Education in the Nineteenth Century* (London: Routledge and Kegan Paul, 1970), 22.

2. John Darby, *Conflict in Northern Ireland: The Development of a Polarized Community* (Dublin: Gill and Macmillan, 1976), 123.

3. Akenson, 23.

4. Akenson, 87.

5. "Fifth Report of the Commissioners of National Education in Ireland, for the year 1838," in *Reports of the Commissioners of National Education in Ireland from 1834 to 1845 inclusive*, 134; cited in E. M. McHugh, "A Study of History as a School Subject in Ireland in the Nineteenth Century," M.A. thesis, The Queen's University of Belfast, 1978, 71; McHugh's citation was found in James Peter Corken, "The development of the teaching of Irish history in Northern Ireland in its political and institutional context," M.A. thesis, The Queen's University of Belfast, 1989, 12.

6. The Anglican Church became the state church in England in 1533 at the time of the Reformation, and thus subsequently became the state church in Ireland. The point that the nineteenth-century Anglican Church saw the mixed schools as a threat comes from Lyons. F. S. L. Lyons, *Ireland since the Famine* (London: Fontana, 1985), 83.

7. According to Akenson, the case for this was argued by making a differentiation between "vested" and "nonvested" schools. "Nonvested" schools were those which had not relied upon the commissioners for any funding for their school buildings, and such schools reserved greater rights of control of who came onto the premises. Akenson, 186.

8. Akenson, 215.

9. Kevin O'Neill, lecture, Boston College, January 30, 1997.

10. J. C. Beckett, *The Making of Modern Ireland* (London: Faber and Faber, 1966), 280.

11. Dominic Murray, *Worlds Apart: Segregated Schools in Northern Ireland* (Belfast: Appletree Press, 1985), 14-15.

12. Akenson, 381.

13. Sean Farren, *The Politics of Irish Education 1920-1965* (Belfast: The Institute of Irish Studies, The Queen's University of Belfast, 1995), 22.

14. T. J. Morrissey, *Towards a National University, William Delaney S.J., 1835-1924* (Dublin: Wolfhound Press, 1983) chapter XVIII; cited in Farren, 22.

15. Report of the Commissioners of Intermediate Education, 1991-1920; cited in Farren, 22.

16. The 1920 partition agreement created a Boundary Commission that was to review the border between North and South in 1925. Many expected that the delivery of this report would force a further debate on partition.

17. Corken, 46.

NOTES TO CHAPTER 6

1. Prior to 1969, district councils were seen as the worst examples of discrimination in Northern Ireland. Since 1969, their power has been, and remains, severely circumscribed. Moreover, whereas various local authority bodies in education and health previously were composed of majorities of elected politicians, after reforms in the 1970s, the proportion of elected representatives was reduced and ministry or agency appointees were put in their place. Both nationalists and unionists have argued at different times that these appointees were "yes" men and women, "Alliance" types—in other words, too middle of the road to represent either community. The government and the boards deny this, but others have argued that a "new class of public figure has emerged over the last two decades . . . which gains preferment not because of its standing with the electorate but precisely because of its immunity from popular pressure. Such a political class is less likely to strike up partisan positions which might frustrate the smooth implementation of public business." Arthur Aughey, "Local government," in Arthur Aughey and Duncan Morrow, eds., *Northern Ireland Politics* (London: Longman, 1996), 98.

2. The GCSE was created in 1986. Before then there were two possible school-leaving exams for sixteen-year-olds, the CSE and the GSE, the former considered the exam for low achievers. The creation of the GCSE was a decision by the authorities to judge everyone by the same standard.

3. Alan Smith, "Education and the Peace Process in Northern Ireland," CAIN website.

4. In spite of the discussion of the history curriculum, proposals in the Assembly for curriculum reform during the brief reign of the Sunningdale government in 1974 got nowhere. Assembly 3: 657, 8 May 1974; cited in James Peter Corken, "The Development of the Teaching of Irish History in Northern Ireland in Its Political and Institutional Context," unpublished M.A. thesis, The School of Education, The Queen's University of Belfast, October 1989, 124.

5. The recognition of the connection between public policy and community relations was slow in coming in all areas of life, not just education. Speaking of the creation of the Community Relations Commission in the early 1970s, Duncan Morrow says, "it represented the first public acknowledgment that community divisions in Northern Ireland were endemic and therefore central to public policy." Duncan Morrow, "In Search of Common Ground," in Arthur Aughey and Duncan Morrow, eds., *Northern Ireland Politics* (London: Longmans, 1996), 62.

6. One person interviewed credited this change at DENI to the new minister for education, Brian Mawhinney, who "bludgeoned them into change." (Mawhinney

was the only member of the British Cabinet with responsibilities for Northern Ireland during direct rule who had been born in Northern Ireland. Though he earned
greater respect in Northern Ireland for this reason, he in fact represented the English
constituency of Peterborough.) Others have attributed DENI's change of policy to
the hunger strikes of the early 1980s and the increased level of despair about the conflict.

7. John Darby, D. Batts, S. Dunn, J. Harris, and S. Farren, *Education and Community in Northern Ireland, Schools Apart?* (Coleraine: University of Ulster, 1977).

8. Dominic Murray, *Worlds Apart: Segregated Schools in Northern Ireland*
(Belfast: Appletree Press, 1985).

9. Alan Smith, "Education and the Conflict in Northern Ireland," in Seumas
Dunn, ed., *Facets of the Conflict in Northern Ireland* (London: Macmillan, 1995),
170.

10. DENI Circular 82/21: "The Improvement of Community Relations: The Contribution of Schools." It was issued to all teachers in June 1982, which was not the
normal policy for DENI circulars.

11. The term had been used earlier in materials published by the Schools Cultural
Studies Project and UNESCO.

12. Alan Smith, *Education for Mutual Understanding* (Belfast: H.M.S.O., 1988).

13. Northern Ireland Curriculum Council, *Cross Curricular Themes—Consultation
Report* (Belfast: Northern Ireland Curriculum Council, 1989); cited in Alan Smith and
Alan Robinson, *Education for Mutual Understanding: Perceptions and Policy* (Col-
eraine: Center for the Study of Conflict, 1992), 13.

14. Seumas Dunn, J. Darby, K. Mullan, *Schools Together?* (Coleraine: Centre for
the Study of Conflict, 1984).

15. See Gordon Allport, *The Nature of Prejudice* (Reading, Mass.: Addison-Wesley,
1954); Y. Amir, "Contact hypothesis in ethnic relations," *Psychological Bulletin,* 1969,
71, 319-43; H. Tajfel, "The roots of prejudice: cognitive aspects," in P. Watson, ed.,
Psychology and Race (Chicago: Aldine, 1973); Miles Hewstone and Rupert Brown,
eds., *Contact and Conflict in Intergroup Encounters* (Oxford: Blackwell, 1986); W. G.
Stephan and C. W. Stephan, *Intergroup Relations* (Madison, Wisc.: Brown and Benchmark, 1996).

16. See A. E. S. Spencer, "Arguments for an Integrated School System in Northern Ireland," in Robert Osborne, Robert Cormack, and R. Miller, eds., *Education and
Policy in Northern Ireland* (Belfast: PRI, 1987).

17. Alan Smith and Alan Robinson, *Education for Mutual Understanding—
Perceptions and Policy* (Coleraine, Northern Ireland: Center for the Study of Conflict,
1992), 25.

18. R. M. Fraser, *Children in Conflict* (London: Secker and Wartburg, 1973), argued that integrated schools would break down community barriers; K. Heskin,
Northern Ireland: A Psychological Analysis (Dublin: Gill and Macmillan, 1980), argued that integrated schools would strengthen a "silent majority" that supported reconciliation. Gallagher argues that these views had an "air of unreality" because they
were based on research in the United States where arguments for desegregation focused on the issue of equality, whereas in Northern Ireland the push for school de-

segregation focuses on social integration. Anthony Gallagher, "Education in a Divided Society," *The Psychologist: Bulletin of the British Psychological Society* 5 (August 1992): 353-56.

19. Cecil Linehan took the principal responsibility for creating All Children Together. The Education (NI) Order 1977, allowing state schools to convert to integrated schools, was the first big achievement of this organization.

20. Northern Ireland Information Service, "Integrated Schools' Contribution to Community Reconciliation," December 7, 1998. http://alexandra14.nio.gov.uk/981207e-nio.htm

21. Anne Hovey, "As Easy as Abc . . . The Anti-Bias Curriculum," and Frank Wright, "Integrated Education and Political Identity," in Chris Moffat, ed., *Education Together for a Change* (Belfast: Fortnight Educational Trust, 1993), 47 and 182 respectively.

22. Informal talks with Mary McAleese in Boston, October 14, 1996, and in Belfast, November 19, 1996.

23. Standing Advisory Commission on Human Rights, *Report on Fair Employment: Religious and Political Discrimination and Equality of Opportunity in Northern Ireland* (London: H.M.S.O., 1987).

24. Anthony Gallagher, *Majority Minority Review 2: Employment, Unemployment and Religion in Northern Ireland* (Central Community Relations Unit, 1991).

25. Murray, 1985, observed that, because of the nature of the social bifurcation, Protestant schools are more closely tied to the existing network of school administration and education policy than Catholic schools. For Catholic schools, these bodies are seen as outsiders and intruders, and this sets off a vicious cycle where Catholic school authorities refrain from seeking the assistance of the education structure, then blame it for not serving their needs.

26. Alan Smith and Alan Robinson, *Education for Mutual Understanding: The Initial Statutory Years* (Coleraine, Northern Ireland: Centre for the Study of Conflict, University of Ulster, 1996).

27. Department of Education for Northern Ireland, "Towards a Culture of Tolerance, Education for Diversity," 1999.

28. Tony Gallagher and Alan Smith, *The Effects of the Selective System of Secondary Education* (Bangor: Department of Education, 2000).

29. J. Gardner and P. Cowan, *Testing the Test: A Study of the Reliability and Validity of the Northern Ireland Transfer Procedure Test in Enabling the Selection of Pupils for Grammar School Places* (Belfast: Queen's University, 2000).

30. Post Primary Review Body, *Education for the 21st Century* (The Burns Report) (Bangor: Department of Education, 2001).

31. Department of Education Northern Ireland, *Post Primary Review: Report on Responses to Consultation* (Bangor: Department of Education, 2002).

32. Post Primary Review Working Group, *Future Post Primary Arrangements in Northern Ireland: Advice from the Post Primary Review Working Group* (The Costello Report) (Bangor: Department of Education, 2004).

33. All of the Department of Education reports and many associated documents can be found at: http://www.deni.gov.uk/pprb/index.htm.

NOTES TO CHAPTER 7

1. Akenson, *The Irish Education Experiment*, 229-30.

2. Akenson, ibid., 238-39.

3. Lyons, 89.

4. Parliamentary Papers 1854 (525), XV, i, 285; cited in McHugh, 85; cited in Corken, 14.

5. McHugh, 392-94; cited in Corken, 15-16.

6. Parliamentary Papers, 1864 (509), XLVI, 433; cited in McHugh, 87; cited in Corken, 16.

7. The Royal Commission on Primary Education in Ireland, normally referred to as the Powis Commission. Even in its composition (seven Roman Catholics, five Anglicans, and two Presbyterians), this commission reflected the power shift of the previous twenty years.

8. Parliamentary Papers, 1870 (C. 6-III), XXVIII, iv, 1226; cited in McHugh, 94; cited in Corken, 17.

9. Parliamentary Papers, 1870 (C.6-II), XXVIII, ii, 550, cited in McHugh, 94; cited in Corken, 18.

10. Report of the commissioners appointed to inquire into National Education in Ireland; Parliamentary Papers, 1870 (C.6), XXVIII, Pt. I, 525; cited in McHugh, 405; cited in Corken, 19.

11. Corken, 193-94.

12. John Magee, "The Teaching of Irish History in Irish Schools," *The Northern Teacher* 10 (Winter 1970) 1: 15.

13. Lyons, 89.

14. Parliamentary Papers, 1870m (C. 6-II), XXVIII, iii, 680; cited in McHugh, 95-96; cited in Corken, 18.

15. Parliamentary Papers, 1870 (C. 6-II), XXVIII, iii, 524; cited in McHugh, 94; cited in Corken, 18.

16. Magee, 15.

17. Magee, 15.

18. Magee, 15-16.

19. P. W. Joyce, *A Child's History of Ireland* (Dublin: Gill and Macmillan, 1899), 5.

20. Sean Farren, "Nationalist-Catholic Reaction to Educational Reform in Northern Ireland, 1920-30," *History of Education* 15 (1986) 1:28; cited in Corken, 41.

21. Final Report of the Departmental Committee on the Educational Services in Northern Ireland. Belfast: H.M.S.O, 1923, 53; cited in Corken, 42.

22. Ibid., 55; cited in Corken, 42.

23. The Boundary Commission was to give its verdict on the final division between North and South in 1925. Prime Minister James Craig told the House of Commons on March 14, 1922, "We may take it for granted that the Boundary Commission is still the predominant danger confronting the loyalists of Ulster. . . . I can say that this whole matter has, from the start, given me more anxiety than any other problem that has ever confronted me with regard to Ulster." Commons 2:9-10, 14 March, 1922; cited in Corken, 42.

24. Final Report of the Departmental Committee, 83; cited in Corken, 197, note 19.

25. Ibid., 53; cited in Corken, 41.

26. Ministry of Education, the examination papers issued at the intermediate examinations held by the Ministry of Education for Northern Ireland in June 1922. English examination; Junior Grade: paper number 15; question 4d; cited by Corken, 43.

27. Massacres committed by Cromwell's troops at Drogheda and Wexford in the 1640s have remained, to this day, open wounds in the Catholic psyche.

28. See NI House of Commons, v. 9 col. 1363, 3 May 1928; cited in Farren, 104.

29. Ministry of Education, Report of the Ministry of Education for the Year 1934-35, 19; cited in Corken, 53.

30. PRONI: Ed. 29-35: S. File 7-13. "Ballycastle Grammar School. Detailed Inspection Reports. 1931-32 and 1947-48." 1935-36: Part II. History. No page reference. Cited in Corken, 54-55.

31. Corken, 57-60.

32. Magee.

33. PRONI: Ed. 29-80: S. File 27-13 "R.B.A.I. Special Inspection Reports 1942-1952." 1951-52: Part II. History. 11; and PRONI: Ed. 29-147: S. File 50-13. "Friends School Lisburn. Special Inspection Reports. 1942-43 and 1951-52." 1951-52: Part II. History. 6; cited in Corken, 89.

34. Commons XXXIII: 244-45, 14 March 1949; cited in Corken, 75.

35. Commons XXXIII: 556, 5 April 1949; cited in Corken, 75.

36. Commons 40: 2837, 20 November 1956; cited in Corken, 83.

37. PRONI: Ed. 29-153: S. File 52-13. "Londonderry St. Columbs College. Detailed Inspection Reports 1933-34 and 1953-54." 1953-54: Part II. History. 10; cited in Corken, 89.

38. Response to a question put to John Hume by the author at a lecture at Boston College, March 10, 1997.

39. Eamonn McCann, *War and an Irish Town* (Middlesex: Penguin, 1974), 16; cited in Corken, 89.

40. Bernadette Devlin, *The Price of My Soul* (New York: Knopf, 1969).

41. Parliamentary Papers, 1825 (C-II), XII, 86; cited in McHugh, 462; cited in Corken, 25.

42. Parliamentary Papers, 1870 (C-II), XXVII, iii, 679; cited in McHugh, 55; cited in Corken, 25.

43. This point was made by one of the teachers interviewed for this study.

44. Commons 67: 1869, 15 November 1967; cited in Corken, 114.

45. On this occasion, civil rights marchers who had walked from Belfast to Derry/Londonderry were attacked with stones thrown by off-duty B-specials at Burntollet just as they were approaching their destination.

46. Commons 73: 263, 8 May 1969; cited in Corken, 102.

47. Commons 74, 1951, 4 December 1969; cited in Corken, 102.

48. Ibid.

49. Commons 75: 229-30, 12 February 1970; cited in Corken, 104.

50. Commons 76: 176, 7 May 1970; cited in Corken, 104-5.

51. *Irish Times*, 13 March 1970; cited in H. Rex Cathcart, "Teaching Irish History," The Wiles Week Open Lecture, 1978 (Belfast: The Queen's University of Belfast Teachers' Centre, 1978), 9.

NOTES TO CHAPTER 8

1. A colloquial description of the difference between the two groups' understandings of Irish history is "poor us" vs. "why a British Prime Minister fell." Liam Kennedy has coined the term "MOPE" (Most Oppressed People on Earth) to describe a mentality that, he says, has taken over the mind-set of Catholics. One Protestant historian said to me, "Unionists in Northern Ireland have the MOPE problem as well."

2. Magee, 15.

3. Interview with Vivian McIver, Belfast, May 1996.

4. Interview with Jonathan Bardon, May 6, 2004.

5. Malcolm Skilbeck, "Education and Cultural Change," *Compass: Journal of the Irish Association for Curriculum Development* 5 (May 1976) 2: 16.

6. Anthony D. Buckley and Mary Catherine Kenney, *Negotiating Identity: Rhetoric, Metaphor and Social Drama in Northern Ireland* (Washington, D.C.: Smithsonian Institution Press, 1995), 214.

7. T. W. Moody, "Irish History and Irish Mythology," *Hermathena* 124 (1978): 7-24. The article is reprinted in Ciaran Brady, ed., *Interpreting Irish History: The Debate on Historical Revisionism* (Dublin: Irish Academic Press, 1994), 71-86.

8. Claude Lévi-Strauss, *Structural Anthropology* (London: 1969); cited in Brady, 8.

9. This opinion is Brady's. Brady, 8.

10. Queen's University in Belfast, founded as Queen's College in 1849 and made an independent university in 1908, was Northern Ireland's single university at the time of partition. The first structured course in Irish history was offered by T. W. Moody in the 1930s. J. C. Beckett was awarded a chair in Irish history in December 1958. In 1963, Beckett's chair was made permanent. Harkness succeeded Beckett.

11. David Harkness, "History and the Irish" (Belfast: Queen's University of Belfast, 1976), 14-15.

12. Ibid.

13. Harkness would use his position to implement this vision through his support of a Schools History Competition initiated by the Churches Central Committee for Community Work. This body, formed in 1971, in 1975 held a conference on "The Teaching of History—A Basis of Understanding or a Cause of Disruption?" The theme of the conference was that "proper" teaching of Irish history could be a basis of understanding. Subsequently the same body sponsored several history essay competitions, on the Siege of Derry and the Siege of Drogheda. Harkness also went on to work on history teaching projects with the Council of Europe.

14. H. Rex Cathcart, "Teaching Irish History," The Wiles Week Open Lecture (Belfast: The Queen's University of Belfast Teachers' Centre, 1978), 13.

15. Many of these points come from D. George Boyce, "Revisionism and the Revisionist Controversy," chapter 1 of D. George Boyce and Alan O'Day, *Modern Irish History: Revisionism and the Revisionist Controversy*, 5-6.

16. Roy Foster, "We Are All Revisionists Now," *The Irish Review* 1 (1986): 1, 5.

17. Cited in M. A. G. O'Tuathaigh. "Irish Historical Revisionism," in Brady, *Interpreting Irish History*, 311.

18. Ibid., 314.

19. These points come from Brady, 24-31.

20. Jonathan Bardon, Rex Cathcart, and Robert Kee have supplied historical background for a number of TV and radio broadcasts on history in Northern Ireland.

21. Conor Cruise O'Brien and Joe Lee publish regularly on the op-ed pages of the main papers in the South. Historians in the North are not given as much of a public platform, but their work is not unacknowledged in the media.

22. F. S. L. Lyons and Liam de Paor have worked on textbooks in the South. Jonathan Bardon authored *A History of Ulster* (Belfast: The Blackstaff Press Ltd., 1992) after ERO, to provide teachers with the background material they would need to teach Northern Ireland history.

23. See for example, Daniel Bar-Tal's analysis of Israeli textbooks for a catalog of phrases that support problematic "societal beliefs."

24. Lorna Hadkins, "Textbooks," *Community Forum* 1 (Spring 1971) 1: 7. Hadkins, a Welsh researcher, was based at the Institute of Education at Cambridge and the London University Institute of Education.

25. Ibid., 8.

26. Ibid.

27. See Magee, 17. The purpose of the European Association of Teachers was to make "members aware of the serious reappraisal of the purposes of history teaching that was going on in other countries and especially of the efforts made by teachers' organizations and official agencies to remove from school textbooks the distorted judgments and prejudices engendered by recent rivalries."

28. The period of the formation of the Republic, particularly the civil war, has until recently remained a topic the people of the South have preferred not to uncover. This is in part why the movie *Michael Collins* was considered so significant. It is interesting that the decision in the 1960s to include 1916-1921 for study in schools stopped short of 1921-1923, the most ignominious period.

29. *Ferment and Change 1485 to 1660*, and *The Age of Revolutions 1660-1815*.

30. Corken, 110-11.

31. The History of Ireland series: *Celts and Normans, Conquest and Colonization*, and *The Birth of Modern Ireland*. (Dublin: Gill and Macmillan), 1969.

32. John Darby, "History in the Schools," *Community Forum* 3 (1974): 37-42.

33. Ibid., 38.

34. Ibid.

35. Ibid.

36. Corken, 129-30.

37. See chapter 5.

38. Sandra Gillespie and Gerry Jones, *Northern Ireland and Its Neighbours since 1920* (London: Hodder and Stoughton, 1995).

39. See, for example, Rex Cathcart, *The Most Contrary Region: The BBC in Northern Ireland, 1924-1984* (Belfast: Blackstaff Press, 1984); and Liz Curtis, *Ireland, The Propaganda War: The Media and the "Battle for Hearts and Minds"* (London: Pluto Press, 1985).

40. Cathcart, 1.

41. Interview of Vivian McIver by Peter James Corken, March 1988; cited in Corken, 112.

42. Magee, 21.

43. Peter Rogers, *The New History: Theory Into Practice* (London: The Historical Association, 1979).

44. This phrase is quoted from the project's mandate in Alan Smith and Alan Robinson, *Education for Mutual Understanding: Perceptions and Policy*, 11.

45. Interview with Alan Robinson, School of Education, University of Ulster at Coleraine, May 9, 1997.

46. Carmel Gallagher and Alan McCully, "The Contribution of Curriculum Enquiry to Educational Policies in Northern Ireland—The Schools Council History Project," unpublished paper given to me by Carmel Gallagher.

47. The General Certificate of Education (GSCE) is, as of 1988, the basic school leaving exam in the United Kingdom. Students usually take it at age sixteen.

48. Carmel Gallagher and Alan McCully.

49. Department of Education, *Primary Education: Teachers' Guide* (Belfast: H.M.S.O., 1974).

50. Northern Ireland Council for Educational Development, *History Guidelines for Primary Schools* (Belfast: Learning Resources Unit, Stranmillis College, 1984).

51. Public exams are created and administered by the Northern Ireland Council for the Curriculum, Examinations and Assessment (CCEA). However, schools can opt to use other U.K. exam boards if they so choose. Since ERO, schools that choose other exam boards have to use boards that include Irish history on their history exams. Information in this section relates to the CCEA's exams.

52. William Smyth, "Irish History in Secondary (Intermediate) Schools in Northern Ireland: A Survey of Extent, Teaching Methods, Qualifications of Teachers and Pupils' Attitudes," unpublished M.A. thesis, The Queen's University of Belfast, March 20, 1974, 94-95.

53. N.I.S.E.C., Chief Examiner's Report for G.C.S.E. History 1988, 1; cited in Corken, 148.

54. I am grateful to Alan Smith for a number of these points about teacher training.

NOTES TO CHAPTER 9

1. Ann Low-Beer, "School History, National History, and the Issue of National Identity," *International Journal of History Teaching and Research*, 3, 1. See also Nicholas Tate, "The End of History? Could You Recognize Alfred the Great? Probably Not If You're a History Student," *The Guardian*, July 27, 1999.

2. Helen Brocklehurst and Robert Phillips, eds., *History, Nationhood and the Question of Britain* (Basingstoke: Palgrave Macmillan, 2004), xxviii.

3. Interview with Jonathan Bardon, Belfast, May 6, 2004.

4. Interview with Carmel Gallagher, Belfast, May 6, 2004.

5. History was an optional subject at this age level in England, Scotland, and Wales, a consideration that may have made the decision easier in Northern Ireland.

6. On January 30, 1972, British paratroopers fired on a crowd of unarmed civilians demonstrating against the newly announced British policy of internment. Fourteen people died. The inquiry that followed exonerated the paratroopers. Prime Minister Tony Blair has opened a new inquiry.

7. K. C. Barton and A. W. McCully, "History, Identity, and the School Curriculum in Northern Ireland: An Empirical Study of Secondary Students' Ideas and Perspectives," in press, *Journal of Curriculum Studies*: 24-25.

8. Pearse was the leader of the republican Easter Rising in 1916. He and fourteen of his fellow fighters were subsequently executed by the British authorities.

9. Alan McCully, Nigel Pilgrim, Alaeric Sutherland, and Tara McMinn, "'Don't Worry, Mr. Trimble. We Can Handle It.' Balancing the Rational and the Emotional in the Teaching of Contentious Topics," *Teaching History* 102 (March 2002): 7.

10. Louis Oppenheimer and Ilse Hakvoort, "Will the Germans Ever be Forgiven? Memories of the Second World War Four Generations Later," in Ed Cairns and Mícheál D. Roe, eds., *The Role of Memory in Ethnic Conflict* (Basingstoke: Palgrave Macmillan, 2003), 101.

11. Ed Cairns, C. A. Lewis, O. Mumcu, and N. Waddell, "Memories of Recent Ethnic Conflict and the Relationship to Social Identity," *Peace and Conflict: Journal of Peace Psychology* 4 (1998) 13-22.

12. Keith C. Barton, Alan W. McCully, and Margaret Conway, "History Education and National Identity in Northern Ireland," *International Journal of History Teaching and Research* 3 (January 2003) 1: www.ex.ac/historyresource.

13. Ibid.

14. The authors of the study underline that two-thirds of the pupils at the thirteen to fourteen age level still do not link ideas about history with community identifications. It is important to recognize, therefore, "that national, political and religious issues do not dominate the way they conceptualize their connection to history, but are simply one source of identification among many." They do not address the possibility that the *reason* the fourteen-year-olds are more conscious of ideas about history linking in with sectarianism is that it is at this year that students begin to study the Home Rule movement and partition. But they do suggest that the current curriculum may not be designed in a way that best serves the needs of students according to their age and level of development. See also K. C. Barton and Alan McCully, "History Education and National Identity in Northern Ireland."

15. They do not consider that the statistics might be worse if schools did not have the curriculum they have.

16. K. C. Barton and A. W. McCully, "History and Identity among Secondary Students in Northern Ireland."

17. Andrew Roberts, "US 'clarifies' Irish history," *The* [Irish] *Sunday Times*, October 13, 1996, 5 and 23.

18. *Speak Your Piece: Exploring Controversial Issues—A Guide for Teachers, Youth and Community Workers* (Belfast: Channel Four Schools, c1995), 2.

19. Interview with Roger Austin, University of Ulster at Coleraine, May 6, 1997.

20. McCully et al., "'Don't Worry, Mr. Trimble,'" 7–9.

21. Ibid., 7.

22. Ibid.

NOTES TO CHAPTER 10

1. John Whyte, *Interpreting Northern Ireland,* 258-59.

2. The founding in 1928 of the journal *Annales d'Histoire Sociale et Economique* by French historians Marc Bloch, Lucien Fabvre, and Fernand Braudel was the start of the "Annales" school of history writing, which aimed to shift the writing of history away from political and diplomatic history and the stories of great men and toward social and economic history and the life of ordinary people.

3. Brian Walker, *Dancing to History's Tune: History, Myth and Politics in Ireland* (Belfast: The Institute of Irish Studies, The Queen's University of Belfast, 1996), 133.

4. "A substantial part of this rise in interest [in local studies] can be attributed not just to the alienating effects of the modern world in general, but most particularly to some people's desire to understand how Ulster society has reached its present stage." Brian Turner, "The Twisting Rope—Local Studies in Ulster," *The Irish Review* 8 (Spring 1990); cited in Walker, 132.

5. Walker, 132.

6. Virginia Crossman and Dympna McLoughlin, "A Peculiar Eclipse: E. Estyn Evans and Irish Studies," *The Irish Review* 15 (Spring 1994): 79-96.

7. E. Estyn Evans, *Ulster: The Common Ground* (Mullingar: Lilliput, 1984), 7; cited in Crossman and McLoughlin, 94.

8. The Institute's mandate, Evans wrote, was to "stimulate and coordinate research in those subjects which have particular Irish interest and which find common ground in the physical and human environment of the region served by Queens." Cited in a letter to the author from the current director of the Institute, Brian Walker, November 19, 1998.

9. Interview with William Crawford, Development Officer for the Federation of Ulster Local Studies, Belfast, April 28, 1997.

10. The Fabian Society, led by Sidney and Beatrice Webb, aimed to spread socialist principles by gradual (i.e., political) rather than revolutionary means.

11. Interview with Jack Johnston, Dungannon, May 8, 1997.

12. Ibid.

13. Willie Carlin, speaking at a one-day conference at the Public Records Office of Northern Ireland, "Telling Our Story—A Celebration of People's History in Ulster 1991–1997," May 3, 1997.

14. See Roger Austin, ed., *Essays on History Teaching in Northern Ireland* (Coleraine, Northern Ireland: The Resource Centre, Faculty of Education, University of Ulster at Coleraine, 1985), especially John Moulden, "The Use of Local Knowledge

and Original Documents with Older Primary School Children," and Terence Duffy, "The New History in Practice: An Experiment in Evidence-based Local History."

15. Teachers were allowed to give more than one answer to the question "If history should teach a sense of belonging, how would you describe that sense of belonging?" Therefore we cannot say that a certain percentage of teachers gave any particular answer. We can say that certain answers cropped up more often than the others—"belonging to one's locality" came first, and "European" identity came a close second.

16. Whyte, 68-69.

17. Ian Adamson, *The Ulster People: Ancient, Medieval and Modern* (Belfast: Pretani Press, 1991), 60.

18. The most recent popular expression of this important narrative is Thomas Cahill, *How the Irish Saved Civilization: The Untold Story of Ireland's Heroic Role from the Fall of Rome to the Rise of Medieval Europe* (New York: Doubleday, 1995).

19. Adamson, 37.

20. Jonathan Bardon, *A History of Ulster* (Belfast: The Blackstaff Press, 1992), 14.

21. H. J. Morgan, "Deceptions of demons," *Fortnight* (September 1993): 34-36.

22. Brian Lambkin, "Navan Fort and the Arrival of 'Cultural Heritage,'" *Emania* 11 (1993). This and the next two references were cited in Michael Hall, *The Cruthin Controversy* (Belfast: Island Publications, 1994), 8.

23. James Ferris, in a review of Stephen Bruce's *The Red Hand, The Linen Hall Review* (Winter 1992).

24. John Hunter, "Now, Councillor, Yer Talkin' Sense," *The Irish News,* January 28, 1994.

25. Michael Hall, *Ulster's Protestant Working Class,* Island Pamphlets 9 (Newtownabbey, Co. Antrim: Island Publications, 1994), 25-26.

26. Michael Hall, *Shankill Think Tank: A New Beginning*, Island Pamphlets 13, (Newtownabbey, Co. Antrim: Island Publications, 1996).

27. Proinsias Mac Cana, "Mongán Mac Fiachna and *Immram Brain*," in *Eriu* XXIII (1972); quoted in Michael Hall, *Shankill Think Tank: A New Beginning,* 7.

28. Michael Hall, *The Cruthin Controversy*, Island Pamphlets 7 (Newtownabbey, Co. Antrim: Island Publications, 1994). Hall has published a book and several additional pamphlets on the subject: *Ulster: The Hidden History* (Belfast: Pretani Press, 1986, 1989); *Ulster's Scottish Connection,* Island Pamphlets 3 (Newtownabbey, Co. Antrim: Island Publications, 1993); *Ulster's Shared Heritage,* Island Publications 6 (Belfast: Island Publications, 1993).

29. Roy Foster, "History and the Irish Question," in Ciaran Brady, ed., *Interpreting Irish History: The Debate on Historical Revisionism* (Dublin: Irish Academic Press, 1994), 138.

30. Anthony Buckley compares Adamson's vision with Irish nationalism—both argue for a comprehensive concept of identity that transcends the plural nature of Irish (and Ulster) society. Anthony Buckley, "'We're Trying to Find our Identity': Uses of History among Ulster Protestants," in Elizabeth Tonkin, Maryon McDonald, and Malcolm Chapman, eds., *History and Ethnicity* (London: Routledge, 1989), 194.

31. John Whyte, *Interpreting Northern Ireland* (Oxford: Clarendon, 1990), 67-69. Whyte cites the results of three important surveys: Richard Rose, *Governing without Concensus: An Irish Perspective* (London: Faber and Faber, 1971); E. Moxon-Browne, *Nation, Class and Creed in Northern Ireland* (Aldershot: Gower, 1983), including supplementary figures supplied to Whyte by Moxon-Browne; and David J. Smith, *Equality and Inequality in Northern Ireland*, part 3, *Perceptions and Views*, PSI Occasional Paper no. 39 (London: Political Studies Institute, 1987), with further data not appearing in the report supplied to Whyte by Smith.

32. Hall, *Falls Think Tank*, 17.

33. Buckley, 194; Morgan, 35.

34. Buckley describes various Ulster unionist factions' uses of history and shows how Adamson's differs particularly from that of the fundamentalists (i.e., Paisley and the Democratic Unionist Party). Adamson's vision is more attractive to official unionists and to the UDA because these groups are antagonistic to fundamentalism. Buckley, 189-94.

35. Whyte, 67-69.

36. Britain has been brought before the European Commission and the Court of Human Rights more than any other Council of Europe member, mainly because of Northern Ireland, though with limited success for the plaintiffs.

37. Ian Paisley has also held seats in both parliaments at once.

38. John Hume, *Personal Views: Politics, Peace and Reconciliation in Northern Ireland* (Dublin: Town House, 1996), 59.

39. See Richard Kearney and Robin Wilson, "Northern Ireland's Future as a European Region: Submission to the Opsahl Commmission," *The Irish Review* 15 (1994): 51. See also Hume, 132, for a brief allusion to the importance of Maastrict in setting up the Committee of the Regions.

40. *Protestant Telegraph,* December 1994, 3.

41. Interview with Roger Austin, University of Ulster at Coleraine, May 6, 1997.

42. Council for Cultural Cooperation, "History Teaching and European Awareness," report of conference held in Delphi, Greece, May 11-14, 1994 (Strasbourg: Council of Europe, 1995), especially 9.

43. Liam Kennedy, "Out of History: Ireland, That 'Most Distressful Country,'" in *Colonialism, Religion and Nationalism in Ireland* (Belfast: The Institute of Irish Studies, 1996).

44. Walker, 34-56.

45. Frank Wright, *Northern Ireland: A Comparative Analysis* (Dublin: Gill and Macmillan), 1987.

NOTES TO CHAPTER 11

1. Alan Smith, "Citizenship Education in Northern Ireland: Beyond National Identity?" *Cambridge Journal of Education* 33 (2003) 1: 22.

2. Northern Ireland Curriculum Council, 1990.

3. Alan Smith and Alan Robinson, *Education for Mutual Understanding: The Initial Statutory Years* (Coleraine: University of Ulster, 1996).

4. *Integrating Education* (Belfast: Department of Education, 1998).

5. *Education for Diversity* (Belfast: Department of Education, 1999).

6. Alan Smith and Alison Montgomery, *Values in Education in Northern Ireland* (Northern Ireland Council for the Curriculum, Examinations and Assessment, 1997). The research was supported by finance from the Gordon Cooke Foundation.

7. Anthony Gallagher and Alan Smith, "Attitudes to Academic Selection, Integrated Education and Diversity within the Curriculum," in A. M. Gray, K. Lloyd, P. Devine, G. Robinson and D. Heenan, eds., *Social Attitudes in Northern Ireland. The Eighth Report* (London: Pluto Press, 2002).

8. This "cohort study" of 3,000 pupils, conducted for CCEA by the National Foundation for Educational Research, covered the seven-year period from 1996 to 2003.

9. Cited in Alan Smith and Murray Print, "Editorial," *Cambridge Journal of Education* 33 (2003) 1: 6.

10. European Commission, *Education and Active Citizenship in the European Union* (Luxembourg: Office of Official Publications of the European Communities, 1998).

11. F. Audigier, *Teaching about Society, Passing on Values. Elementary Law in Civic Education. A Secondary Education for Europe* (Strasbourg: Council of Europe Publishing, 1996).

12. Council of Europe, *Education for Citizenship: The Basic Concepts and Core Competences.* (Council of Europe, DECS/CIT (98), 7 def. 1998).

13. "The Curriculum Framework," Section 3.3—"The Aim, Objectives and Key Elements," in *Pathways: Towards a More Coherent, Enjoyable, Motivating and Relevant Curriculum for Young People Aged 11-14* (Northern Ireland Council for the Curriculum, Examinations and Assessment, 2003), 27.

14. *Pathways*, 69.

NOTES TO CHAPTER 12

1. Mícheál D. Roe and Ed Cairns, "Memories in Conflict: Review and a Look to the Future," in Ed Cairns and Mícheál D. Roe, eds., *The Role of Memory in Ethnic Conflict* (Basingstoke: Palgrave Macmillan, 2003), 177.

2. Another elaboration of the *divergent interpretations* model is one that was proposed for the Croatian education system by the Transnational Foundation. The plan envisaged a "three-version" history, one version written by Croatian historians, another by Serb historians inside Croatia, and the third by a mixed, international group that identifies agreements and disagreements between the two. The three versions were to be published together. Jan Oberg, "Reconciliation through a History and School Book Commission—in Croatia and Elsewhere," Transnational Foundation PressInfo 40, June 24, 1998 (Lund, Sweden: Transnational Foundation for Peace and Future Research).

3. The Orange Order is a fraternal order that has been very significant in creating cohesion in the unionist community and, in the view of nationalists, has reinforced unionist domination.

4. Graffiti in the residential areas of the two communities has developed into an evolved art form, where large paintings on the gable walls of row houses or on billboards depict elements of the narratives of the respective groups.

5. Anthony D. Buckley and Rhonda Paisley, *Symbols* (Belfast: Cultural Traditions Group of the Community Relations Council, 1994).

6. Anthony D. Buckley and Mary Catherine Kenney, *Negotiating Identity: Rhetoric, Metaphor and Social Drama in Northern Ireland* (Washington, D.C.: Smithsonian Institution Press, 1995), 225-26.

7. This point comes from Joyce Appleby, Lynn Hunt, and Margaret Jacob, *Telling the Truth about History* (New York: W. W. Norton, 1994), 257.

8. Falk Pingel, "Plural Societies: history teaching and the dilemma of a national curriculum," manuscript subsequently published in *Yesterday and Today* 25 (May 1993): 16-21.

9. Ibid.

10. Ibid., 4.

11. Emile Potenza, South African historian and textbook author, quoted in Bob Drogin, "Reversing Apartheid's Lessons," *Los Angeles Times*, February 11, 1997, A10.

12. Pingel, 7.

13. Ibid.

14. Tom Hennessey and Robin Wilson, *With All Due Respect: Pluralism and Parity of Esteem* (Belfast: Democratic Dialogue, Report No. 7, 1997), 6.

15. Voting can pass on the basis of *parallel consent,* which means over 50 percent of voting Assembly members from each community, or by *weighted majority,* which means 60 percent of voting Assembly members, including at least 40 percent from each community.

16. Charles Taylor, *Multiculturalism and "The Politics of Recognition,"* with commentary by Amy Gutmann, ed., et al. (Princeton: Princeton University Press, 1992).

17. This concept and those that follow come from Milton Bennett, "Towards Ethnorelativism: A Developmental Model of Intercultural Sensitivity," in Michael Paige, ed., *Education for the Intercultural Experience,* 2nd ed. (Yarmouth, Maine: Intercultural Press, 1993).

18. Ibid.

19. Norman Porter, *The Elusive Quest: Reconciliation in Northern Ireland* (Belfast: The Blackstaff Press, 2003), 58.

20. Roe and Cairns coin this term in *The Role of Memory in Ethnic Conflict.*

21. Daniel Bar-Tal emphasizes that conflicts that have persisted for generations have far greater power to affect the mind-sets of the protagonists because over decades, perhaps centuries, groups have the chance to selectively create collective memories, and then the collective memory becomes institutionalized. Daniel Bar-Tal, "Collective Memory of Physical Violence," in Ed Cairns and Mícheál D. Roe, eds., *The Role of Memory in Ethic Conflict.*

NOTES TO AFTERWORD

1. Edna Longley, "Multi-Culturalism and Northern Ireland," in Edna Longley and Declan Kiberd, *Multi-Culturalism: The View from the Two Irelands* (Armagh: Center for Cross Border Studies and Cork University Press, 2001).

2. Cornel West, "Black, White and Brown," dialogue between Cornel West and Henry Louis Gates, Jr., *New York Times Book Review,* May 16, 2004, 35.

3. So far the only memorial that has resonance for both communities is a book that lists every person killed in the Troubles, with a short biography. D. McKittrick, S. Kelters, B. Feeney, C. Thornton, eds. *Lost Lives* (London: Trafalgar Square, 1999). All other monuments to the conflict are partisan. The Bloomfield Commission, charged with finding ways to recognize the pain and suffering arising from the Troubles, acknowledged that a physical memorial to the victims of the conflict would be difficult to achieve any time soon and recommended various nonphysical provisions such as community services and counseling for the victims. Sir Kenneth Bloomfield, *We Will Remember Them: Report of the Northern Ireland Victims Commissioner*, April 1998.

4. See Martha Minow, *Between Vengeance and Forgiveness: Facing History after Genocide and Mass Violence* (Boston: Beacon Press, 1998).

Bibliography

Sources Relating to History Teaching and Textbooks

Austin, Roger, ed. *Essays on History Teaching in Northern Ireland*. Coleraine, Northern Ireland: The Resource Center, Faculty of Education, University of Ulster, 1985.

Ballard, Martin, ed. *New Movements in the Study and Teaching of History*. Bloomington, Ind.: Indiana University Press, 1970.

Berghan, Volker, and Hanna Schissler, eds. *Perceptions of History: International Textbook Research on Britain, Germany and the United States*. Oxford: Berg Publishers, 1987.

Billington, Ray Allen. *The Historians' Contribution to Anglo-American Misunderstanding*. London: Routledge and Kegan Paul, 1966.

Bourdillon, Hilary, ed. *History and Social Studies—Methodologies of Textbook Analysis, Report of the Educational Research Workshop Held in Braunschweig (Germany) 11-14 September 1990*. Amsterdam: Swets & Zeitlinger, 1992.

Council of Europe. *Education for Citizenship. The Basic Concepts and Core Competences.* (Council of Europe, DECS/CIT [98], 7 def. 1998).

Council of Europe, Council for Cultural Cooperation. *History, Democratic Values and Tolerance in Europe: the Experience of Countries in Democratic Transition.* Report of conference held in Sofia, Bulgaria, October 1994. General Rapporteur, David Harkness. Strasbourg: The Council of Europe, 1995.

Council of Europe, Council for Cultural Cooperation. "History Teaching and European Awareness." Report of conference held in Delphi, Greece, 11-14 May, 1994. General Rapporteur, David Harkness. Strasbourg: Council of Europe, 1995.

Dance, E. H. *History for a United World*. London: George G. Harrap, 1971.

———. *History the Betrayer: A Study in Bias*. Westport, Conn.: Greenwood Press, 1975.

De Puig, Luis Maria. "History and the learning of history in Europe: Report of the Committee on Culture Education." Strasbourg: Council of Europe, 1996.

Education Advisory Committee of the Parliamentary Group for World Government. *Cyprus School History Textbooks: A Study in Education for International Misunderstanding.* London: World Security Trust, 1967.

Ferro, Marc. *The Use and Abuse of History, or How the Past is Taught.* London: Routledge & Kegan Paul, 1981.

Fitzgerald, Frances. *America Revised: History Schoolbooks in the Twentieth Century.* Boston: Little, Brown, 1979.

Gallagher, Carmel. "History Teaching and the Promotion of Democratic Values and Tolerance." A handbook for teachers. Strasbourg: Council of Europe, Council for Cultural Cooperation, 1996.

Höpken, Wolfgang. "Preliminary Observations and Conclusions." In *History, Democratic Values and Tolerance in Europe: The Experience of Countries in Democratic Transition.* Sofia, Bulgaria, 19-22 October 1994. Strasbourg: The Council of Europe, 1995.

International Commission for the Teaching of History, ed. Georg Eckert. *World History Teachers in Conference: Index of References.* New York: Pergamon Press, Macmillan, 1964.

Jalal, Ayesha. "Conjuring Pakistan: History as Official Imagining." *International Journal of Middle East Studies* 27 (1995): 73-89.

Jelavich, Charles. *South Slav Nationalisms: Textbooks and Yugoslav Union before 1914.* Columbus: Ohio State University Press, 1990.

Low-Beer, Ann. "School History, National History, and the Issue of National Identity." *International Journal of History Teaching and Research,* 3, 1.

McDairmid, Garnet, and David Pratt. *Teaching Prejudice: A Content Analysis of Social Studies Textbooks Authorized for Use in Ontario.* Curriculum Series 12. The Ontario Institute for Studies in Education, 1971.

Oberg, Jan. "Reconciliation Through a History and School Book Commission—in Croatia and Elsewhere." Transnational Foundation PressInfo 40, June 24, 1998. Lund, Sweden: Transnational Foundation for Peace and Future Research.

Pingel, Falk. "Plural Societies: History Teaching and the Dilemma of a National Curriculum." *Yesterday and Today* 25 (May 1993).

———. *UNESCO Guidebook on Textbook Research and Textbook Revision.* Paris: UNESCO, 1999.

Pronay, Nicholas, and Keith Wilson, eds. *The Political Re-education of Germany and Her Allies after World War II.* Beckenham, Kent: Croom Helm, 1985.

Rosandic, Ruzica, and Vesna Pesic, eds. *Warfare, Patriotism, Patriarchy: The Analysis of Elementary School Textbooks.* Belgrade: Centre for Anti-War Action and Association MOST, 1994.

Roy, Simon, Clermont Gauthier, and Maurice Tardif. "Evolution Des Programmes D'Histoire de 1861 à nos Jours." Cahiers du LABRAPS. Université Laval, Séries d'Etudes et de Documents, Vol. 11, 1992.

Salman, Lucy M. "Study of History below the Secondary School." In "The Study of History in the Schools, Being the Report to the American Historical Association by the Committee of Seven." Annual Report of the American Historical Association, 1898.

Schissler, Hanna. "Perceptions of the Other and the Discovery of the Self." In *Perceptions of History: International Textbook Research on Britain, Germany and the*

United States, edited by Volker Berghan and Hanna Schissler. Oxford: Berg Publishers, 1987.

Schüddekopf, Otto-Ernst. *History Teaching and History Textbook Revision.* Strasbourg: Council for Cultural Cooperation of the Council of Europe, 1967.

UNESCO. *Bilateral Consultations for the Improvement of History Textbooks.* Educational Studies and Documents, No. 4, 1953.

——. *The Historiography of Southern Africa.* The General History of Africa: Studies and Documents, #4, 1980.

——. *Multilateral Evaluation of History and Social Studies Teaching Material.* Report of a UNESCO project on Multilateral Evaluation of Secondary School History and Social Studies teaching material and curricula in light of the UNESCO recommendations of 1974. Conducted by the Finnish National Commission for UNESCO, 1983.

——. *Teaching for International Understanding, Peace and Human Rights*, 1984.

——. UNESCO International Textbook Research Network Newsletter No. 1.

——. UNESCO International Textbook Research Network Newsletter No. 2.

Valkenier, Elizabeth Kridl. "Teaching History in Post Communist Russia." *The Harriman Institute Forum* 6 (April 1993) 8.

Vincent, Sylvie, and Bernard Arcand. *The Image of the Amerindian in Quebec Textbooks.* London: International Organization for the Elimination of All Forms of Racial Discrimination, 1984.

Walshe, Peter. Review of *History in Black and White: An Analysis of South African School History Textbooks* by Elizabeth Dean, Paul Hartmann, and May Katzen. In *International Journal of African Historical Studies* 18 (1985) 4: 748-51.

Northern Ireland/ Ireland Sources

Adamson, Ian. *The Ulster People: Ancient, Medieval and Modern.* Belfast: Pretani Press, 1991.

Akenson, Donald Harman. *Education and Enmity: The Control of Schooling in Northern Ireland, 1920-50.* London: Routledge and Kegan Paul, 1970.

——. *Small Differences: Irish Catholics and Irish Protestants, 1815-1922, An International Perspective.* Kingston: McGill-Queen's University Press, 1988.

——. *The Irish Education Experiment: The National System of Education in the Nineteenth Century.* London: Routledge and Kegan Paul, 1970.

Arthur, Paul and Keith Jeffery. *Northern Ireland since 1968.* Oxford: Blackwell, 1996.

Arthur, Paul. Interview with Margaret Smith, Washington, D.C., July 6, 1998.

Aughey, Arthur. "Local government." In *Northern Ireland Politics*, edited by Arthur Aughey and Duncan Morrow. London: Longman, 1996.

Austin, Roger. Interview with Margaret Smith, University of Ulster at Coleraine, May 6, 1997.

Bardon, Jonathan. *A History of Ulster.* Belfast: The Blackstaff Press, 1992.

——. Interview with Margaret Smith, Belfast, November 28, 1996.

——. Interview with Margaret Smith, Belfast, May 6, 2004.

Barton, Keith C., and A. W. McCully, "History, identity, and the school curriculum in Northern Ireland: An empirical study of secondary students' ideas and perspectives." In press, *Journal of Curriculum Studies*. 2004.

Barton, Keith C., Alan W. McCully, Margaret Conway. "History Education and National Identity in Northern Ireland." *International Journal of History Teaching and Research*. January 2003. www. ex. ac/historyresource.

Beckett, J. C. *The Making of Modern Ireland*. London: Faber and Faber, 1966.

———. "The Study of Irish History." New Lecture Series, No. 13. Belfast: The Queen's University of Belfast, 1963.

Bew, Paul, Peter Gibbon, and Harry Patterson. *Northern Ireland 1921-1996*. London: Serif, 1996.

Bloomfield, David. *Peacemaking Strategies in Northern Ireland*. New York: St. Martin's Press, 1997.

Bloomfield, Kenneth. *We Will Remember Them: Report of the Northern Ireland Victims Commissioner*. April 1998.

Boyce, D. George. "Past and Present: Revisionism and the Northern Ireland Troubles." In *The Making of Modern Irish History: Revisionism and the Revisionist Controversy,* edited by D. George Boyce and Alan O'Day. London: Routledge, 1996.

———. "Revisionism and the Revisionist Controversy." In *Modern Irish History: Revisionism and the Revisionist Controversy*, edited by D. George Boyce and Alan O'Day. London: Routledge, 1996.

Brady, Ciaran, ed. *Interpreting Irish History: The Debate on Historical Revisionism*. Dublin: Irish Academic Press, 1994.

———. *God Save Ulster! The Religion and Politics of Paisleyism*. Oxford: Oxford University Press, 1986.

Bruce, Steve. "Cultural Traditions: A Double-Edged Sword?" *Causeway* Autumn 1994: 21-24.

Buckley, Anthony. "'We're Trying to Find Our Identity': Uses of History among Ulster Protestants." In *History and Ethnicity*, edited by Elizabeth Tonkin, Maryon McDonald, and Malcolm Chapman. London: Routledge, 1989.

Buckley, Anthony D., and Mary Catherine Kenney. *Negotiating Identity: Rhetoric, Metaphor and Social Drama in Northern Ireland*. Washington, D.C.: Smithsonian Institution Press, 1995.

Buckley, Anthony D., and Rhonda Paisley. *Symbols*. Belfast: Cultural Traditions Group of the Community Relations Council, 1994.

Cahill, Thomas. *How the Irish Saved Civilization: The Untold Story of Ireland's Heroic Role from the Fall of Rome to the Rise of Medieval Europe*. New York: Doubleday, 1995.

CAIN Web Service (Conflict Archive on the Internet). http://cain.ulst.ac.uk. 1996-2004.

Carlin, Willie. Informal talk at a one-day conference at the Public Records Office of Northern Ireland, "Telling Our Story—A Celebration of People's History in Ulster 1991–1997," May 3, 1997.

Cathcart, H. Rex. "Teaching Irish History." The Wiles Week Open Lecture. Belfast: The Queen's University of Belfast Teachers' Centre, 1978.

――. *The Most Contrary Region: The BBC in Northern Ireland, 1924-1984.* Belfast: Blackstaff Press, 1984.

Chapman, Malcolm. *The Celts: The Construction of a Myth.* Basingstoke: Macmillan Press, 1992.

Community Relations Council. *Annual Report, 1991.* Belfast: Community Relations Council, 1991.

Corken, James Peter. "The Development of the Teaching of Irish History in Northern Ireland in Its Political and Institutional Context." Unpublished M.A. thesis, The Queen's University of Belfast, 1989.

Crawford, William. Interview with Margaret Smith, Belfast, April 28, 1997.

Crossman, Virginia, and Dympna McLoughlin. "A Peculiar Eclipse: E. Estyn Evans and Irish Studies." *The Irish Review* 15 (Spring 1994): 79-96.

Crozier, Maurna, ed. *Cultural Traditions in Northern Ireland: Varieties of Irishness.* Proceedings of the Cultural Traditions Group Conference, 3-4 March 1989. Belfast: The Institute of Irish Studies, 1989.

――. Interview with Margaret Smith, Belfast, June 13, 1996.

Curtis, Liz. *Ireland, the Propaganda War: The Media and the "Battle for Hearts and Minds."* (London: Pluto Press, 1985).

Darby, John, D. Batts, S. Dunn, J. Harris, and S. Farren. *Education and Community in Northern Ireland, Schools Apart?* Coleraine, Northern Ireland: University of Ulster, 1977.

Darby, John. "History in the Schools." *Community Forum* 3 (1974): 37-42.

――. *Conflict in Northern Ireland: The Development of a Polarized Community.* Dublin: Gill and Macmillan, 1976.

Davis, Richard. *Mirror Hate: The Convergent Ideology of Northern Ireland Paramilitaries, 1966-1992.* Aldershot: Dartmouth, 1994.

Department of Education for Northern Ireland. Circular 82/21. "The Improvement of Community Relations: The Contribution of Schools." 1982.

――. *Education for Diversity.* Belfast: Department of Education, 1999.

――. http://www. deni.gov.uk/pprb/index.htm. 2004.

――. *Integrating Education.* Belfast: Department of Education, 1998.

――. *Post Primary Review: Report on Responses to Consultation.* Bangor: Department of Education, 2002.

――. "Irish History in the Classroom: Research, Resources and Realisation." Seminar held at Cultra Manor, Holywood, 18-21 September, 1986. Bangor: Educational Development Division, Rathgael House, 1986.

――. *Primary Education: Teachers' Guide.* Belfast: H.M.S.O., 1974.

Devlin, Bernadette. *The Price of My Soul.* New York: Knopf, 1969.

Dunn, S., and A. Smith. *Inter School Links.* Coleraine, Northern Ireland: Centre for the Study of Conflict, University of Ulster, 1989.

Dunn, Seumas, J. Darby, and K. Mullan. *Schools Together?* Coleraine, Northern Ireland: Centre for the Study of Conflict, New University of Ulster, 1984.

English, Richard. "'Cultural Traditions' and Political Ambiguity." *The Irish Review* 15 (Spring 1994).

――. Interview with Margaret Smith, The Queen's University of Belfast, November 21, 1996.

Evans, E. Estyn. *Ulster: The Common Ground*. Mullingar: Lilliput, 1984.

Fanning, Ronan. "The Great Enchantment." In *Interpreting Irish History: The Debate on Historical Revisionism,* edited by Ciaran Brady. Dublin: Irish Academic Press, 1994.

Farren, Sean. "Nationalist-Catholic Reaction to Educational Reform in Northern Ireland, 1920-30." *History of Education* 15 (1986) 1.

——. *The Politics of Irish Education 1920-1965*. Belfast: The Institute of Irish Studies, The Queen's University of Belfast, 1995.

Ferris, James. Review of Steve Bruce's *The Red Hand: Protestant Paramilitaries in Northern Ireland*. *The Linen Hall Review,* Winter 1992.

Foster, John Wilson. "Strains in Irish Intellectual Life." In *On Intellectuals and Intellectual Life in Ireland*, edited by Liam O'Dowd. Belfast: The Institute of Irish Studies, The Queen's University of Belfast, 1996.

Foster, Roy. "Varieties of Irishness." In *Cultural Traditions in Northern Ireland: Varieties of Irishness*, edited by Maurna Crozier. Proceedings of the Cultural Traditions Group Conference, 3-4 March 1989. Belfast: The Institute of Irish Studies, The Queen's University of Belfast, 1989.

——. "History and the Irish Question." In *Interpreting Irish History: The Debate on Historical Revisionism*, edited by Ciaran Brady. Dublin: Irish Academic Press, 1994.

——. "We Are All Revisionists Now." *The Irish Review* 1 (1986).

——. *Modern Ireland 1600-1972*. London: Penguin Books, 1989.

Fraser, R. M. *Children in Conflict*. London: Secker and Wartburg, 1973.

Fulton, Sean, and Anthony Gallagher. "Teacher Training and Community Relations in Northern Ireland." In *Teacher Education in Plural Societies: An International Review,* edited by Maurice Craft. London: The Falconer Press, 1996.

Gallagher, Anthony. "Education in a Divided Society." *The Psychologist: Bulletin of the British Psychological Society* 5 (1992).

——. Majority Minority Review 2: *Employment, Unemployment and Religion in Northern Ireland*. Central Community Relations Unit, 1991.

Gallagher, Anthony, and Alan Smith. *Research into the Effects of the Selective System of Secondary Education*. Bangor: Department of Education, 2000.

——. "Attitudes to Academic Selection, Integrated Education and Diversity within the Curriculum." In *Social Attitudes in Northern Ireland: The Eighth Report*, edited by A. M. Gray, K. Lloyd, P. Devine, G. Robinson, and D. Heenan. London: Pluto Press, 2002.

Gallagher, Carmel. Interview with Margaret Smith, Belfast, May 6, 2004.

Gallagher, Carmel, and Alan McCully. "The Contribution of Curriculum Enquiry to Educational Policies in Northern Ireland—The Schools Council History Project." Unpublished paper.

Gardner, J., and P. Cowan. *Testing the Test: A Study of the Reliability and Validity of the Northern Ireland Transfer Procedure Test in Enabling the Selection of Pupils for Grammar School Places*. Belfast: Queen's University, 2000.

Gillespie, Sandra, and Gerry Jones. *Northern Ireland and Its Neighbours since 1920*. Belfast: Hodder and Stoughton, 1995.

Hadkins, Lorna. "Textbooks." *Community Forum* 1 (Spring 1971) 1.

Hall, Michael. *The Cruthin Controversy*. Island Pamphlets 7. Newtownabbey, Co. Antrim: Island Publications, 1994.

——. *Falls Think Tank: Ourselves Alone? Voices from Belfast's Nationalist Working Class*. Island Pamphlets 15. Newtownabbey, Co. Antrim: Island Publications, 1996.

——. *Shankill Think Tank: A New Beginning*. Island Pamphlets 13. Newtownabbey, Co. Antrim: Island Publications, 1996.

——. *Ulster: The Hidden History*. Belfast: Pretani Press, 1986, 1989.

——. *Ulster's Protestant Working Class*. Island Pamphlets 9. Newtownabbey, Co. Antrim: Island Publications, 1994.

——. *Ulster's Scottish Connection*. Island Pamphlets 3. Newtownabbey, Co. Antrim: Island Publications, 1993.

——. *Ulster's Shared Heritage*. Island Publications 6. Newtownabbey, Co. Antrim: Island Publications, 1993.

Harkness, David. Interview with Margaret Smith, Belfast, June 6, 1996.

——. "History and the Irish." Belfast: The Queen's University of Belfast, 1976.

Hayes, Maurice. Conference Chairman's Introduction, Proceedings of Cultural Traditions Group Conference, March 1990. In *Cultural Traditions in Northern Ireland: Varieties of Britishness*, edited by Maurna Crozier. Belfast: The Institute of Irish Studies, The Queen's University of Belfast, 1990.

Hennessey, Tom, and Robin Wilson. *With All Due Respect: Pluralism and Parity of Esteem*. Democratic Dialogue No. 7. Belfast: Democratic Dialogue, 1997.

Heskin, K. *Northern Ireland: A Psychological Analysis*. Dublin: Gill and Macmillan, 1980.

Hovey, Anne. "As Easy as Abc . . . The Anti-Bias Curriculum." In *Education Together for a Change*, edited by Chris Moffat. Belfast: Fortnight Educational Trust, 1993.

Hume, John. Lecture at Boston College, Boston, March 10, 1997.

——. *Personal Views: Politics, Peace and Reconciliation in Northern Ireland*. Dublin: Town House, 1996.

Hunter, John. "Now, Councillor, Yer Talkin' Sense." *The Irish News,* January 28, 1994.

Johnston, Jack. Interview with Margaret Smith, Dungannon, Northern Ireland, May 8, 1997.

Joyce, P. W. *A Child's History of Ireland*. Dublin: Gill and Macmillan, 1899.

Kearney, Richard, and Robin Wilson. "Northern Ireland's Future as a European Region: Submission to the Opsahl Commission." *The Irish Review* 15 (1994).

Kennedy, Liam. "Out of History: Ireland, That 'Most Distressful Country.'" In his book *Colonialism, Religion, and Nationalism in Ireland*. Belfast: The Institute of Irish Studies, The Queen's University of Belfast, 1996.

Lambkin, Brian. "Navan Fort and the Arrival of 'Cultural Heritage.'" *Emania* 11 (1993).

Logue, Peter. *Speak Your Piece: Exploring Controversial Issues—A Guide for Teachers, Youth and Community Workers*. Belfast: Channel Four Schools, c1995.

Longley, Edna. "Multi-Culturalism and Northern Ireland." In *Multi-Culturalism: The View from the Two Irelands,* edited by Edna Longley and Declan Kiberd. Armagh: Center for Cross Border Studies and Cork University Press, 2001.

Lustick, Ian. *State-building Failure in British Ireland and French Algeria*. Berkeley,

Calif.: Institute of International Studies, University of California, 1985.

Lyons, F. S. L. *Culture and Anarchy in Ireland, 1890-1939*. Oxford: Clarendon Press, 1979.

——. *Ireland since the Famine*. London: Fontana, 1973.

Magee, John. "The Teaching of Irish History in Irish Schools." *The Northern Teacher* 10 (Winter 1970) 1.

McAleese, Mary. Informal talks with Margaret Smith in Boston, October 14, 1996, and in Belfast, November 19, 1996.

——. Address to Headmasters of Independent Schools, November 10, 1995. Unpublished speech.

McCann, Eamonn. *War and an Irish Town*. Middlesex: Penguin Books, 1974.

McCully, Alan. *Seminar Report: The Teaching of History in a Divided Community, Northern Ireland*, 4-9 October, 1997. Strasbourg: Council of Europe, Central Bureau for Educational Visits and Exchanges. Circulated in draft form, 1998.

McCully, Alan, Nigel Pilgrim, Alaeric Sutherland, and Tara McMinn. "'Don't Worry, Mr. Trimble. We Can Handle It': Balancing the Rational and the Emotional in the Teaching of Contentious Topics." *Teaching History* (March 2002).

McEwen, Alex, and John Salters. "Integrated Education: The Views of Parents." In *After the Reforms: Education and Policy in Northern Ireland*, edited by Robert Osborne, Robert Cormack, and Anthony Gallagher. Aldershot: Avebury, c1993.

McGarry, John, and Brendan O'Leary. "Five Fallacies: Northern Ireland and the Liabilities of Liberalism." *Ethnic and Racial Studies* 8 (October 1995) 4.

——. *Explaining Northern Ireland*. Oxford: Blackwell, 1985.

McHugh, E. M. "A Study of History as a School Subject in Ireland in the Nineteenth Century." Unpublished M.A. thesis, The Queen's University of Belfast, 1978.

McIver, Vivian. Interview with Margaret Smith, Belfast, May 1996.

McKittrick, D., S. Kelters, B. Feeney, and C. Thornton, eds. *Lost Lives*. London: Trafalgar Square, 1999.

Miller, David. *Queen's Rebels: Ulster Loyalism in Historical Perspective*. Dublin: Gill and Macmillan, 1978.

Moffat, Chris, ed. *Education Together for a Change*. Belfast: Fortnight Educational Trust, 1993.

Morrissey, T. J. *Towards a National University, William Delaney S.J., 1835-1924*. Dublin: Wolfhound Press, 1983.

Morrow, Duncan. "In search of common ground." In *Northern Ireland Politics*, edited by Arthur Aughey and Duncan Morrow. London: Longmans, 1996.

Moxon-Browne, E. *Nation, Class and Creed in Northern Ireland*. Aldershot: Gower, 1983.

——. "National Identity in Northern Ireland." In Peter Stringer and Gillian Robinson, eds., *Social Attitudes in Northern Ireland: The First Report, 1990-1991*. Belfast: The Blackstaff Press, 1991.

Murray, Dominic. *Worlds Apart: Segregated Schools in Northern Ireland*. Belfast: Appletree Press, 1985.

Murray, Karl W. "The 36th (Ulster) Division, and the Battle of the Somme, 1916." In *The Great War 1914-1918*. April 1996. http://users.tibus.com/the-great-war/sommewww. htm. (26 May 2004).

N. I. S. E. C., Chief Examiner's Report for G. C. S. E. History, 1988.

Northern Ireland Council for Educational Development. *History Guidelines for Primary Schools*. Belfast: Learning Resources Unit, Stranmillis College, 1984.

Northern Ireland Curriculum Council. *Cross Curricular Themes—Consultation Report*. Belfast: Northern Ireland Curriculum Council, 1989.

Northern Ireland Council for the Curriculum, Examinations and Assessment. "The Curriculum Framework," Section 3. 3—"The Aim, Objectives and Key Elements," in *Pathways: Towards a More Coherent, Enjoyable, Motivating and Relevant Curriculum for Young People Aged 11-14*. Northern Ireland Council for the Curriculum, Examinations and Assessment, 2003.

Northern Ireland Information Service. "Integrated Schools' Contribution to Community Relations." 1998. http://alexandra14.nio.gov.uk/981207e-nio.htm.

O'Brien, Conor Cruise. *The Shaping of Modern Ireland*. Toronto: University of Toronto Press, 1960.

O' Tuathaigh, M. A. G. "Irish Historical Revisionism." In *Interpreting Irish History: The Debate on Historical Revisionism,* edited by Ciaran Brady. Dublin: Irish Academic Press, 1994.

Porter, Norman. *The Elusive Quest: Reconciliation in Northern Ireland*. Belfast: The Blackstaff Press, 2003.

Post Primary Review Body. *Education for the 21st Century*. (The Burns Report). Bangor: Department of Education, 2001.

Post Primary Review Working Group. *Future Post Primary Arrangements in Northern Ireland—Advice from the Post Primary Review Working Group* (The Costello Report). Bangor: Department of Education, 2004.

Press Association. "Action Demanded over Catholic Unemployment." *UTV*. 20 February 2003. http://u.tv/newsroom/indepth.asp?id=29170&pt=n (26 May 2004).

Richardson, Norman. *Roots, If Not Wings! Where Did EMU Come From?* Keynote address at the conference "EMU in Transition," Newcastle, Co. Down, 19 May 1992.

Riddell, Peter. Informal notes taken at the conference "Burying the Past—Justice, Forgiveness and Reconciliation in the Politics of South Africa, Guatemala, East Germany and Northern Ireland" held at Oriel College, Oxford, 14-16 September 1998.

Roberts, Andrew. "US 'clarifies' Irish history," *The* [Irish] *Sunday Times*, October 13, 1996, 5 and 23.

Robinson, Alan. Interview with Margaret Smith, School of Education, University of Ulster at Coleraine, May 9, 1997.

Rogers, P. J. "The Nine Years' War." In *Teaching History 8-13*. Belfast: The Teachers' Centre, The Queen's University of Belfast, 1979.

———. *The New History: Theory into Practice*. London: The Historical Association, 1979.

Rose, Richard. *Governing without Concensus: An Irish Perspective*. London: Faber and Faber, 1971.

Ruane, Joseph, and Jennifer Todd. *The Dynamics of Conflict in Northern Ireland: Power, Conflict, and Emancipation.* Cambridge: Cambridge University Press, 1996.

Skilbeck, Malcolm. "Education and Cultural Change." *Compass: Journal of the Irish Association for Curriculum Development* 5 (May 1976) 2: 16.

Smith, Alan. "Citizenship Education in Northern Ireland: Beyond National Identity?" *Cambridge Journal of Education* 33 (2003) 1.

——. "Education and the Conflict in Northern Ireland." In *Facets of the Conflict in Northern Ireland*, edited by Seumas Dunn. London: Macmillan, 1995.

——. "Education and the Peace Process in Northern Ireland." Paper presented to the Annual Conference of the American Education Research Association, Montreal: 1999.

——. *Education for Mutual Understanding.* Belfast: H.M.S.O., 1988.

Smith, Alan, and Seumas Dunn. *Extending Inter School Links: An Evaluation of Contact between Protestant and Catholic Pupils in Northern Ireland.* Coleraine, Northern Ireland: Centre for the Study of Conflict, University of Ulster, 1990.

Smith, Alan, and Alison Montgomery. *Values in Education in Northern Ireland.* Northern Ireland Council for the Curriculum, Examinations and Assessment, 1997.

Smith, Alan, and Alan Robinson. *Education for Mutual Understanding: The Initial Statutory Years.* Coleraine, Northern Ireland: Centre for the Study of Conflict, University of Ulster, 1996.

——. *Education for Mutual Understanding: Perceptions and Policy.* Coleraine, Northern Ireland: Centre for the Study of Conflict, University of Ulster, 1992.

Smith, David J. *Equality and Inequality in Northern Ireland*, Pt. 3, "Perceptions and Views." PSI Occasional Paper no. 39. London: Political Studies Institute, 1987.

Smyth, William. "Irish History in Secondary (Intermediate) Schools in Northern Ireland; A Survey of Extent, Teaching Methods, Qualifications of Teachers and Pupils' Attitudes." Unpublished M.A. thesis, The Queen's University of Belfast, 20 March 1974.

Spencer, A. E. S. "Arguments for an Integrated School System in Northern Ireland." In *Education and Policy in Northern Ireland*, edited by Robert Osborne, Robert Cormack, and R. Miller. Belfast: PRI, 1987.

Standing Advisory Commission on Human Rights. *Report of Fair Employment: Religious and Political Discrimination and Equality of Opportunity in Northern Ireland.* London: H.M.S.O., 1987.

Todd, Jennifer. "Northern Irish Nationalist Political Culture." *Irish Political Studies* 5 (1990): 31-44.

——. "Two Traditions in Unionist Political Culture." *Irish Political Studies* 2 (1987): 1-26.

Turner, Brian. "The Twisting Rope—Local Studies in Ulster." *The Irish Review* 8 (Spring 1990).

Walker, Brian. *Dancing to History's Tune: History, Myth and Politics in Ireland.* Belfast: The Institute of Irish Studies, The Queen's University of Belfast, 1996.

Whyte, John. *Interpreting Northern Ireland.* Oxford: Clarendon Press, 1990.

Wright, Frank. "Integrated Education and Political Identity." In *Education To-gether for a Change*, edited by Chris Moffat. Belfast: Fortnight Educational Trust, 1993.

———. *Northern Ireland: A Comparative Analysis*. Dublin: Gill and Macmillan, 1987.

General Sources

Abrahamson, Irving, ed. *Against Silence: The Voice and Vision of Elie Wiesel*. New York: Schocken, 1984.

Allport, Gordon. *The Nature of Prejudice*. Reading, Mass.: Addison-Wesley, 1954.

Amir, Y. "Contact hypothesis in ethnic relations." *Psychological Bulletin*. 1969.

Anderson, Benedict. *Imagined Communities*. London: Verso, 1983.

Appleby, Joyce, Lynn Hunt, and Margaret Jacob. *Telling the Truth About History*. New York: W. W. Norton, 1994.

Arendt, Hannah. *The Human Condition: A Study of the Central Conditions Facing Modern Man*. Garden City, N.Y.: Doubleday Anchor Books, 1959.

Audigier, F. *Teaching about Society, Passing on Values: Elementary Law in Civic Education. A Secondary Education for Europe*. Strasbourg: Council of Europe Publishing, 1996.

Azar, Edward, E. "The Theory of Protracted Social Conflict and the Challenge of Transforming Conflict Situations." *Monograph Series in World Affairs* 20 (M2). 1983.

———. "Protracted International Conflicts: Ten Propositions." *International Interactions* 12 (1985) 1.

———. *The Management of Protracted Social Conflict*. Hampshire, England: Dartmouth, 1990.

Banks, Marcus. *Ethnicity: Anthropological Constructions*. London: Routledge, 1996.

Bar-Tal, Daniel. "Collective Memory of Physical Violence." In *The Role of Memory in Ethic Conflict,* edited by Ed Cairns and Mícheál D. Roe. Basingstoke: Palgrave Macmillan, 2003.

Barth, Frederik. "Introduction." In his book *Ethnic Groups and Boundaries*. Boston: Little, Brown, 1969.

Bennett, Milton. "Towards Ethnorelativism: A Developmental Model of Intercultural Sensitivity." In *Education for the Intercultural Experience*, 2nd ed., edited by Michael Paige. Yarmouth, Maine: Intercultural Press, 1993.

Bloom, William. *Personal Identity, National Identity and International Relations*. Cambridge: Cambridge University Press, 1990.

Boutros-Ghali, Boutros. *An Agenda for Peace: Preventive Diplomacy, Peacemaking and Peace-keeping*. Report of the Secretary General pursuant to the statement adopted by the Summit Meeting of the Security Council on 31 January 1992. New York: United Nations, 1992.

Brocklehurst, Helen, and Robert Phillips, eds. *History, Nationhood and the Question of Britain*. Basingstoke: Palgrave Macmillan, 2004.

Bromley, Yulian. "The Term *Ethnos* and Its Definition." In *Soviet Ethnology and Anthropology Today*, edited by Yulian Bromley. The Hague: Mouton, 1974.

Bruner, J. S. *The Process of Education*. Knopf: Vintage Books, 1960.

Buergenthal, Thomas, and Harold Maier. *Public International Law in a Nutshell*. St. Paul, Minn.: West Publishing Co., 1989.

Burg, Steven L. "Nationalism and Civic Identity: Ethnic Models for Macedonia and Kosovo." In *Cases and Strategies for Preventive Action*, edited by Barnett R. Rubin. New York: Council on Foreign Relations and the Twentieth Century Fund, The Century Foundation Press, 1998.

Burns, James MacGregor. "Wellsprings of Political Leadership." *The American Political Science Review* LXXI (March 1977).

Burton, John. *Conflict: Resolution and Provention*. New York: St. Martin's Press, 1990.

——. *Resolving Deeply-Rooted Conflict: A Handbook*. Lanham, Md.: University Press of America, 1987.

Cammett, John. *Antonio Gramsci and the Origins of Italian Communism*. Stanford, Calif.: Stanford University Press, 1967.

Cairns, Ed, C. A. Lewis, O. Mumcu, and N. Waddell. "Memories of Recent Ethnic Conflict and the Relationship to Social Identity." *Peace and Conflict: Journal of Peace Psychology* 4 (1998) 13-22.

Cairns, Ed, and Mícheál D. Roe, *The Role of Memory in Ethnic Conflict*. Basingstoke: Palgrave Macmillan, 2003.

Carnegie Endowment for International Peace. "History Teaching and School Text-books in Relation to International Understanding." Reading List No. 29, March 4, 1931.

Carr, David. *Time, Narrative and History*. Bloomington: Indiana University Press, 1986.

Chartier, Roger. "Intellectual History or Sociocultural History? The French Trajectories." In *Modern European Intellectual History: Reappraisals and New Perspectives*, edited by Dominick LaCapro and Steven L. Kaplan. Ithaca, N.Y.: Cornell University Press, 1982.

Colley, Linda. *Britons: Forging the Nation 1707-1837*. London: Pimlico, 1992.

Connor, Walker. "Terminological Chaos." In his book *Ethnonationalism: The Quest for Understanding*. Princeton: Princeton University Press, 1994.

——. Lecture, Weatherhead Center for International Affairs, Harvard University, April 22, 1998.

Curti, Merle. *Peace or War: The American Struggle, 1636-1936*. New York: W. W. Norton, 1936.

Drogin, Bob. "Reversing Apartheid's Lessons." *Los Angeles Times*, February 11, 1997: A1 and A10.

Emerson, Rupert. *Empire to Nation*. Cambridge, Mass.: Harvard University Press, 1960.

Eriksen, Thomas Hylland. *Ethnicity and Nationalism: Anthropological Perspectives*. London: Pluto Press, 1993.

European Commission. *Education and Active Citizenship in the European Union*. Luxembourg: Office of Official Publications of the European Communities, 1998.

Foner, Eric. *Who Owns History? Rethinking the Past in a Changing World*. New York: Hill and Warg, 2002.

Friberg, Mats. "The Need for Unofficial Diplomacy in Identity Conflicts." In *Yugoslavia Wars*, edited by Tonci Kuzmanic and Arno Truger. Ljubljana, Slovenia: Peace Institute, 1992.

Friedman, Jonathan. "The Past in the Future: History and the Politics of Identity." *American Anthropologist* 94 (1992) 4: 855.

Gardner, Howard, in collaboration with Emma Laskin. *Leading Minds: An Anatomy of Leadership.* New York: Basic Books, 1995.

Geertz, Clifford. "The Integrative Revolution—Primordial Sentiments and Civil Politics in the New States." In his book *Old Societies and New States: The Quest for Modernity in Asia and Africa.* New York: The Free Press, 1965.

Gellner, Ernest. *Nations and Nationalism.* Ithaca, N.Y.: Cornell University Press, 1983.

Glaser, Barney G., and Anselm L. Strauss. *Grounded Theory: The Discovery of Strategies for Qualitative Research.* Chicago: Aldine, 1967.

Glazer, Nathan, and Daniel Patrick Moynihan. *Ethnicity: Theory and Experience.* Cambridge, Mass.: Harvard University Press, 1975.

Goodall, Sir David. "Terrorists on the Spot." *The Tablet,* 25 December 1993/1 January 1994: 1676.

Gramsci, Antonio. *Collected Works, L'Opera di Antonio Gramsci.* Turin: Einaud, 1947.

———. *Vol. III—Intellettuali e L'organizzazione della cultural.* 1949.

Graves, Robert, and Raphael Patai. *Hebrew Myths: The Book of Genesis.* Garden City, N.Y.: Doubleday, 1969.

Gurr, Ted Robert. *Minorities at Risk.* Washington, D.C.: The United States Institute of Peace, 1993.

Helm, P. J. *History of Europe, 1450-1660.* London: G. Bell and Sons, 1961.

Hewstone, Miles, and Rupert Brown, eds. *Contact and Conflict in Intergroup Encounters.* Oxford: Blackwell, 1986.

Hobsbawn, Eric. *Nations and Nationalism since 1780.* Cambridge: Cambridge University Press, 1990.

Hobsbawn, Eric, and Terence Ranger, eds. *The Invention of Tradition.* Cambridge: Cambridge University Press, 1983.

Horowitz, Donald. *A Democratic South Africa?* Berkeley, Calif.: University of California Press, 1991.

———. *Ethnic Groups in Conflict.* Berkeley: University of California Press, 1985.

Horowitz, M. J. *Stress Response Syndromes.* New York: Jason Aronson, 1976.

Ignatieff, Michael. "On Civil Society: Why Eastern Europe's Revolutions Could Succeed." *Foreign Affairs* (March/April 1995): 128-136.

Isaacs, Harold. *Idols of the Tribe.* Cambridge, Mass.: Harvard University Press, 1975.

Ivor, Wayne. *Can History Textbooks Be Analyzed Systematically? A Methodological Inquiry.* Unpublished doctoral thesis, Department of Sociology, American University, Washington, D.C., 1971.

Katz, Daniel. "Nationalism and Conflict Resolution." In *International Behavior: A Social-Psychological Analysis,* edited by Herbert Kelman. New York: Holt, Rinehart and Winston, 1965.

Kelly, George. *A Theory of Personality: The Psychology of Personal Constructs.* New York: W. W. Norton, 1955.

Kelman, Herbert C. "Nationalism, Patriotism and National Identity: Social-Psychological Dimensions." In *Patriotism in the Lives of Individuals and Nations*, edited by Daniel Bar-Tal and Ervin Staub. Chicago: Nelson-Hall Publishers, 1997.

———. "Negotiating National Identity." *Negotiation Journal* (October 1997): 336.

———. "Patterns of Personal Involvement in the National System: A Social-Psychological Analysis of Political Legitimacy." In *International Politics and Foreign Policy: A Reader in Research and Theory*, rev. ed., edited by James N. Rosenau. New York: The Free Press, 1969.

———. "The Place of Ethnic Identity in the Development of Personal Identity: A Challenge for the Jewish Family." In *Coping with Life and Death: Jewish Families in the Twentieth Century*, edited by Peter Y. Medding. Studies in Contemporary Jewry: An Annual, XIV. New York: Oxford University Press, Published for the Avraham Harman Institute of Contemporary Jewry, 1998.

Kennedy, Paul. "The Decline of Nationalistic History in the West." *Journal of Contemporary History* 8 (1973) 1: 92.

Kinchloe, Joe L., and Shirley R. Steinberg. *Changing Multiculturalism*. Buckingham: Open University Press, 1997.

Kupchan, Charles. "Introduction: Nationalism Resurgent." In *Nationalism and Nationalities in the New Europe*, edited by Charles Kupchan. Ithaca: Cornell University Press, 1995.

Lally, Conor. *Sunday Tribune*, October 13, 1996, 3.

Leach, Edmund. *Political Systems of Highland Burma*. London: Athlone, 1954.

Lederach, Jean Paul. *Building Peace: Sustainable Reconciliation in Divided Societies*. Washington, D.C.: United States Institute of Peace, 1997.

Lemarchand, René. *Burundi: Ethnic Conflict and Genocide*. Cambridge and New York: Woodrow Wilson Center Press and Cambridge University Press, 1994.

Lijphart, Arend. *Democracy in Plural Societies*. New Haven: Yale University Press, 1977.

———. *Patterns of Democracy: Government Forms and Performance in Thirty-Six Countries*. New Haven: Yale University Press, 1999.

Lund, Michael S. "Underrating Preventive Diplomacy." *Foreign Affairs* (July/August 1995): 160-63.

Mack, John E. "Cultural Amplifiers." Working paper presented to the Committee on International Affairs at the Fall Meeting of the Group for the Advancement of Psychiatry, White Plains, New York, November 10-12, 1984.

———. "The Psychodynamics of Victimization." In *The Psychodynamics of International Relationships,* Vol. I, edited by Vamik Volkan, Demetrios Julius, and Joseph Montville. Lexington, Mass.: Lexington Books, 1991.

Malinowski, Bronislaw. "Myth in Primitive Psychology." In his book *Magic, Science and Religion and Other Essays*. Garden City, N.Y.: Doubleday Anchor Books, 1954.

———. "The Foundations of Faith and Morals." In his book *Sex, Culture, and Myth*. New York: Harcourt, Brace, 1962.

Maxwell, Joseph. *Qualitative Research Design*. Thousand Oaks, Calif.: Sage, 1996.

Minow, Martha. *Between Vengeance and Forgiveness: Facing History after Genocide and Mass Violence*. Boston: Beacon Press, 1998.

Montville, Joseph. "Epilogue: The Human Factor Revisited." In *Conflict and Peacemaking in Multiethnic Societies*, edited by Joseph Montville. New York: Lexington Books, 1991.

Moore, Barrington. *Injustice: The Social Bases of Obedience and Revolt*. New York: Pantheon Books, 1978.

Morgan, H. J. "Deceptions of Demons." *Fortnight* (September 1993): 34-36.

New York Times, January 30, 1998, A1.

Northrup, Terrell. "The Dynamic of Identity in Personal and Social Conflict." In *Intractable Conflicts and Their Transformation*, edited by Louis Kriesberg, Terrell Northrup, and Stuart Thorson. Syracuse: Syracuse University Press, 1989.

O'Brien, Jay. "Toward a Reconstitution of Ethnicity: Capitalist Expansion and Cultural Dynamics in Sudan." *American Anthropologist* 88 (1986): 905.

O'Neill, Kevin. Lecture, Boston College, Boston, January 30, 1997.

Oppenheimer, Louis, and Ilse Hakvoort. "Will the Germans Ever be Forgiven? Memories of the Second World War Four Generations Later." In *The Role of Memory in Ethnic Conflict*, edited by Ed Cairns and Mícheál D. Roe. Basingstoke: Palgrave Macmillan, 2003.

Otto, Walter F. *Die Gestalt und das Sein: Gesammelte Abhandlungen über den Mythos und seine Bedeutung für die Menschheit* [Image and Existence: Collected Essays on Myth and Its Meaning for Mankind]. Dusseldorf-Koln: Eugen Diedricks Verlag, 1955.

Parekh, Bhikhu. *The Future of Multi-Ethnic Britain*. London: Profile Books, 2000.

Patai, Raphael. *Myth and Modern Man*. Englewood Cliffs, N.J.: Prentice Hall, 1972.

Pearson, Raymond. "Improving History: Nationalism and the Historian." Unpublished lecture, 1996.

Peel, John. "The Cultural Work of Yoruba Ethnogenesis." In *History and Ethnicity*, edited by Elizabeth Tonkin, Maryon McDonald, and Malcolm Chapman. London: Routledge, 1989.

Renan, Ernest. "Qu'est-ce qu'une nation?" In *Oeuvres Complètes* 1. Edition définitive, edited by Henriette Psichari. Paris: Calmann-Levy, 1947.

Renshon, Stanley Allen. "The Role of Personality Development in Political Socialization." In *New Directions in Political Socialization*, edited by David C. Schwartz and Sandra Kenyon Schwartz. New York: Free Press, 1975.

Roe, Mícheál D., and Ed Cairns. "Memories in Conflict: Review and a Look to the Future." In *The Role of Memory in Ethnic Conflict*, edited by Ed Cairns and Mícheál D. Roe. Basingstoke: Palgrave Macmillan, 2003.

Rothman, Jay. *Resolving Identity-Based Conflict in Nations, Organizations, and Communities*. San Francisco: Jossey-Bass, 1997.

Said, Edward. *Cultural Imperialism*. New York: Knopf, 1993.

Seton-Watson, Hugh H. *Nations and States*. London: Methuen, 1977.

Shafer, Boyd. *Nationalism: Myth and Reality*. New York: Harcourt, Brace, 1955.

Shriver, Donald. *An Ethic for Enemies: Forgiveness in Politics*. New York: Oxford University Press, 1995.

Sites, Paul. *Control: The Basis of Social Order*. New York: Dunellen Publishers, 1973.

Smith, Alan, and Murray Print. "Editorial." *Cambridge Journal of Education* 33 (2003) 1.

Smith, Anthony D. *The Ethnic Origin of Nations*. Oxford: Blackwell, 1986.

Snyder, Jack. "Nationalism and the Crisis of the Post-Soviet State." In *Ethnic Conflict and International Security*, edited by Michael E. Brown. Princeton: Princeton University Press, 1993.

Stedman, Stephen John. "Alchemy for a New World Order: Overselling 'Preventive Diplomacy.'" *Foreign Affairs* (May/June 1995): 14-20.

Stephan, W. G., and C. W. Stephan. *Intergroup Relations*. Madison, Wisc.: Brown and Benchmark, 1996.

Tajfel, Henri. *Human Groups and Social Categories*. Cambridge: Cambridge University Press, 1981.

———. "The Roots of Prejudice: Cognitive Aspects." In *Psychology and Race*, edited by P. Watson. Chicago: Aldine, 1973.

———, ed. *Social Identity*. Cambridge: Cambridge University Press, 1982.

Tamir, Yael. *Liberal Nationalism*. Princeton: Princeton University Press, 1993.

Tate, Nicholas. "The End of History? Could You Recognize Alfred the Great? Probably Not If You're a History Student." *The Guardian*, July 27, 1999.

Tavuchis, Nicholas. *Mea Culpa: A Sociology of Apology and Reconciliation*. Stanford, Calif.: Stanford University Press, 1991.

Taylor, Charles. *Multiculturalism and "The Politics of Recognition."* With commentary by Amy Gutmann, ed., et al. Princeton: Princeton University Press, 1992.

Thompson, Leonard. *The Political Mythology of Apartheid*. New Haven: Yale University Press, 1985.

Tudor, Henry. *Political Mythology*. London: Pall Mall Press, 1972.

Van Evera, Stephen. "The Cult of the Offensive and the Origins of the First World War." In *Military Strategy and the Origins of the First World War*, edited by Steven Miller et al. Princeton: Princeton University Press, 1991.

———. "Hypotheses on Nationalism and War." *International Security* 18 (Spring 1994) 4: 26-33.

———. "Primed for Peace: Europe After the Cold War." *International Security* 15 (Winter 1990/91) 3: 23.

Volkan, Vamik. *Bloodlines*. New York: Farrar, Straus and Giroux, 1997.

———. "Bosnia-Herzegovina: Ancient Fuel of Modern Inferno." *Mind and Human Interaction* 7 (August 1996).

———. *Cyprus: War and Adaptation*. Charlottesville: University Press of Virginia, 1979.

———. "Psychoanalytic Aspects of Ethnic Conflicts." In *Conflict and Peacemaking in Multiethnic Societies*, edited by Joseph Montville. New York: Lexington Books, 1991.

———. "The Psychodynamics of Victimization." In *The Psychodynamics of International Relationships*, Vol. I., edited by Vamik Volkan, Demetrios Julius, and Joseph Montville. Lexington, Mass.: Lexington Books, 1991.

Washington, James M., ed. *A Testament of Hope: The Essential Writings of MLK, Jr.* San Francisco: Harper and Row, 1986.

Weber, Max. *Economy and Society: An Outline of Interpretive Sociology,* edited by Gunther Roth and Claus Wittich. Berkeley, Calif.: University of California Press, 1978.

West, Cornel, and Henry Louis Gates, Jr. "Black, White and Brown." *New York Times Book Review,* May 16, 2004, 35.

Williams, Gwynn A. "Gramsci's concept of *Egemonia*." *Journal of the History of Ideas* XXI (1960).

Index

251

textbooks, Northern Ireland/Irish
history, 220n19; Catholic school
policy and, 118; Clarke, Randall
and *A Short History of Ireland:
From 1485 to the Present Day*
(1941), 115, 117; Gillespie, Sandra,
and Gerry Jones and *Northern
Ireland and Its Neighbours since
1920*, 135, 146, 207n24, 224n38;
Herring, Ivor and *History of
Ireland* (1937), 115, 117; Joyce, P.
W. and *A Child's History of Ireland*
(1897), 111; nineteenth-century
basic reading series, *The First Book
of Lessons,* etc., and, 108–9; and
the reformed curriculum of the
1990s, 132–35, 141, 146;
smokescreen problem and, 178;
"Ulster history" controversy and,
115–17. *See also* curriculum
development projects
Thatcher, Margaret/Thatcher government,
53, 100, 144, 145, 198, xviin3
Treaty of Amsterdam (1997), 174
Trimble, David, 85, 225n9, 226n20,
226n22
Troubles. *See* historical events and
personalties of significance in group
narratives, Troubles (began 1968)

Ulster: 36th Ulster Division, 60–61;
historical narrative of Ian Adamson,
118, 161–65, 227n17, 227n19,
227n30, 228n34; historical narrative

of Michael Hall, 118, 163–64,
227n22, 227n25–28, 228n32;
"Ulster" as a form of identity, 74,
157, 161–65
Ulster Special Constabulary, 47, 49–50
Ulster Workers' Council Strike (1974),
53, 165
UNESCO. *See* textbook revision,
organizations involved in promoting
Unionism, as political philosophy, 45
United Nations Decade for Human
Rights Education (1995–2004), 175
United Nations General Assembly Plan
of Action for the Decade, 175
U.S. State Department, 102

Volkan, Vamik, 31, 211n41–n43,
211n46–51, 212n57

Whyte, John, 157, 161, 214n6, 226n1,
227n16, 228n31, 228n35
Wilson, Harold and Wilson government,
53, 213n10
World War I, 24, 46, 60, 133, 167,
205n10
World War II, 24, 47, 49, 86, 166;
textbook revision/history writing
and, 3, 4, 5, 10; as a topic in the
classroom, 147–48, 150
Wright, Frank, 66–67, 168, 215n16,
219n21, 228n45

Yeats, William Butler. *See* Irish
language, Gaelic League (1893)

About the Author

Margaret E. Smith is Assistant Professor in the School of International Service at American University and Academic Director of American University's Washington Semester Program in Peace and Conflict Resolution. She earned her doctorate from the Fletcher School of Law and Diplomacy, Tufts University, and she has a master's degree in history from Boston University. She has taught history, international relations, and conflict resolution at Tufts University, the University of Massachusetts in Boston, Mount Ida College, and the College of the Holy Cross.